The Literar

Tales of Literacy fo

The Literary Agenda

Tales of Literacy for the 21st Century

MARYANNE WOLF
with Stephanie Gottwald

OXFORD
UNIVERSITY PRESS

Great Clarendon Street, Oxford, OX2 6DP,
United Kingdom

Oxford University Press is a department of the University of Oxford.
It furthers the University's objective of excellence in research, scholarship,
and education by publishing worldwide. Oxford is a registered trade mark of
Oxford University Press in the UK and in certain other countries

© Maryanne Wolf 2016

The moral rights of the author have been asserted

First Edition published in 2016

Impression: 1

All rights reserved. No part of this publication may be reproduced, stored in
a retrieval system, or transmitted, in any form or by any means, without the
prior permission in writing of Oxford University Press, or as expressly permitted
by law, by licence or under terms agreed with the appropriate reprographics
rights organization. Enquiries concerning reproduction outside the scope of the
above should be sent to the Rights Department, Oxford University Press, at the
address above

You must not circulate this work in any other form
and you must impose this same condition on any acquirer

Published in the United States of America by Oxford University Press
198 Madison Avenue, New York, NY 10016, United States of America

British Library Cataloguing in Publication Data

Data available

Library of Congress Control Number: 2016932270

ISBN 978-0-19-872417-9

Printed in Great Britain by
Clays Ltd, St Ives plc

Links to third party websites are provided by Oxford in good faith and
for information only. Oxford disclaims any responsibility for the materials
contained in any third party website referenced in this work.

Series Introduction

The Crisis in, the Threat to, the Plight of the Humanities: enter these phrases in Google's search engine and there are 23 million results, in a great fifty-year-long cry of distress, outrage, fear, and melancholy. Grant, even, that every single anxiety and complaint in that catalogue of woe is fully justified—the lack of public support for the arts, the cutbacks in government funding for the humanities, the imminent transformation of a literary and verbal culture by visual/virtual/digital media, the decline of reading...And still, though it were all true, and just because it might be, there would remain the problem of the response itself. Too often there's recourse to the shrill moan of offended piety or a defeatist withdrawal into professionalism.

The Literary Agenda is a series of short polemical monographs that believes there is a great deal that needs to be said about the state of literary education inside schools and universities and more fundamentally about the importance of literature and of reading in the wider world. The category of "the literary" has always been contentious. What *is* clear, however, is how increasingly it is dismissed or is unrecognized as a way of thinking or an arena for thought. It is skeptically challenged from within, for example, by the sometimes rival claims of cultural history, contextualized explanation, or media studies. It is shaken from without by even greater pressures: by economic exigency and the severe social attitudes that can follow from it; by technological change that may leave the traditional forms of serious human communication looking merely antiquated. For just these reasons this is the right time for renewal, to start reinvigorated work into the meaning and value of literary reading for the sake of the future.

It is certainly no time to retreat within institutional walls. For all the academic resistance to "instrumentalism", to governmental measurements of public impact and practical utility, literature exists in and across society. The "literary" is not pure or specialized or self-confined; it is not restricted to the practitioner in writing or the academic in studying. It exists in the whole range of the world which is its subject-matter: it consists in what non-writers actively receive from writings when, for example, they start to see the world more imaginatively as a result of reading novels and begin to think more carefully about human personality. It comes from literature making available much of human life that would not otherwise be existent to thought or recognizable as knowledge. If it is true that involvement in literature, so far from being a minority aesthetic, represents a significant contribution to the life of human thought, then that idea has to be argued at the public level without succumbing to a hollow rhetoric or bowing to a reductive world view. Hence the effort of this series to take its place *between* literature and the world. The double-sided commitment to occupying that place and establishing its reality is the only "agenda" here, without further prescription as to what should then be thought or done within it.

What is at stake is not simply some defensive or apologetic "justification" in the abstract. The case as to why literature matters in the world not only has to be argued conceptually and strongly tested by thought, it should be given presence, performed and brought to life in the way that literature itself does. That is why this series includes the writers themselves, the novelists and poets, in order to try to close the gap between the thinking of the artists and the thinking of those who read and study them. It is why it also involves other kinds of thinkers—the philosopher, the theologian, the psychologist, the neuroscientist—examining the role of literature within their own life's work and thought, and the effect of that work, in turn, upon literary thinking. This series admits and encourages personal voices in an unpredictable variety of individual approach and expression, speaking wherever possible across countries and disciplines and temperaments. It aims for something more than intellectual assent: rather the literary sense of what it is like to feel the thought, to embody an idea in a person, to bring it to being in a narrative or in aid of adventurous reflection. If the artists refer to their own works, if other thinkers return to ideas that have marked much of their working life, that is not their vanity nor a failure of originality. It is what the series has asked of them: to speak out of what they know and care about, in whatever language can best serve their most serious thinking, and without the necessity of trying to cover every issue or meet every objection in each volume.

Philip Davis

Contents

List of Figures	ix
1. Introduction	1
2. A Linguist's Tale	12
3. A Child's Tale	37
4. A Neuroscientist's Tale of Words	66
5. The Deep Reading Brain	109
6. A Second Revolution in the Brain	141
7. A Tale of Hope for Non-Literate Children	163
Epilogue	188
Acknowledgments	189
Selected Bibliography	193
Index	195

List of Figures

2.1.	Chinese characters for *bear* and *bear exhibit*	29
2.2.	Korean *bear*	33
4.1.	Diotima's brain	84
4.2.	Diotima's visual system	87
4.3.	Phonological and semantic processes with George Eliot	95
5.1.	Full reading brain circuit with St Thomas Aquinas	137

1
Introduction

"Nothing is unaltered in the brain."[1] So begins the epic poem, *Mozart's Third Brain*, by Swedish poet Göran Sonnevi, and so begins our narrative about what it means to be literate—cognitively, linguistically, socially, emotionally, and neurologically. Literacy alters the brain in profoundly transformative ways, which alters the person, which alters the species, which alters humanity itself. There is little more important for the future of our species' intellectual development.

The history of how we came to be a literate species only six millennia ago still contains as much mystery as fact. There are clues to the mystery of its origins to be found in ancient places like the Wadi el Hol (Gulch of Terror) where Egyptian hieroglyphs have been discovered that might have preceded the Sumerian script, long thought to be our first writing system. By contrast, the rapidly unfolding science of the reading brain may well outpace what we know of its history. We have much to learn from both our past and our present as we move from a deeply literate culture into a digital culture insufficiently cognizant of the contributions of past forms of literacy and of the changes digital reading will bring.

What we know about our past and what we are learning about the present reading brain can help us address three issues that will be leitmotifs in this book: what it means to be literate or non-literate in human development; how the future of the expert reading brain is intimately connected to *what* and *how* we read and write; and what the effects of a digital "screen culture" may be for the development of children and adults in literate and in non-literate environments. In a world where almost 200 million children and 600 million adults will never attain anything approaching true literacy, the waste of human potential is incalculable. The reality, however, is that we are on the cusp of being able to change that waste in ways unimaginable only a decade ago, if we possess the will to do so.

In this book I wish to bring together research from multiple disciplines to shed light on how literacy develops; what happens when it does not; and how literacy transforms brain, mind, and culture in highly significant, deeply consequential ways. For this I will be using "tales" from literature and from cognitive neurosciences, psycholinguistics, developmental sciences, education, philosophy, and technology. To ensure that this material, particularly on the reading brain and language, will be accessible, I have prepared three somewhat unusual introductory chapters that will acquaint the reader with core concepts from psycholinguistics about language, from child development about language and reading development, and from neuroscience about the reading brain. Few reading-related neurons will be left unturned by the end of these pages; and, it is our hope, few children will be left to remain illiterate by 2040. This is our literacy agenda.

Working assumptions

> Though threatened with extinction, we who are today's readers don't know what reading is.[2]
>
> Alberto Manguel, *A History of Reading*

Few people—whether linguist, educator, or writer—understand the importance of reading and literacy better than Alberto Manguel. It is, therefore, all the more striking to encounter his perspicacious assessment of how little most people understand what reading is. We wish to contribute to changing this assessment in this book and in work that we describe here. But before we do, a few basic assumptions are needed to ground our approach and to make concrete why an understanding of reading and literacy at this moment in our history is critical for all of us.

The first assumption begins with how we use the often interchangeably used terms *reading* and *literacy* and how both of these terms will be distinguished from the term *literary*. For our purposes, *literacy* refers to the attainment by an individual or a society of the full panoply of reading and writing skills. *Reading* refers more specifically to the multiple perceptual, cognitive, linguistic, affective, and physiological processes involved in the act of decoding and comprehending written language. For our purposes here, it is not as important as in other contexts if these two terms become conflated.

What is more important here is to underscore that for us reading is not just about "decoding" the information before our eyes. Rather, reading is ultimately about an encounter between a reader and another mind that leads to *thinking beyond ourselves*. Philip Davis, in his introduction to the Literary Agenda series, made an important distinction between the "literal" and the "literary" that also helps to clarify the important leap between decoding text and entering into an exchange with text and author. He wrote that "the *'literary'* offers to human discourse something more than the opinionated, the informative, the finished and the explicit—an extra dimension achieved in the processes of thinking out into language, with both its hesitations and its surprises; in the contextual feeling of a thought—its nuance, resonance and richness for further development; and thus in the increased capacity for realization and discovery."[3] It is this capacity for realization, insight, and discovery that is the apex of the reading act and our goal for literacy around the world.

In similar vein, Marcel Proust once wrote, "we always like to be taken out of ourselves a little, to *travel*, when we read."[4] It is an apt metaphor for what we do both as individual readers—*we travel a little beyond ourselves*; and as societies—we learn to travel beyond the shifting borders of our cognitive capacities and cultural domains. Literacy allows us, indeed invites us, to use the backdrop of our previous knowledge in order to go beyond it to somewhere new, beyond both author and the readers themselves. It is within the process of transforming individuals into literate beings, that society itself is transformed. Through processes whose examination will reveal as much about the brain's design as the reader's skills, literacy propels the ever deepening expansion of thought, as whatever is read becomes integrated with what is known, felt, inferred, hoped, and imagined by the reader. That is our starting point in this book.

The second assumption here concerns the simple insight I came to years ago: *we were never born to read*. The brain that reads is not a given.[5] Literacy is a cultural invention, which means that there is no genetic program that can dictate its design—a reality with many implications and consequences. The first implication is that because the acquisition of reading is not biologically determined (like language or taste), there exists no one, ideal, universal design. Rather, the brain of an individual reader will be shaped by its environment in particular ways, beginning with the writing system, the manner taught, the medium, and the unique development of that individual's expertise and preferences over the lifespan.

How this relatively new cultural invention came to shape our brain in the process of its acquisition is a still undertold story. It is less known not because it is less studied, as you will see in these pages, but in part because it continues to unfold like a slippery thing under our very fingertips as we become, many of us, digital readers. The development of a "brain that reads" represents one of the more astonishing manifestations of the brain's plastic ability to form new circuits from older, genetically programmed circuits that underlie vision and language, cognition and emotion. This plasticity—with its intrinsic ability to adapt and reflect the environmental milieu—contains within itself the foreknowledge of change.

Joseph Epstein's admonition, that "we are what we read," is as physiologically real as it is figuratively correct for an individual.[6] When we learn to read, our brain has to create a totally new circuitry that reflects many important influences, beginning with the type of writing system to be learned. Our addendum to Joseph Epstein is that we are also "'*how*' we read." That is, the very ways we learn to read—for example, on print or digital mediums—will influence the formation of the reading brain circuit in ways we do not yet fully understand, but that are imperative to research in this moment of cultural change.

A second implication amplifies these social consequences. Because literacy is not genetically programmed in the young of our species, between 50 and 70 million children (the exact figure is still uncertain) on the planet may never become literate through no fault of their own. They are often called the "pastoral children" who simply have no access to schools or teachers. Another 150 to 200 million children have such inadequate schooling that they will never reach literacy beyond the third grade level.

Yet another implication is less obvious. Again, because there is no biologically given, ideal program for reading, the brain that learns to read "deeply" cannot be assumed, either in otherwise totally literate children, or in literate adults. During our present transition, with its emergence of a "digital reading brain," unknown changes have begun to accompany the co-occurring emergence of a new reading style—one that is able to integrate multiple sources of information, but that often appears fragmented, less focused, and potentially less able to attain previously achieved depths of concentration, comprehension, and even immersion in reading. It is critical to understand this form of the reading brain, lest it begin to threaten the very kind of intelligence that has flourished from the historical development of sophisticated, expert reading. There are many unresolved questions at this moment in our transition from a literate to a digital culture: helping to articulate the critical questions is a major goal in this book where we hope to illumine the role of literacy in the arc of human development, and how this transition will impact what we think of as the "literary" dimension in our lives.

The third assumption concerns an unusual method of approaching the study of literacy. We believe that an important way of envisioning what it means to be literate involves the study of peoples who are like one another in every typical way—from social-cultural to intellectual factors—except that some of these individuals acquired literacy, and the others did not, for no reasons save the chance environment where they were born.

We want to know, therefore, what happens when groups of human beings never acquire literacy, particularly with regard to their strengths, capacities, and differences in the use of language. With Socrates as a timeless example of a person who was not fully literate and indeed who eschewed literacy, we want to preface any aspect of our exploration of non-literate peoples with the following statement. We are uninterested in any examination of literate and non-literate peoples that either explicitly or implicitly aims through comparison to show that a literate mind is "better" than a non-literate mind. Rather, we want to deepen our understanding of literacy by learning the *unique, additive* properties of literacy through a comparison with its absence in non-literate peoples who possess their own unique cognitive capacities.

Such is the case with a group of former revolutionaries in Colombia studied by Manuel Carreiras, Director of the Basque Center on Cognition, Brain, and Language.[7] His group studied forty-two former revolutionaries who had never learned to read, but who in peacetime were given the opportunity to become literate through adult literacy courses. By comparing brain scans of those revolutionaries who became literate versus those who chose not to, Carreiras and his team found significant differences for those subjects who became literate in areas of the brain important for visual and linguistic processes. Studies like these help us to understand how becoming literate as an adult strengthens new, never before experienced connections between vision and language areas of the brain, just as it would in young children who learn to read.

Structure of the book

Before we begin, a word about pronouns here will be helpful. The "I" refers to the first author, whose past and present work on the reading brain serves as the foundation for this book. The "we" refers to the collaborative work with members of the Center for Reading and Language Research, particularly linguist Dr Stephanie Gottwald, whose work with me spans the writing of several books and multiple research projects, in particular, the global literacy project described in the last chapter of the book. She supplied much of the content of the third chapter on child language, which we wrote together, and she "looked over my shoulder" on the last chapter.

With a nod to Chaucer's *Canterbury Tales*, the book itself will be divided into three conceptual sections. In the first section, based on research in psycholinguistics, child development, and cognitive neuroscience, there will be several tales that give particular perspectives on the various aspects of oral language; on the development of oral and written language in literate and non-literate children; and on the reading brain. More specifically, an overview of language in Chapter 2 ("A Linguist's Tale") presents what we hope will be an entertaining "linguistic primer" that provides the reader with the "vocabulary" of language and reading development, so as better to appreciate the critical importance of specific aspects of early language development for the development of literacy.

In Chapter 3 ("A Child's Tale") we use the science of language and reading to understand some of the differences in the development of a literate versus a non-literate child. We will consider how the literate world changes everything from children's play to the need for ever more demanding varieties of linguistic sophistication for work and leisure. What was sufficient for the demands of a non-literate environment is alarmingly inadequate for both the present literate world and the emerging digital world. We will consider how this reality creates a vast and growing divide between the literacy haves and have-nots.

My earlier attempt to describe the reading brain in some detail for the lay audience was found in *Proust and the Squid: The Story and Science of the Reading Brain*. Chapter 4 ("A Neuroscientist's Tale of Words") will, to be sure, involve new additions to this research, but in a rather unusual way that has as much to do with Plato and Walter Benjamin as with neuroscience. The purposes of this last "primer" chapter are threefold. First, I wish to provide a foundation for understanding the changes to the present and future literate brain. Second, I hope to illumine how much goes on beneath the surface of our brains when we read either a single word or a poem by Yeats or Keats, whose names will never be pronounced the same despite every surface reason that they should be. Third, I envision this material as the best preparation for what I consider the heart of reading, which will be the material in Chapter 5. Using examples in literature from Emily Dickinson to Thomas Mann to Marilynne Robinson, I hope to illustrate what I have come to call the "deep reading" processes, their variousness and their essential role in the formation of an expert reading circuit, that is the basis for a literary mind. Although I will endeavor to buttress my thoughts on deep reading with work in the cognitive neurosciences, this chapter is not so much about the brain that reads as about how reading propels our best thoughts.

Indeed, at no time in this book—that owes its very foundation to work in the neurosciences—do I differ from a statement made by Philip Davis, a professor of literature: "In all its youthful mix of imitations, possibilities, and even fantasies, brain imaging is no more and no less than one...part of a greater aspiration that must do its exploratory work at various levels and by diverse methods. The aspiration is to find what unrecognized or neglected powers the mind employs...in the most personal forms of reading."[8] I am a scholar of words who has found their study usually enhanced, and occasionally limited by the efforts of my field of cognitive neuroscience to depict their physiological reality. But more than anything else, I am uplifted by the collective efforts of varied fields to use our growing knowledge of written words to preserve their inestimable role in the evolution of our species.

Such a statement contains, like the first hint of autumn, a harbinger of concern. With knowledge of deep reading and the present reading brain as the foundation, the sixth chapter represents the denouement of this book in which many concerns will be raised about future reading brains. In it everything from the earlier chapters prepares the readers to evaluate for themselves a cognitive neuroscience-based framework for understanding the affordances of print and screen culture for new readers (young and old). Within that framework, three extremely important questions will be raised: first, what is the reality of our culture's *digital habits* from the earliest years on? Second, what are the consequences of these digital habits for the *nature of attention*? Specifically, what are the relationships between *how we attend* and *how and what we read* (e.g. decisions about text length and complexity for both reader *and* writer)? And third, given the immediacy and overwhelming volume of easily accessed information, what are our relationships to our culture's *information overload*, and its effects on *knowledge and learning*?

Ongoing research from child development, cognitive science, technology, and philosophy will be employed to create a kind of first algorithm of the critical factors necessary to evaluate: first, what needs to be sustained for the preservation of some of our most important human values; and second, what needs to be advanced to ensure that every child will acquire the skills necessary for the twenty-first century. Throughout the chapter I will discuss the implications of digital culture on the literary mind, on writing, and on text. By the end of Chapter 6 and throughout Chapter 7, the earlier direction of this book will change, like the tacking of a sailboat to harness the wind. Here we will consider the leaps in cognition and perception that can be *gained* in a transition from a more literate, print-based culture to a pervasively digital, screen-based culture.

Thus, the third and most unusual part of the book represents a cerebral turnabout in which we examine the positive affordances of the digital medium for the "democratization of knowledge" and the acquisition of literacy. It will describe an ongoing attempt to use insights from research on the literate- and digital-reading brain to address the issue of global literacy in non-literate children. We will examine how the sum of this knowledge may help usher in new forms of literacy for pastoral children who might otherwise remain non-literate members of society, and also for those children whose impoverished environment has not prepared them for full literacy.

More specifically, insights from the earlier chapters will be used to describe one of the most positive, indeed hopeful applications of our knowledge about the reading brain. I will describe a radical study of a digitally based, learning-to-read experience, conducted by a team of researchers and technology experts from our Center for Reading and Language Research at Tufts University, the MIT Media Lab in Boston (with technology design expert Tinsley Galyean and robotics scientist Cynthia Breazeal), and Georgia State University in Atlanta (with eminent methodologist and neuropsychologist Robin Morris). Chapter 7 will document how children in remote regions of Ethiopia, settlement schools in South Africa, and preschools in Uganda, India, and the rural United States are learning pre-reading skills from digital tablets designed to encourage the development of oral and written language in young children.

The growth of the children's social, linguistic, and cognitive skills in these different environments is providing an unexpected source of information about what occurs in literacy's early acquisition when there are no or few teachers available. Although our deployments in these areas were initiated as an attempt to bring literacy to remote places in the world, this work provides us with an unanticipated petri dish for studying the emergence of literacy and its consequences in a group of children who have never seen symbolic text. As such, it has given our group a new, unexpected vehicle for studying over the next decade how access to literacy can become a means of increasing the health, economic development, and educational achievement of children both in developing regions of the world and also in our own backyard.

The final goal in this project will be beyond the reach of our present data. We wish to understand if technology can be used in these settings in such a way that children reach not just basic pre-literacy skills, but achieve what reading scholar and my former teacher Jeanne Chall often called the "transition from learning to read to reading to learn."[9]

Within the context of this ongoing work, we are confronted with questions that go beyond our prior knowledge, even as we build upon it. For example, we know that literacy can open the mind of a child to whole new areas of learning and that the very process of becoming literate can contribute to the new reader's creativity, personal growth, and critical thought. We also know that developing such forms of thinking in a society can fuel discovery, productivity, and innovation, which, in turn, can drive economic growth, public health, and the well-being of that society.

What we do not know is whether we can germinate the process of learning to read in such a way that it encourages more sophisticated forms of reading in the absence of a teacher, by only self- and child-driven learning. If we can prove that children can learn to read well through this approach, we estimate that 100 million children could, with concerted global efforts, become literate in the next generation, with implications that give increased hope for the species' development. If we cannot prove this, we hope in the process to contribute to efforts to find what will. If H. G. Wells is correct that "human history becomes more and more a race between education and catastrophe,"[10] then this initiative provides new hope that together we can contribute to bringing new and educated members in our world to that "race." As Pope Francis stated, "Without a solution to the problems of the poor, we cannot resolve the problems of the world."[11]

An overarching goal of this book, therefore, will be to bring to life—linguistically, cortically, cognitively, emotionally, and societally— what it means to become literate for a child, an individual, and human society. From this view, literacy represents one of the most powerful cultural inventions that the species has ever created. Furthermore, if the act of reading goes beyond the species' biological endowment, it increases in the process the species' intelligence, and perhaps, its survival. By addressing both the known and unknown promise of literacy across time, across mediums, and, perhaps most unexpectedly, across vastly different cultures, my hope at the time of writing this book is that the unfolding story of a literacy initiative begun in tiny, remote villages and overcrowded slums in distant places of our world will underscore the profound, *intellectual transformation* that literacy propulses and why we must never lose it as we move ever forward.

Notes

1. Göran Sonnevi, *Mozart's Third Brain*, trans. Rika Lesser (New Haven, CT: Yale University Press, 2012), p. 1.
2. Alberto Manguel, *A History of Reading* (New York: Penguin Press, 1996).

Introduction

3. Philip Davis, Proposal for Literary Agenda series (Oxford: Oxford University Press, 2014).
4. Marcel Proust, *Days of Reading* (London: Penguin Books, 2009), p. 86.
5. Maryanne Wolf, *Proust and the Squid: The Story and Science of the Reading Brain* (New York: HarperCollins, 2007). Hereafter cited as Wolf, 2007.
6. Joseph Epstein, "You Are What You Read," *Wall Street Journal* (November 16, 2012). <http://www.wsj.com/articles/SB10001424052970203846804578102932194914110>.
7. Manuel Carreiras, Mohamed L. Seghier, Silvia Baquero, Adelina Estévez, Alfonso Lozano, Joseph T. Devlin, and Cathy J. Price, "An Anatomical Signature for Literacy," *Nature* 461, no. 7266 (October 15, 2009): pp. 983–6. doi:10.1038/nature08461. See also Stanislas Dehaene, Laurent Cohen, Jose Morais, and Regine Kolinsky, "Illiterate to Literate: Behavioural and Cerebral Changes Induced by Reading Acquisition," *Nature Reviews* 16 (2015): pp. 234–44. Hereafter cited as Dehaene, 2015.
8. Philip Davis, *Reading and the Reader: The Literary Agenda* (Oxford: Oxford University Press, 2013), p. 5. Hereafter cited as Davis.
9. Jeanne S. Chall, Vicki A. Jacobs, and Luke E. Baldwin, *The Reading Crisis: Why Poor Children Fall Behind* (Cambridge, MA: Harvard University Press, 1991), p. 14.
10. Herbert George Wells, *The Outline of History: Being a Plain History of Life and Mankind* (New York: Macmillan, 1921).
11. Jim Yardley and Simon Romero, "Pope's Focus on Poor Revives Scorned Theology," *New York Times* (May 23, 2015). Hereafter cited as Pope Francis. <http://www.nytimes.com/2015/05/24/world/europe/popes-focus-on-poor-revives-scorned-theology.html>.

2
A Linguist's Tale

"The Franklyn's Prologue"

But sires by cause I am a burel man
At my bigynnyng first I yow biseche
Haue me excused of my rude speche
I lerned neuere rethorik certeyn
Thyng that I speke it moot be bare and pleyn

But, sirs, because I am a simple man,
Right at the very start I would beseech
That you excuse my ignorant form of speech.
I've never studied rhetoric, no way,
So plain and bare must be what I've to say.

Geoffrey Chaucer, *Canterbury Tales*[1]

It is fitting that we begin this chapter and indeed the formal part of this book with an excerpt from the *Canterbury Tales*. One glance at Chaucer's Franklyn, who six centuries later still bemoans his plain, "rude speche" and lack of "rethorik," shows both how different our spoken language and written language have become and also how much remains of our Middle English roots. *Beowulf*, on the other hand, represents our best-known example of written Old English and would be almost indecipherable, except by English literature majors and those who have studied its varied roots, as Irish poet Seamus Heaney's translation and his writing about this translation make beautifully clear.[2] Although the poem may well date back centuries earlier, a time-traveler to tenth-century England would be both frustrated and intrigued at the extent to which the language we call English has changed its pronunciation and spelling systems, even though a core of basic words and many aspects of grammar remain the same.

A Linguist's Tale

The interdigitation of these *word fossils* alongside the "new" words, which came from over a millennium of conquests, cultural shifts, cross-linguistic influences, and technological inventions, has produced an oral and written language whose roots and parts bear the stamp of many centuries, cultures, and languages. Words from Old and Middle English, French, German, Latin, and Greek, as well as from the newest influx of words based on our technologies, have commingled to produce a dynamic, thriving, changing written language that wears its history on its sleeve: that is, the very spelling of its words. An understanding of this living language and how our words carry within them the history of our language is essential to an understanding both of literacy and of the changing reading brain.

This chapter will introduce terms and concepts about language and literacy that come from linguistics, psycholinguistics,[3] and cognitive neuroscience.[4] Our goal is to provide a working vocabulary that will serve the reader as a foundation for the rest of the book. With this said, we wish to follow the worried example of another researcher who had to introduce basic linguistic concepts only partially known to his readership. He graciously invoked Doris Lessing's preface to the *Golden Notebook*,[5] where she exhorted her readers to *skip whatever was necessary to keep their interest going*!

A linguistic primer for oral and written language

My friend and colleague, linguist Ray Jackendoff, wrote a singularly elegant, very scholarly book, *Foundations of Language*,[6] in which he used one simple sentence about a little star and a big star to illustrate many of the extraordinary properties of language. Most recently, he wrote one of the most whimsically written and accessible works of erudition I have ever read on the topic of language and thought, *A User's Guide to Thought and Meaning*.[7] With no small amount of time with his tongue held firmly in cheek, he created a new genre for discussing some of the most complex issues about language and consciousness, and for describing what a *cognitive perspective* on both entails. With his permission we shamelessly follow his lead, albeit with just one word and with far more modest goals.

We will begin with the word *bear*. With over one million possible words in the English lexicon, it may be surprising that I wish to redeploy the word *bear*, which I have used as an example for one thing or another upon many occasions. The reality is that *bear* is one of my favorite (and easiest) words to illustrate multiple linguistic concepts, and in the process, bring to life what poets knew long before contemporary linguistics: the world that is contained in every word.

Analyze what you know about this single word, and you'll have your own bird's eye perch from which to view many of the different linguistic systems important to language study by linguists, psycholinguists, educators, and neuroscientists. There are five major linguistic systems that are basic to an understanding of the many dimensions contained within a spoken or written word: *phonology, morphology, syntax, semantics,* and *pragmatics*. An additional system, *orthography*, is necessary for written words, but as we will see later, in the mind of the fully literate individual, what one *hears* while processing oral language is influenced by what one *sees* almost automatically.

All these linguistic systems play pivotal roles in the acquisition, development, and sometimes demise of oral and written language. To keep all six systems handily in memory, we use the underloved, nocturnal "possum" as an acronym and aide-memoire for this approach: P for phonology and pragmatics; O for orthography; S for semantics; S for syntax; M for morphology. As for the <u>, well—it stands for *und*, which means *and*, at least in German. Naming a linguistic approach after an oft-misunderstood possum (Pogo Possum does come to mind!) may seem a poor aesthetic judgment, but memory research tells us that we recall novel, and sometimes downright silly things better than more sensible ones. Our hope is that this marsupial mnemonic will help keep the major language systems in memory. Later on, we will chronicle the gradual amalgamation of all of these systems in a child's reading, along with the potential impediments that any or all of these systems could bring to reading acquisition.

Phonology

> The brain is just the weight of God,
> For Heft them Pound for Pound
> And they will differ if they do
> Like Syllable from Sound.
>
> Emily Dickinson[8]

In the beginning is sound: the sound of the human voice—its melody, rhythm, sonority, stresses, and pauses, all of which help the ear discriminate the large and small units of speech, our *syllables* and *phonemes*. These units of sound are integral to everything we do and think, and they have more layers and tacit rules than meets the eye—or ear. Phonology involves the study of all of these layers in the sound system of a language, as well as the rules governing how phonemes form syllables and words. Many people understandably confuse or conflate phonology, phonemes, and *phonetics* with the more frequently heard word, *phonics*, and indeed all these words share the same Greek root, *phon*, for sound. Phonics, however, refers to a method of teaching reading that emphasizes the sounds represented by letters and letter patterns, and is something very separate from the rest of these linguistic terms, which are our principal foci here.

Our chosen word *bear* is made up of a particular sequence of tiny individual sounds, called *phonemes*. Each spoken language has its own particular, limited set of phonemes. English has approximately forty-four to forty-six phonemes with the "approximate" based on the regional and dialectal differences that influence this number. By contrast, Italian has thirty phonemes and the Hawaiian language has only twelve, which is why that language contains so many words with unusual-sounding repetitions of syllables and phonemes. The colorful Hawaiian state fish, *humuhumunukunukuapua'a*, is my personal favorite. Some phonemes are unique to a particular language. For example, the multiple African click sounds—which are made by moving your tongue rapidly down from the roof or palate of your mouth—are unique to certain African languages like Hottentot in Southwest Africa and in Xhosa, one of the official languages of South Africa. Many believe that the click sounds were present in the first human languages. Numerous phonemes, like our common vowel sounds, are shared across multiple languages.

Four tiers of sound

> Human speech is like a cracked kettle on which we beat crude rhythms for bears to dance to, while we long to make music that will melt the stars.
>
> Gustave Flaubert, *Madame Bovary*[9]

Ray Jackendoff describes four levels or *tiers* that make up a word's sounds. We like to think of the first tier as *melody*—that is, the word's *prosodic* structure. Perhaps we may never attain what Flaubert recognizes as part of the yearning of humans, but it is the case that music or melody is the first aspect of language that babies hear in speech, at least as early as six weeks before they are born, and one of the first things they produce after they come into the world. Prosody or melody is the aspect of speech that is conveyed by the rhythm, intonation, and *stress patterns* in our pronunciation. There were wonderfully clever experiments by French scientist Jacques Mehler and his colleagues[10] that show that prenatal babies hear and recognize the prosodic contours of their mother's speech in the womb, much like we would be able to hear the muffled ups and downs of conversations from in the next room.

Further, both four-day-old newborn humans *and* our little tamarin monkey cousins can recognize and respond to the rhythm and melody of their own language and not respond to those of another language. A creative dissertation study by Juan Toro[11] showed that this capacity extends to another mammalian species—rats. Just by using the rhythmic contours of Dutch vs Japanese, the rats could detect which language was which—for a nice reward, of course. Such experiments indicate how very much the child is learning prenatally about this earliest phonological tier, which can be processed by several mammals. The first dimension of language, therefore, is melody.

In one-syllable words like *bear*, stress and intonation are not so obvious, but in multi-syllable words and sentences, they can be key. They both help convey not only a word's correct pronunciation, but also at times the speaker's underlying message. For example, in "No one guessed that the bear had eaten the zookeeper," it is the stress on *bear*, *eat*, and *zoo* that provides extra clarifying information to the listener. These stress patterns in oral language also help listeners and readers detect the second tier in a word's phonological structure, the *syllabic* structure. Each syllable has a *nucleus*, a *rhyme*, and an *onset*. The nucleus is usually the vowel that the syllable revolves around, and a rhyme is almost always just what it sounds like—the vowel-consonant pattern that rhymes in any word (e.g. the <ear> in *bear*, and the <ap> in *trap*). The onset is the first phoneme or phoneme cluster that precedes the rhyme (e.g. <b> in *bear* and <tr> in *trap*).

British researchers Usha Goswami and Jenny Thomson[12] demonstrate how important it is for young children who are first learning to read to be able to use stress information to detect the syllable boundaries in words. They have found that children at risk for reading disabilities have particular difficulty detecting some of the important acoustic information in what is called the *speech amplitude envelope* that helps us perceive phonemes in words. Their research highlights the layers of tacit knowledge important for producing or perceiving sounds in words for children learning to read with or without extra challenges like dyslexia.

The third and fourth tiers involve the *segmental* structure, including the phonemes and their distinctive features. Each phoneme in every language has a set of distinctive features used to categorize it—like whether it makes a voiced (e.g. /b/) or unvoiced sound (e.g. /p/), or where the phoneme is articulated (e.g. at the front or back of the mouth). The feature of voicing depends on how and when air is vibrated across our vocal folds. For /b/ the vocal folds start vibrating very early into the next vowel at around 20 milliseconds; for /p/ the vibrations occur later. Try putting your hand on your throat as you make a /p/ or a /b/. In voiced sounds like /b/, you can feel vibrations in your throat, while in unvoiced sounds like /p/, you should not be able to feel any vibrations.

To visually transcribe these individual sounds, there is a *phonetic* system that can be used to depict every human phoneme. Thus *bear* becomes /b/+/ɛ/+/r/. Notice that the /r/ makes what is called an r-controlled vowel, that is actually something between one and two sounds. When a voiced /r/ follows a vowel, it changes the sound of the vowel considerably more than an unvoiced letter like /t/ (e.g. *bat*). Words aren't a matter of a strict, serial production of one discrete sound following another; rather, spoken words follow a system for *connecting* their sounds in such a way that each phoneme affects the one following it. There are important phonological rules in each language that speakers are unaware of, but that govern how phonemes work together to form words in speech. The reality we will return to, especially in a child's development, is that the way we speak has rules we never knew we followed.

To illustrate, a major principle in how phonemes are connected to form words is called *coarticulation*. It describes the reality of how phonemes are "shingled together" to make continuous speech, an apposite description first made by Isabelle Liberman, Don Shankweiler, and their colleagues at Haskins Laboratory.[13] The process of shingling phonemes together changes how each one sounds. Consider the /b/ sound in *bear*, compared to the /b/ sound in *boot*. The latter /b/ causes our lips to round to prepare for the further rounding of the lips in /oo/. Coarticulation may sound simple, but it quickly becomes complicated during reading acquisition when the teacher asks children to "sound out" or give the sounds of the letters in a word. It also becomes complicated when you are first learning a foreign language and all the speech sounds appear fused and indecipherable. And it becomes very complicated indeed, if, like our Greek ancestors, you want to create a writing system capable of representing every sound inside all our words.

The problems caused by coarticulation are more than outweighed, however, by the overwhelming advantages it bestows on language: it is the glue within a *combinatorial* system that enables a relatively small number of phonemes to produce a huge number of possible combinations of sound patterns for words. There was a most unusual invention by Georg Harsdoerffer[14] called the "thought ring" in which five movable rings composed of different German phonemes could combine to produce 97,209,600 words. Although we remain unconvinced about the precision of Harsdoerffer's number of possible German words, his ambitious concept provides a bizarrely appropriate illustration of the combinatorial principle of phonemes in any language.

Imagine how different our languages would be if each word had to be represented by a single different sound. This is exactly the case with our cousins the vervet monkeys who make a different sound or call for each of their predators: eagle, snake, leopard, etc. It would be incredibly difficult for us if we had to make, much less remember, a different sound per word. Without this combinatorial capacity in our phonological system, our vocabulary possibilities would be immensely narrowed, with many implications for the rest of our language use.

Morphology

> livingly
> here
> a livingly free mysterious

> dreamsoul floatstands
> oak by birth by maple
> pine...
>
> e. e. cummings, *Complete Poems 1913–1962*[15]

The poet e. e. cummings probably made more creative use of morphemes, the smallest meaningful parts of a language, than any other modern writer except Lewis Carroll, whom we will also discuss a little later. Morphology refers to the system of rules for how words are formed. Morphemes can be stems like <bear>, prefixes that precede the stem (e.g. *over*bearing), or suffixes that follow the stem (e.g. bear*able*). Many of our English prefixes and suffixes are derived from Latin and Greek. The Tagalog language in the Philippines even has *infixes* inside the stem. Most of us are unaware that we too have some rather creative infixes in English, some of which may come as a surprise. For example, there is a word-that-cannot-be-said that begins with an <f>, that rhymes with *duck*, and that is sometimes—that is, on the rarest of occasions—used by my sons as an infix in some of their words. In an otherwise learned book on word formation, Mark Aronoff[16] spends no small amount of time expounding on words with this same infix—like fan-f—in'-tastic. All to say, morphology appears to be as dynamic as every other aspect of language.

But back to tamer things, like *bears*, for example, which has two morphemes: *bear*, and <s>. The <s> in *bears* is a morpheme that can convey either plurality, if it is used with a noun, or the present tense, if used with a verb; or even possession, if used with an apostrophe—like *bear's*. The phonological aspect within the morpheme <s> has a surprise or two. Unlike what you might think at first, the <s> in *bears* is not pronounced like an /s/, but always as /z/. This is because of *tacit* phonological rules which only linguists are aware of, but that every native speaker uses without a thought. These rules determine how the phoneme <s> is pronounced, based on whatever phoneme precedes it. All vowels and voiced consonants like <d>, <b>, <g>, <m>, and <r> require a /z/ pronunciation, while consonants which are not voiced (e.g. <f>, <k>, <p>, <t>) require an /s/ sound. Thus we have *lions* and *tigers* and *bears* with the /z/ pronunciation, and *cats* and *aardvarks* with the /s/.

If you think you, who are very informed adults, never knew this before, just consider what the irrepressible linguist Jean Berko Gleason[17] found with little children using her infamous "wug" test of morphological knowledge. Picture in your mind one prototypical little bird that is named a "wug." Now imagine two of them. What do you have now? You have two "_____" (fill in the blank). Chances are very, very good that you, like every four-year-old, pronounced "wugs" with a /z/. This is because we internalize morpho-phonological rules like these as we learn language, even though we may have little to no awareness of this knowledge.

Morphology is tremendously important to an understanding of reading's development because it conveys information related not only to phonology, but also to the semantic component (the system for meaning), and to the grammatical system. For example, the addition of little morphemes like <s> and <ed> can change the grammatical parts of speech (e.g. from *bat* to *batted*), while suffixes (like <able>) and prefixes (like <un>) can change both the word's part of speech and meaning (e.g. from *bear* to *unbearable*). For early readers morphemes provide extremely important input because they immediately provide clues to meaning and function which, in turn, increase their comprehension and fluency. Very importantly, when learned well, morphemes become processed as visual chunks, rather than single letters. Thus, the word *unbearable*, which is composed of three different morphemes, is processed as a composite of three visual units. The young reader who is confronted with nine letters can be overwhelmed by the word's length; but, if the child has come to see the morphemes <un> and <able> as visual units with discrete meanings, the word is both read far faster and understood more quickly. A knowledge of morphemes is one of the great secret weapons in the arsenal of the fluent readers of the world, and most of them never know it.

In reality, a knowledge of morphemes is a part of the earliest aspects of language's development, as child linguists like Roger Brown[18] and his many students cleverly demonstrated over the years. Very young children have already acquired fourteen basic morphemes in the English language, many of them by two years of age. For these toddlers, it is part of what "comes for free" in language development, as Boston linguist Rebecca Kennedy often describes it to her students, and as Jean Berko Gleason famously illustrated with her "wugs."

Syntax

Syntax refers to the grammar of a language and its rules for sentence formation. Syntax gives language and thought an organizational scaffolding so that all speakers of a given language can understand what is or is not a sentence in that language. The twentieth century's renaissance of interest in linguistics and what came to be called cognitive science emerged in large part because of eminent MIT linguist Noam Chomsky's then revolutionary ideas about the role of syntax in language. In his modestly titled *Syntactic Structures*,[19] Chomsky described the *generative* capacity of language embodied in our ability to use a finite number of utterances to produce an infinite number of sentences. This generativity is based in large part on two properties: the *combinatorial* property which allows endless combinations of words in our sentences; and the *recursive* property which allows us to embed words, phrases, or clauses within sentences ad infinitum and still understand their relationships. Take the following example of both properties:

> The bear that ate the zookeeper who fed him dog food made of animal parts is now in an upstairs exhibit, which basically amounts to a bear's solitary confinement, which should be taboo for any living creature, but which seems, nevertheless, to encourage hordes of crowds who come to gape at the man-eating bear, which etc., etc.

Steven Pinker, a prolific cognitive scientist and language scholar whose book, *The Better Angels of our Nature*, presented the case for the decline of violence, might well shudder at our recursive bear example on several grounds. Nevertheless, we invoke him here because no one so memorably described this generative aspect of language and thought: "Because human thoughts are *combinatorial* and *recursive*, breathtaking expanses of knowledge can be explored with a finite inventory of mental tools."[20]

What underlies such an extremely productive capacity has been a heated topic of no small speculation over recent years. For example, Chomsky and evolutionary psychologists Marc Hauser and W. Tecumseh Fitch[21] hypothesized that the origins of such mental computations might be found in such early capacities as animals' navigation abilities. Their concept was that our ability to navigate the grammatical thickets in language might stem from our ancestors' abilities to navigate spatially. Such a concept is a distant kin to Dehaene and Cohen's notion of *neuronal recycling*,[22] in which cognitive processes like reading are based on earlier human functions like identifying the features in objects. We will explore the latter, thought-provoking concept later in Chapter 4.

Far better known are Chomsky's original contributions to an understanding of syntax, beginning with his distinction between a *universal* grammar, that has combinatorial and recursive principles shared by all languages, and a grammar that is particular to the individual rules of each spoken language. Chomsky revolutionized the study of language by his assertion that young human children are born with a universal grammar, that is the foundation from which they learn the particular rules of the language in their environment. As one very humble example of a very large topic, in English grammar we place our verbs together in a sentence: *The bear has eaten the very worried zookeeper's dog food*. By contrast, in German grammar many verb forms are divided, with the last verb(s) reserved for the end of the sentence:

> German: Der Baer hat auch den sehr besorgten Tierpfleger gefressen.
> Literal meaning: The bear has also the very worried zookeeper eaten.

These differences in verb use in each language reflect rules dictated by the particular grammar. As we can see from the German verb example, however, there are different intellectual demands associated with different grammatical uses: for example, different uses of short-term memory, sequencing, planning, and a useful capacity for cognitive suspension. We can also see from the last example the importance of context and "priming" for understanding the meaning of a sentence. Because you had just read a long sentence earlier about a man-eating bear, you were "primed" for the otherwise unnatural demise of the zookeeper in the German example.

Noam Chomsky was not the only Chomsky to change our views of language. Carol Chomsky[23] was one of the first investigators to understand that a child continues to develop a rich knowledge of semantics and syntax well past the age of five. In her earlier, groundbreaking work, she found that children up to the age of ten years have degrees of difficulty understanding the following sentences:

1. Maria told Patrick to go to the movies.
2. Maria promised Patrick to go to the movies.
3. Maria asked Patrick to go to the movies.

What makes these sentences difficult for children to understand is determining who is the actor of the second clause—that is, who will go to the movies. Children who were at least five years of age understood the first sentence in which Patrick is going to the movies. However, children as old as ten believed that Patrick was the one going to the movies in the second sentence. And adults and children alike have varying interpretations of the third sentence. This result is interesting because the differences in these sentences lie not just in the semantic meanings of the words *tell, promise,* and *ask*, but in the structure of the sentences that allow either the subject or the direct object or both to be the chief actor of the verb in the second clause. This does not seem to be an issue in verbs that children acquire much earlier, like *give*. Children know very early in development that the verb *give* has to have a *giver*, a recipient, and a *thing* that is given.

This is all to say, the syntactic aspects of our language scaffold our thoughts and provide the structure for their expansion and variousness. The development of our syntactic knowledge undergirds the development of our ability to read ever more complex text, which reflects ever more complex thoughts, one of the critical issues we will return to in Chapter 5.

Semantics

> 'Twas brillig, and the slithy toves
> Did gyre and gimble in the wabe:
> All mimsy were the borogoves,
> And the mome raths outgrabe.
> "Beware the Jabberwock, my son!
> The jaws that bite, the claws that catch!
> Beware the Jubjub bird, and shun
> The frumious Bandersnatch!"
>
> Lewis Carroll, "Jabberwocky"[24]

Lewis Carroll's still astonishing poem "Jabberwocky" evokes our imagination and feelings with largely nonsensical words—that is, words that seem to have no meaning. What makes Carroll's achievement all the more brilliant is that he conveys meaning to the reader with nonsense words that incorporate two important principles: first, the use of unknown but "linguistically legal" (i.e. possible) English morphemes; and second, the placement of nonsense words in syntactic contexts that require a particular, constrained range of meanings. In so doing, Carroll brings to life a very important aspect of the semantic function of language: the capacity to convey meaning not simply through the single word itself, but also through its function within particular syntactic contexts. We might never have a clue what "brillig" means by itself, but within the context of "Jabberwocky," we feel we know just what is meant—like the time of day or the weather that moment.

The semantic system refers to all that is involved in the conceptual meanings conveyed by words and sentences that help us understand our world. This includes the ways words refer to specific objects and concepts; the ways in which words and their referents can be understood in their contexts; and also the realms of meaning not captured by our words. This may seem relatively simple on the surface until a veritable maelstrom of questions about meaning, reference, consciousness, and inference begin to appear—questions that are as much the stuff of philosophy as psychology and linguistics. One of the central contributions that Ray Jackendoff makes in his cognitive perspective on thought and meaning is the light such a perspective throws on the invisible world of thought that lies *beneath our words and that is sometimes hidden by them.*

One of the reasons that we must often work so hard to express our thoughts is that these thoughts have meanings beyond our words, something which Plato tried to capture in his discussion of the inadequacy of words. We will return to Plato's conceptualization of what words can and cannot do, but in this section we wish to emphasize some of the more generous aspects of their nature: for example, the sometimes astonishing capacity for the same word to mean different things, and sometimes to mean totally opposite things.

The true beauty of the word *bear* shines in this moment, because it is what linguists call a *polysemous* word, which means that it has several,

A Linguist's Tale

very different, possible meanings. To add a little more complexity and cerebral fun, some of the meanings for *bear* occupy totally different grammatical categories (e.g. noun, verb, and adjective), which exist within very different semantic fields—that is, words that are connected to each other in meaning. For example, consider the following:

- The runaway bear entered the tent without warning and ate the man's money.
- On that very day the bear market lost the rest of the man's money. The man called his broker who briefly muttered, "Bear with me awhile longer, before doing anything rash."
- The man could bear it no longer, and contemplated the unbearable.

Don't stop. Here are two more in question form: what does the brain of a reader have to do to bring to bear all the factors that bear on choosing an accurate meaning in each of these sentences?

The reality is that you, the reader, have just processed five different meanings of *bear* in the first three sentences, with two subtly different uses of the same meaning in the last sentence. But how does the brain do that? What prepares the developing reading brain to know that the first *bear* is a frightening carnivorous beast; that the second *bear* is a noun–noun compound which has absolutely nothing to do with selling bear meat; that the third and fourth *bears* are verbs that are subtly different variants of meaning that concern the need to endure things; and that the fifth *bear* is a stem with a prefix that makes it mean the opposite of the verb *bear*? How does the young reader know what *it* refers to? How do we infer what *unbearable* refers to, virtually automatically?

Sadly, our brain does not possess its own version of an *Oxford English Dictionary* for us to access at whim. In our opinion, it has something better. When we need to connect the meaning of a spoken or written word to our stored information, we unconsciously *activate* an entire web of meanings, functions, concepts, and relationships among words. The words connected by meaning are often referred to as a "semantic neighborhood" around the selected word. In this sense, as our research teachers daily instruct our youngest would-be readers, "If you know one word really *well*, you know a hundred!" In addition to adding quantity to our lexical stores, semantic knowledge changes our understanding of how words are connected to each other by their syntactic relationships, which contributes to the ever more precise meaning we pursue.

The point is that the minute we go below the surface of what a word means, we enter the labyrinthine network of all the *word* knowledge and *world* knowledge that are activated in our minds. As for the strange word-world that Lewis Carroll ushered us into, we were able to make sense of the unknowable, nonsense words because of this shared word and world knowledge that permeates the poem's structure.

There is a related, still more important point that Ray Jackendoff makes about the mental fecundity involved in the conceptual-semantic realm: it possesses its own form of generativity, where the conceptual meanings within words—that are finite—can lead to a virtually infinite number of possible relationships amongst words and thoughts. This bold if somewhat controversial conceptualization of semantic functions expands Noam Chomsky's views on generativity, which he ascribed solely to the syntactic function of language. In Jackendoff's view, generativity is similarly embodied in the combinatorial capacities contained within several language functions—like semantics and phonology—and not unique to syntax.

Indeed as I have suggested in my earlier work, generativity lies at the core of written language *because* it embodies each of these generative language functions in syntax, phonology, and semantics, and something more elusive still. As described in the first assumption about literacy, written language allows and sometimes propels the reader to go beyond the text to *generate new thoughts*. Such thoughts often represent the coming to awareness of the invisible, unconscious concepts we possess unaware. As I will elaborate later, written language involves a systematic, enlarged cognitive workspace for our unique capacities to assimilate, reconfigure, analyze, synthesize, and sometimes transform information. Within that context I conceptualize reading as one of the most remarkable vehicles for generativity that the species has ever created. We will return with no small purpose to this conceptualization of written language when we consider "deep reading" in later chapters.

For now, despite these expansive properties within the semantic realm, we still haven't directly answered one of the originating questions in this semantic section—what the brain actually does when it encounters a polysemous word with all its multiple meanings. There is a simple answer. It activates them all. And then, after a few milliseconds, it settles down with the most sensible one for the particular context. David Swinney's[25] early, cross-modality priming research with words like *bugs* demonstrates that the brain is cortically prepared for all semantic possibilities from the outset. His work demonstrated that when we read the word *bugs*, we may consciously think of insects and crawling things, but we are also unconsciously activating far more exotic meanings and thoughts like spies and espionage. I think David Swinney would have loved to have tested *bears*. This whole dimension of polysemy is why jokes, poems, and puns work and are the delight of all ages of readers and listeners. Our brain beats us to the punchline every time. The semantic system with all the multiple dimensions barely sketched in this section is a microcosm of how our brain approaches the pluripotentiality contained in even the most humble of words like *bugs* and *bears* and the most far-fetched words like "brillig" and "frumious."

In addition, there are far more ordinary aspects of meaning inherent in things that do not involve words and that are "in your face." As any teenager knows who asks someone for a date and is greeted by a pregnant pause, there are worlds of meaning conveyed in what we don't say, as well as what we say. For this, we turn to another linguistic function, pragmatics.

Pragmatics

Pragmatics refers to an aspect of language that has its own set of rules about usage that are more culturally and contextually based and that have a great deal to do with a speaker's intentions. For example, we can say the same two words, *bear up*, in a sympathetic context to someone going through a difficult time, or as a curt directive to someone searching for the infamous bear "exhibit" up the ramp (I acknowledge that the latter is a bit of a linguist's stretch).

One of the more fascinating aspects of pragmatics and cultural rules concerns what can and cannot be spoken in a given language. Sociolinguist Chip Gidney studies all manner of pragmatic elements in the seven plus languages he speaks fluently, and those languages he studies just for fun. He maintains that in Russian the word *bear* is best avoided in typical oral discourse, because the bear is highly revered and, perhaps, even feared within some Russian traditions.

Indeed the intentional act of <u>not</u> saying a word has a very long history in many cultural traditions. For example, in ancient Egypt the sun god Ra's name could never be uttered, a tradition borne of respect for divinity that can be seen in other religions, including Judaism. A less theological, pragmatics-driven custom is found in Zulu usage in South Africa where a new wife is not to use syllables or words that include the syllables that match any part of her father-in-law's names. Consequently, nicknames are invented to refer to "that person" in conversation, a practice that must make for no small cognitive flexibility and fascinating dinner table exchanges.

Although there are many aspects of pragmatics that contribute to reading, particularly around written conversation in text and metaphorical language, we must regretfully give shorter shrift to the pragmatic contributions than are their due. On that apologetic note, we turn to what distinguishes oral and written language most visibly, the writing system or orthography.

Orthography

The aspects or components of language described till this point characterize both oral and written language. Orthography, however, is unique to written language, even though it influences how speech is processed after a person is literate. Orthography denotes both the type of writing system of a particular language and also the rules each language has for representing and/or spelling its words with its characters or letters. The first orthographies or writing systems illustrate the move from pictured objects to symbol-systems. Symbol drawings like those seen in the evocative cave paintings in France and in the Blombas Cave in South Africa are not classified as an orthography, because to our knowledge they are only pictographic—that is, picture-like approximations of a thing's reality. The earliest signs in Chinese and in our first writing systems were something between pictographic and more abstract *logographic* symbols. Logographic signs are based on the language's morphemes and immediately convey the meanings of persons, objects, actions, etc. There is one pictographic script still used in southern China for the Nakhi language.[26] As a rule, however, most writing systems developed symbols that became increasingly abstract and logographic.

All of the world's different types of writing systems can be categorized according to whether they represent the word, morpheme, syllable, or phoneme, or some combination of these levels, and according to their properties. In logographies like ancient Chinese and the historically related Kanji system in Japanese, the written characters convey meaning at the morpheme level. The word level in any language can be composed of one or several morphemes. As shown in Figure 2.1, *bear exhibit* in Chinese is composed of several morpheme-based characters.

Other writing systems represent information that has nothing to do with the meaning or concepts within words, but rather represent the internal *sound* structure of spoken words. For example, a second Japanese writing system, Kana, conveys information about a word's syllables. This type of writing system is called a *syllabary*. Syllables are the largest, basic spoken segments within words and usually, but not always, are composed of a vowel sound or some combination of consonant plus vowel. For example, *bearing* has two syllables, <bear> and <ing>.

Because syllables are so salient to the young learner, a good question is why many modern writing systems didn't use a syllabary instead of an alphabet. The answer inevitably has to do with the particular syllabic structure of the oral language. Japanese has a very simple, tidy syllabic structure with most syllables following a consonant-vowel or consonant-vowel-nasal combination. So also does Cherokee. When the great Native American leader, Sequoyah, decided to invent a writing system, he used a syllabary which was the orthography best suited for Cherokee's eighty-six syllables. English, as anyone can attest to, has hundreds and hundreds of syllables that range from a

熊-bear

熊展-bear exhibit

Figure 2.1. Chinese characters for *bear* and *bear exhibit*

single vowel (<a>) to consonant-consonant-consonant-vowel-consonant-consonant-consonant (e.g. *stretch*). Thus a syllabary works elegantly for some oral languages like Japanese and Cherokee, but would prove a nightmare for others like English.

Many writing systems were and are combinations of the different levels of analysis and their logographic and phonetic properties. Many people falsely assume that modern Chinese is a purely logographic system with pictographic signs. Chinese became over time a logosyllabic system with some phonetic properties. In fact, most Chinese logographs are no longer pictographic, and as Chinese changed, its characters also began to incorporate more information about the pronunciation or sound structure of the syllables in the words depicted. Many common Chinese logographs have phonetic markers within them called *determinatives*, that convey how a sign is to be pronounced at the syllabic level. The majority of the 3,500 most-used Chinese signs contain this phonetic element.

It is a matter of great interest to me how other phonetic properties found their way into different types of Chinese writing, particularly for women and children. Chinese children learn a tiny alphabet-like system called *pin yin* to help them first learn the concept of how writing conveys our words' sounds. And, a most curious form of an older writing system—used only by women—was completely based on phonetic translations of the sounds of Chinese words. I have described elsewhere the strange story of *nu shu* writing, "female writing," which is poignantly depicted in Lisa See's novel, *Snow Flower and the Secret Fan*.[27] Now extinct, *nu shu* was a kind of writing that was drawn on exquisitely formed ribs of delicately painted fans or sewn into beautiful textiles. It was used only within a special *laotong* relationship between two women, after marriages—that were often difficult—had been arranged for them. *Nu shu* writing is a poignant reminder of the powerful role that writing has played in many lives across many writing systems.

Like Chinese, the English writing system hides many mysteries in its similarly historical mix of linguistic units and features. At its surface, English represents the third major type of writing system, the *alphabet*, where written symbols (called *graphemes*) represent the smallest individual sounds or phonemes within the spoken language. The *alphabetic principle* represents one of the most cognitively sophisticated sets of insights about the relationship between oral and written language. The alphabet is based on three central concepts: 1) that words are composed of small units of sounds (i.e. phonemes); 2) that visual symbols (i.e. graphemes) can be created to represent those sounds; and 3) that there are precise rules governing this correspondence between graphemes and phonemes (i.e. grapheme–phoneme correspondence rules or letter–sound rules).

There are many kinds of alphabets. Modern Hebrew and Arabic represent systems which convey largely consonant-based information, although "pointed Hebrew" gives children additional information about vowels up until the time they are launched as readers. I have written at some length about the fascinating connections between ancient Hebrew scripts and the history of the Greek alphabet. Suffice to say here, that Greek is not the first true alphabet, but is the first almost "perfect" one, where each phoneme has a corresponding letter. Since the creation of the Greek alphabet, most alphabetic systems have had, in principle, a letter for every phoneme, whether consonant or vowel, but many alphabet systems are less than perfect. An absolutely perfect correspondence would go both ways, where each sound in the oral language has only one grapheme or grapheme pattern to express, and each grapheme or grapheme pattern can always be pronounced one way with one sound that it represents.

Morphology expert Marcia Henry[28] observes that English has forty-six plus phonemes and 1,120 ways to represent them! The <ea> in our trusty *bear* is a perfect example of English's many imperfect correspondences between phonemes and graphemes. Just consider the following <ea>-filled sentence which came to me literally in a *dream* long ago, and which I like to use to illustrate the enigma of English with a few newly dreamed up elaborations every time:

> The beautiful bear created a fair, albeit embarrassingly bare, portrait of her beatific earth clan that hung at the rear of the sealed off room, above the hearth, under the beams.

Within this one sentence there are at least seven (seven to nine, depending on your dialect) different pronunciations for <ea>; and four different spellings for the <air> in *bear*. One could go on, but won't, for your sake.

All to say: the English alphabet may not be for the faint of heart, but there are good reasons for this. Most of these reasons have to do with how our writing system developed. The history of English words—indeed the history of any orthography—gets complicated because our languages and writing systems change over time, just as we described at the outset of this chapter. Thus, although it would seem all well and good on the surface to say that Chinese orthography is morpheme-based, and that the English alphabet is phoneme-based, in fact, this does not begin to capture the rich histories in both languages that are depicted in their writing systems and that changed them in the process.

Indeed, English is actually a *morphophonemic* writing system because it represents both morphemes and phonemes in its spelling. This single, albeit complicating, fact is the root cause of many a complaint and frustration to both new and old readers, as George Bernard Shaw made famous with his *ghoti* example.[29]

In reality, English words with many a seemingly vexatious letter like the silent <g> in *sign* are actually *signaling* their morphemic connection to the entire family of words like *signature* and *signatory* and *signal* in which the phoneme <g> *is* pronounced. Many a bewilderingly spelled word is actually demonstrating how English words reflect their history and their connections to an underlying family of semantically and morphemically related words.

I have saved one of the most interesting and most sensible writing systems in the world for my last example of an orthography: Korean *Hangul*. This carefully thought-out writing system was invented wholecloth in the middle of the fifteenth century by a very enlightened ruler, King Sejong. Discouraged by the inability of most of his subjects to learn Korean's older Chinese-influenced writing system, King Sejong set out to create a highly regular alphabet that would render the Korean spoken language in a logical, simple form that could be universally learned. George Bernard Shaw would have loved it. As indelicately described by fifteenth-century scholar Chong In-Ji in the king's manual to Hangul, "The bright can learn it in a single morning and even the not-so-bright can do so within ten days."[30] King Sejong wanted a system that everyone could read, as he explicitly wrote, "without regard to whether they are of noble birth or mean...even *women* and *girls*" (our italics).

If one were to try to design a new writing system today knowing everything we know now about how written language works and particularly how it is acquired, it would have many of the same principles as King Sejong's 500-year-old Hangul. Because Korean's spoken language is full of simple syllables and simple phonemes, Hangul's characters represent these syllables, but in a unique way that uses each Korean phoneme. For example, as seen in Figure 2.2 of the Korean word for *bear*, each scripted syllable consists of two to four graphed phonemes that make up a square, that is to be read left-to-right, top-to-bottom. Thus Korean has sometimes been classified as something between an alphabet and a syllabary, because it uses characters for each phoneme to make up the blocks containing each syllabic unit.

What should temper the ire of any English reader who remains disgruntled with English's irregularity is how the "more perfect" Korean developed over time. As cognitive scientist and reading researcher Charles Perfetti[31] observed, Korean and English share more than one might think in terms of historical word formation. In order to handle just the kinds of expanding vocabulary English has had to assimilate, modern Korean Hangul departed from its almost perfect grapheme–phoneme correspondence to accommodate the growing morphological relationships among new words, many of which were derived from older ones. Thus, just as with the English "sign-signature" example, new Korean words are given spellings that portray their underlying morphological relatedness to other words, rather than being spelled with their potentially perfect grapheme–phoneme relationships.

It is another living example of the morpheme–phoneme "trade-off" and of the ways that language changes over time to accommodate the intellectual and cultural growth of its speakers. The conscious choice of this trade-off in Korean illustrates how critical a role morphological information plays in language change, even when it means sacrificing some degree of regularity in writing and ease in learning.

곰

Figure 2.2. Korean *bear*

Very importantly for later chapters and an understanding of the reading brain, each of these kinds of writing systems has direct analogues in the brain's organization for reading. Each writing system requires something a little different in how the brain organizes itself to read, a fact we will return to in the next chapters.

But first, as a rather unusual method of reviewing several of the linguistic concepts described in this chapter, we will end with a single sentence that rivals Proust's average sentence length.

The linguist's tale of a bear

Once there was a very busy bear who ate a zookeeper and also the money of a man who lost his money in a market which is known for its man-eating practices in many parts of the modern world, which, to be sure, is not saying much if a zookeeper can get eaten by a bear just because he was never informed that the dog food he fed the bear was made of animal parts, including the brains of some animals, which is doubly bad, since some people like Descartes believe that brains contain the human soul, even though others think brains are gelatinous globs of slithy cells, a view you will be soon disabused of in our discussion of the reading brain in Chapter 4.

Notes

1. Geoffrey Chaucer, *The Canterbury Tales: A Complete Translation into Modern English*, trans. Ronald L. Ecker and Eugene J. Crook (Palatka, FL: Hodge & Braddock Publishers, 1993).
2. Seamus Heaney (trans.), *Beowulf: A New Verse Translation* (New York: W. W. Norton & Company, 2001).
3. The study of the psychology of language.
4. The study of how the brain is organized for mental functions that range from language and perception to memory and affect.
5. Doris Lessing, *The Golden Notebook* (New York: Simon & Schuster, 1962), p. xii.
6. Ray Jackendoff, *Foundations of Language* (London: Oxford University Press, 2002).
7. Ray Jackendoff, *A User's Guide to Thought and Meaning* (Oxford: Oxford University Press, 2012).
8. Emily Dickinson, *The Complete Poems of Emily Dickinson* (Boston, MA: Little, Brown, 1960).
9. Gustave Flaubert, *Madame Bovary*, trans. Francis Steegmuller (New York: 1857), pt 1, ch. 12.

10. Jacques Mehler and Emmanuel Dupoux, *What Infants Know* (Cambridge: Blackwell, 1994).
11. Juan M. Toro, Joseph B. Trobalon, and Nuria Sebastian Galles, "The Use of Prosodic Cues in Language Discrimination Tasks by Rats," *Animal Cognition* 6 (2003): pp. 131–6. doi:10.1007/s10071-003-0172-0.
12. Jennifer M. Thomson and Usha Goswami, "Learning Novel Phonological Representations in Developmental Dyslexia: Associations with Basic Auditory Processing of Rise Time and Phonological Awareness," *Reading and Writing* 23, no. 5 (2010): pp. 453–73. doi:10.1007/s11145-009-9167-9.
13. Donald Shankweiler and Isabelle Y. Liberman, "Misreading: A Search for Causes." In James F. Kavanagh and Ignatius G. Mattingly (eds), *Language by Ear and by Eye: The Relationship between Speech and Reading* (Cambridge, MA: MIT Press, 1972), pp. 293–329.
14. Gerhart Hoffmeister, "Georg Philipp Harsdörffer," *The Literary Encyclopedia*, July 14, 2007. <http://www.litencyc.com/php/speople.php?rec=true&UID=11808>.
15. e. e. cummings, *Complete Poems 1913–1962* (New York: Harcourt, Brace and Jovanovich, 1972), no. 658.
16. Mark Aronoff, *Word Formation in Generative Grammar* (Cambridge, MA: MIT Press, 1976).
17. Jean Berko Gleason, "The Child's Learning of English Morphology Revisited." In Diana S. Natalicio and Luiz F. S. Natalicio (eds), *Learning: A Journal of Research in Language Studies* 19, nos. 3–4 (2006): pp. 205–15. doi:10.1111/j.1467-1770.1969.tb00463.x.
18. Roger Brown, *A First Language: The Early Years* (Cambridge, MA: Harvard University Press, 1973).
19. Noam Chomsky, *Syntactic Structures* (The Hague: Mouton, 1957).
20. Steven Pinker, *The Better Angels of our Nature* (New York: Penguin Books, 2011); Steven Pinker, *The Language Instinct* (New York: Harper Perennial, 1997), p. 360.
21. Marc Hauser, Noam Chomsky, and William Tecumseh Fitch, "The Faculty of Language: What Is It, Who Has It, and How Did It Evolve?" *Science* 298, no. 5598 (2002): pp. 1569–79. doi:10.1126/science.298.5598.1569.
22. Stanislas Dehaene, *Reading in the Brain* (New York: Penguin Viking, 2009).
23. Carol Chomsky, "Stages in Language Development and Reading Exposure," *Harvard Educational Review* 42 (1972): pp. 1–33. doi: 10.17763/haer.42.1.h78l676h28331480.
24. Lewis Carroll, "Jabberwocky." In *The Complete Works of Lewis Carroll* (New York: Modern Library, 1896/1936), p. 153.
25. David Swinney and David Hakes, "Effects of Prior Context upon Lexical Access during Sentence Comprehension," *Journal of Verbal Learning and Verbal Behavior* 15 (1976): pp. 681–9. doi:10.1016/0022-5371(76)90060-8.
26. Gerry T. M. Altmann and Andrea Enzinger, *The Ascent of Babel: An Exploration of Language, Mind, and Understanding* (Oxford: Oxford University Press, 1999), p. 231.
27. Lisa See, *Snow Flower and the Secret Fan* (New York: Random House, 2005).
28. Marcia Henry, *Unlocking Literacy: Effective Decoding and Spelling Instruction* (Baltimore, MD: Paul H. Brookes, 2003).

29. For the few of you unfamiliar with this uniquely Shavian diatribe, he said that only in English could "ghoti" spell "fish"! For example, if one combines the pronunciations of "gh" in "laugh"; "o" in "baron"; and "ti" in "tion," it could be pronounced "fish." It is said that Shaw wanted to give a huge reward to anyone who would "clean up" English and make a new, transparent spelling system, which would henceforth be called... "Shavian"! There appear to have been no takers at the time, though there are no end to the various unsuccessful attempts to regularize English spelling.
30. J.-R. Cho and Connie McBride-Chang, "Correlates of Korean Hangul Acquisition among Kindergartners and Second Graders," *Scientific Studies of Reading* 9 (2005): pp. 3–16. doi:10.1207/s1532799xssr0901_2.
31. Charles Perfetti, "The Universal Grammar of Reading," *Scientific Studies of Reading* 7 (2003): pp. 3–24. doi:10.1207/S1532799XSSR0701_02.

3
A Child's Tale

On turning ten

> The whole idea of it makes me feel
> like I'm coming down with something,
> something worse than any stomach ache
> or the headaches I get from reading in bad light-
> a kind of measles of the spirit,
> a mumps of the psyche,
> a disfiguring chicken pox of the soul.
> You tell me it is too early to be looking back,
> but that is because you have forgotten
> the perfect simplicity of being one
> and the beautiful complexity introduced by two.
> But I can lie on my bed and remember every digit.
> At four I was an Arabian wizard.
> I could make myself invisible
> by drinking a glass of milk a certain way.
> At seven I was a soldier, at nine a prince.
> But now I am mostly at the window
> watching the late afternoon light.
> Back then it never fell so solemnly
> against the side of my tree house,
> and my bicycle never leaned against the garage
> as it does today,
> all the dark blue speed drained out of it.
> This is the beginning of sadness, I say to myself,
> as I walk through the universe in my sneakers.
> It is time to say good-bye to my imaginary friends,
> time to turn the first big number.
> It seems only yesterday I used to believe
> there was nothing under my skin but light.
> If you cut me I would shine.

> But now when I fall upon the sidewalks of life,
> I skin my knees. I bleed.
>
> Billy Collins, "On Turning Ten"[1]

It is, for most but not all of us, a wonderful thing to remember childhood. For the very fortunate among us, childhood evokes the most halcyon of memories, particularly, as Marcel Proust described in poignant detail, those days immersed in the "divine pleasure" of a favorite book. Not all childhoods are created equal. Many children never dream of becoming a soldier or a prince, like Billy Collins once did, because they never encountered one, either in their environments or in the books and poems they never heard nor read.

The gap between literate and non-literate children is not an absolute one in this country or any other. Rather it is a continuum with a very large range that is heavily influenced by the single chance fact of where the child is born and grows up. For the approximately 57 million children in the world who are completely non-literate, most, though not all of them, live in places where there are no schools and no hint of written materials. Another 150–200 million live where the schools are so overcrowded and the teachers so overtaxed and under-trained that it is almost as if there is no school. Most of these children are unlikely to acquire anything beyond the most basic of literacy skills.

Most children in the developed world will acquire some degree of reading skills, but with a more insidiously subtle version of the same continuum in which how-and-what you read is also based on how-and-where you live. In the US, for example, there remains a long discussed, seemingly intractable *gap* between the reading skills of many, more privileged European-American students and many, less privileged African-American and Hispanic students. Although there are plentiful anecdotal and individual cases of schools where the gap has been closed, the National Assessment of Educational Progress[2] notes that the gap has changed very little since 1992, in spite of sustained efforts and increased financial attention in many parts of the US. Unlike countries like highest-ranked Finland, which distributes educational resources according to the needs of every individual child over the kindergarten to twelfth grade schooling period,[3] the resources of most US public schools still heavily depend on the taxes

A Child's Tale

within their communities, and the involvement of that community in the schools. The gap that has emerged in the US represents another variation of the Matthew Effect, where the rich get richer and the poor get poorer.[4]

In this chapter we will argue that the present literacy gap begins from the very first day any child is born into a non-literate or semi-literate home, where there is little exposure to print and books, and where little reading ever occurs by an adult or between any member of the household and the child. Within this book's overarching theme, *what it means to be literate*, there is an implicit question—what it means *not* to be literate. As alluded to in our opening chapter, no discussion of literacy can be divorced from cultural factors that are intrinsically untidy and easily misinterpreted. Although these factors are never absent from the authors' consciousness, they remain outside our scholarly goals in this book. Rather, we seek here to understand the *additive* cognitive, linguistic, and affective effects of literacy on the young child's life, in order to better foster what is most important about literacy in all children whatever their cultures or environments. For those reasons, we wish to structure this chapter in terms of a developmental comparison of the first years of life growing up in a literate environment, in comparison to a home where there is no exposure to print. This is a difficult task, for there is much more known about the former than the latter. We do so, however, because the stakes are higher than ever and the Matthew Effect worse than ever for the children of the near future.

Pre-reading can last a very long time

As discussed at some length in several chapters in *Proust and the Squid*, the development of reading passes through various phases from pre-reading through the acquisition and development of fluent comprehension and deep reading skills. One of the most important reading theorists of the twentieth century, Jeanne Chall,[5] proposed six stages for a sequence for these skills that should be mastered in each developmental level of becoming literate. Although the later phases of reading will be interwoven into later chapters, in this chapter on the Child's Tale, we will concentrate on Chall's pre-reading and beginning periods as the backdrop for understanding what happens before the child ever enters kindergarten in a literate environment, but not in a non-literate one.

Two major questions will scaffold this comparison and highlight the *additive effects* of literacy in these two critical moments of a child's life. First, what is learned that is pertinent to oral and written language during the pre-reading stage in both environments? Second, what changes result from the child's acquisition of literacy?

One of the simplest, yet single most important foundations for literacy concerns whether or not a child is *read to* from early on. Indeed studies from Carol Chomsky[6] in the 1970s to Catherine Snow and her colleagues[7] in the recent past show that being read to remains one of the most powerful predictors we have of later reading ability. There is some educational research and some important applications in pediatric medicine that bear on this issue. For example, in a survey conducted by the National Survey of Early Childhood Health, it was found that only 52 per cent of the 2,000 parents in the study read to their children every day, but it gave no detail on when those families began to read to their children. In another smaller study in Ontario, with parents who ranged from low to upper-middle income, some of the parents reported beginning to read to their children sporadically at seven months and regularly at eighteen months of age.[8] To be sure, no studies have been conducted to ascertain whether reading to a seven-month-old means sitting and reading a story to the end, or thumbing through the book till the child finished *chewing* on it. We feel the latter can be as conducive for enjoying a book at this age as the former!

Pediatricians have long understood this. Indeed, they have demonstrated across the country and in some parts of Africa that the simple act of giving young parents (most of whom had little training for their new roles) a small bag of age-appropriate books at every well-visit quickly becomes an invitation to read to their children. Pediatricians Barry Zuckerman and Perri Klass and their associates joined forces to create a national Reach Out and Read (ROaR) program that has had singular success in alerting parents to the importance of reading to the young child.[9] Pam High[10] at the Brown University School of Medicine reported that one of the results of their local ROaR intervention was a change in how many additional books came into the household. Many parents had no idea that reading to a toddler, much less an infant, was even appropriate, much less desirable.

A Child's Tale

Indeed, the natural response of many an unknowing parent is to ask why any sensible parent would read to a baby if the child cannot possibly understand the story or pay attention to it for any length. There are many good answers. Each of them helps to provide an overview of what goes on in an enriched pre-literacy environment. First, decades of research into children's emotional and social development have shown that children not only crave physical contact and attention, they can, in fact, die without it.[11] The human brain, but especially the infant brain, is wired to feel well-being and security from touch and from the human voice. What makes the act of reading so special in the life of the child is the way this natural emotional and tactile interaction becomes linked with it. As *Pat the Bunny* and *Runaway Bunny* become more and more the stuff of routine, the developing infant learns to associate the reading of books with the most fundamental of human feelings—love and comfort.

Over the course of this book, we will be constructing with the reader an understanding of how the reading brain comes into being. It is wonderful to think that the first building blocks of what will become the reading brain circuit are the feelings activated when the beloved parent reads to the child. Although one hates to think of Pavlov's infamous dogs at such a tender moment, it is likely enough that over time the act of reading to one's child contributes to making the very sight of a book associated with pleasure and comfort. (Note: it is probably the case at this moment in the chapter that the twenty-first-century reader cannot suppress the twenty-first-century parents' question—will tablets and laptops do the same thing as a book on a lap? It is an important question, and a tough one. For now, however, we will leave you to your own devices, to return with something of a vengeance to this question in Chapter 6.)

Before going further, we wish to add a personal, additional implication of what it means to connect reading to the sense of touch and the feeling of being loved. We have come to believe that such a fundamental association to literacy can prove to be an emotional lifeline for those children who, years later, may find themselves struggling to learn to read, something that is, at least at the moment, difficult to predict. In our clinical work, both of us have worked with children who have had to endure enormous struggles over many years before they became proficient readers. While it would be difficult to prove, we strongly suspect that the resilience and perseverance that many children show in their efforts to learn to read may represent a by-product of their earliest, powerful, and positive associations with reading.

A second reason why reading to one's child is important concerns the role of *joint or shared attention* discovered from research on learning and language development in infants. Simply put, infants pay very close attention to the objects that adults point to or look at. Reading to an infant provides a superb opportunity for *sustained joint attention*. The young child and her typically doting reading partner share a narrative, look at and examine the illustrations, and, often as not, create a kind of dialogue with the book's content as the focus. Children learn a great deal more than you might think as a function of social engagement over a book. When parents point something out to a one-year-old, they are assisting in the young child's overwhelming task of determining the relevance or importance of an idea or object. There is much to learn and pay attention to in what William James famously called the "buzzing, teeming" life of an infant. The world of books helps them learn many of what Winnie the Pooh famously called Very Important Things.

Thus, the acts of paying close attention and hearing a story have great implications not only for a child's emotional attachment to reading, but also for a child's cognitive and linguistic development. Lest we forget, children are very busy with the process of becoming native speakers of an oral language all the while that one is reading to them. Those who study language acquisition disagree, sometimes fiercely, about how much linguistic knowledge is "wired" into our neuronal networks and what must be gained from exposure. What is never argued is that exposure to literature gives each child a tremendously expanded and elaborated view of words and sentences, both more than and different from everyday speech.

To illustrate some of those differences, let's take one of the most frequently asked questions by parents of young children related to reading: why does their child want to read the same book over and over again? While it is true that reading *Goodnight Moon*[12] for the thousandth time might tax the patience of even the most devoted parents, the commonality of this behavior among young children is revealing on multiple fronts. (Both of your authors can still recite *Goodnight Moon* from memory, which continues to embarrass and secretly please their four collective offspring!) The reality is that children love repetition, and repetition is a perfect recipe for giving them the "multiple exposures" to things they need to learn, from sounds to symbols. The young brain is busily constructing neuronal networks that are dedicated to these sounds, words, images, objects, faces, and other important sensory stimuli that make up their environment. Each time this brain is exposed to a phoneme or group of phonemes in a word, for example, the better "represented" that phoneme or word is and the more connected it is becoming to its meaning(s) and functions.

Thus, children are wired to thrive on what might seem to adults the sheer tedium of frequently repeating patterns. Reading or written language gives this exposure "for free," as Becky Kennedy lovingly describes it. Repetition aids not only the setting down of representations of information, but also the discovering of patterns in what they see and touch and hear. Both repetition (which sets down information) and the discovery of patterns in this information are key contributors to developing forms of thought processes like analogy and inference and to exponential increases of knowledge. Consider the fact that each time the child hears *Goodnight Moon*, she mines something new that had not been clear or fully formed as a concept from previous readings. She gradually sees, for example, that the little mouse appears in one different place after another. It is a revelation!

Of equal, albeit immeasurable importance, each reading conveys continuously developing layers of linguistic knowledge for the developing brain. Word knowledge exists on a continuum. As each word is acquired in the young child's lexicon, it moves from the barest familiarity to an in-depth knowledge of that word with all manner of associations and contexts.[13] Most babies do not know that *good night moon* is made of three words, two of which make up one of the "polite forms" of the language, and one of which is a noun referring to a thing in nature. But after many a reading, they are beginning to parse this; furthermore, they are using this linguistic knowledge to build out from. Rereading quite literally deepens children's knowledge of words with each exposure. All to say, every parent should resolve to repeat, reread, and not . . . skip! You will be detected.

From a linguistic perspective, going below the surface of Margaret Wise Brown's classic story also provides a glimpse into what children learn about language that they will not be able to learn if not exposed to literature. At the first reading of a story, to be sure, there may seem very little that the child would likely comprehend or remember about its rather unlikely narrative. That simply does not matter in the beginning of the written language knowledge continuum. A story like *Goodnight Moon* is pleasurable from its very first reading because of the broad sound patterns and rhythms in the verse.

> In the great green room
> There was a telephone
> And a red balloon
> And a picture of
> The cow jumping over the moon

From the outset, there is rhythm that seems immediately familiar, even if it is the first time heard. *Goodnight Moon* soothes both parent and child with the predictability of its rhythm, rhymes, repetitions of words and sounds, and ever so gentle alliteration. These audible patterns do more than soothe. They spotlight particular units of sound, the *phonemes* in words. This highlighting is, in Pooh's famous terms, A Very Useful Thing for young children who are trying to figure out "what means what" in their environment's otherwise constant stream of speech sounds. (Think of your own experiences when hearing a foreign language.) More specifically, when we read the /gr/ sound of "great green room," the typical reader automatically, unconsciously gives those elements slight emphases; further, we read them slightly louder than the other words and insert pauses between the words. Most readers do something similar with the *and* at the beginning of lines 3 and 4. The next seven lines begin with the word *and*, which moves an invisible cognitive spotlight across all the objects in the room, while the child silently, effortlessly learns each of them.

The brain of a young child is wired, if you will, to attend to the sounds represented by patterns in whatever spoken language they are surrounded by. Just like the unconscious ways a mother or an older child automatically exaggerates the prosody of their voices when speaking to a young child (this is called "motherese"), reading stories aloud to a child reinforces and felicitously *exaggerates* the patterns in their spoken language. To our knowledge there is no word for this "readerese," but it happens over and over again when we read to the young child.

In the process the child gradually receives increased exposure to elements that occur in less emphasized fashion in spoken language. For example, humans rarely employ rhyme or alliteration when speaking to others, but in written language these elements occur very frequently and serve as *phoneme-spotlights*. Children's literature, therefore, creates an invisible, tiny sound laboratory where the line between music and speech is blurred and the little phonemes of oral language are better heard. The advantages of such a frequently repeated experience are not only that children learn to listen carefully and patiently for the auditory surprises in the sounds of the words in the story, but their brains become more skilled at storing and "representing" the smaller and smaller pieces of the sound stream. It is the perfect preparation for later matching those stored phoneme representations to visual symbols—letters—when it is time to learn to read.

Thus, when children from six months to six years are exposed to the various sounds and rhythms awash in children's literature, they are better prepared for the task of decoding the words in the text when they begin to read. Some of the most fascinating older research that began in England on this topic almost three decades ago illustrated how exposure to the rhymes of Mother Goose and other similar children's materials made a significant difference in later reading performance.[14] This only makes linguistic sense. One of the single most important predictors of reading performance is a child's awareness of phonemes. There is little that consolidates this phoneme knowledge more for the young child than *hearing* words that rhyme and play with the ear and mind. Later on, there is little that propels this same knowledge even further than *reading* the words that contain these phonemes. It is a wonderful example of the great, continuously reciprocal relationship between the various interrelated aspects of oral and written language.

There is more. The particular language of books presents children with examples of words and sentence structures that they are unlikely to hear in spoken language. Most of us have a tendency to be fairly simple and, well, fairly redundant in our everyday speech patterns. We talk about everyday matters among ourselves and rarely use more than the most common 4,000–5,000 words. We also rely heavily on declarative sentences, sentence fragments, and questions. It might be said that in certain developmental periods, and in certain circles, there are even *less* complex structures occurring in speech (variations of the original Valley Girl speech in California come readily to mind). The point is that in ordinary speech, we can understand and create many more patterns than those sentence types, but we just don't do so very frequently. The language of stories and poems and books gives exposure to different syntactic patterns than oral language and in the process pushes conceptual development as well. Compound sentences do more than link two thoughts, they give practice to the act of connecting thoughts—analogical thinking by any other term. Such connections, in turn, often lead to new thoughts. As we described briefly in the last chapter, the syntactic structure of our written sentences often reflects the complexity of our thoughts. Written language *pushe*s that complexity in the most subtle and gentle of ways in childhood's stories that grow in complexity themselves.

Think back to an example in your own life when you were asked to read something totally outside your ordinary discourse—like the work of Shakespeare with words and phrase structures that were totally new to you. Shakespeare introduced hundreds of new uses for old words, along with whole new words and phrases, into common usage: from words like *gossip*, to phrases like *in a pickle* and *strange bedfellows*, to lines that are iconic in our oral and written language—"To be or not to be," "If music be the food of love." The scholar F. Max Mueller[15] estimated that Shakespeare used 15,000 different words in his works, more than triple or quadruple a typical speaking vocabulary. Reading Shakespeare as an expert reader, whatever the age, semantically and syntactically expands the horizons of every reader and goes well beyond the limits of typical spoken language.

Reading to a child is an early microcosm of this later experience. Think back to the beloved story of *Winnie the Pooh*. It is a beautiful example of how a story can employ sentence structures never heard in conversations.

> Here is Edward Bear, coming downstairs now, bump, bump, bump, on the back of his head, behind Christopher Robin. It is, as far as he knows, the only way of coming downstairs, but sometimes he feels that there really is another way, if only he could stop bumping for a moment and think of it.[16]

Because adult readers so readily comprehend what is happening in these sentences, the complexity of the language may not be obvious. But ask yourself this question, what does the *it* in the second sentence represent? Typically, we understand pronouns to stand in for a person or a thing. At a bare minimum, *it* should refer to a noun or phrase that was present in a previous utterance. But here, *it* represents the idea of *a way of coming down the stairs*, which is not mentioned until after the *it* appears. Now let's observe the second use of *it*, which occurs in the same sentence. Here *it* stands in for *another way*, best understood as another way of coming down the stairs. Both of these uses of this simple, unassuming pronoun are actually syntactically and cognitively complex. The reader and the listener have to envision, with very little explicit explanation, how Edward Bear is going down the stairs, and also try to imagine some other way of coming down the stairs which is also unspecified.

To be exposed to these sentences over several readings of *Winnie the Pooh* opens up new possibilities for the use of one of English's most common pronouns, which a child would be unlikely to hear when talking to parents or peers. Understanding the complex language world of children's literature when being read to is a vital precursor to the comprehension of words and sentences in text that children will later read independently.

There is rich and ample evidence that children who have been read to by the people around them will possess richer vocabularies than children growing up in non- or less literate homes. A landmark study by Todd Hart and Betty Risley[17] exposed the vast gap in vocabulary knowledge as a result of the sheer quantity of words that children hear in homes with a good deal of language being spoken, versus homes where children hear less language. Children raised by parents with professional backgrounds are estimated to hear approximately 48 million instances of various words by the time they reach four years of age. In contrast, children raised by parents with far less education hear only 13 million instances of words in this same time period. This study, which is more cited in studies of vocabulary knowledge than any study we know, amplifies the importance of semantic knowledge as a contributor to academic knowledge.

What is less often discussed or cited are the differences in the *quality* and topics of those conversations. Hart and Risley found that children in professional homes heard 750,000 times before the age of four that they were "right," and 250,000 times that they were "wrong." In the homes of families on public assistance the children heard 250,000 times that they were wrong, and 125,000 times that they were right.

There are no quick judgments that apply here. The parent who has just come home from her second job will use language as often as not to warn and/or protect the well-being of her child. There will be far less time to elaborate any interesting question by the child, or to commend them for it, much less to have the time to read to them. As stewards of the next generations of children, however, we have to confront the implications of such data not only for vocabulary growth (and what it portends), but also for social-emotional development. There are various studies that show a child's willingness to speak and to participate in activities like show-and-tell in kindergarten will reliably predict their later academic success. If young children for five years are more frequently told they are doing something wrong than right, the likelihood of their "willingness" to show their knowledge when they enter school is decreased.

There is, to our minds, a too-little discussed *gap* between the child who enters kindergarten primed with the confidence and assurance to ask many questions and tell stories, and the child who has never been told that his once-too-many questions and his wild stories are the "stuff as dreams are made on."[18] The quantity and content of oral and written language in the lives of young children will have an impact far beyond the first years. From a linguistic perspective, we do not need another study to keep proving that the vocabulary knowledge young children possess in kindergarten predicts their performance years later at the end of high school.[19] For the families of children from impoverished language backgrounds, this prediction underscores the devastating, lasting implications of what occurs far earlier than when their children enter the kindergarten doors. The gap begins five years before.

There is a highly related issue that is almost as important as language development, that also comes from the books of childhood: the developing capacity to take on another person's perspective and imagine the thoughts of others. Some of the most loved children's literature from *George and Martha* and *Frog and Toad* to *Charlotte's Web* provide this affectively and cognitively expanded experience inside

A Child's Tale

literature. Indeed, one of the essential precursors to the comprehension of text involves being able to understand how another person may think and feel. Underlying this ability are what is referred to as "Theory of Mind" and its correlative, *empathy*, as we will discuss more in Chapter 5. A great deal of research has been conducted on the developmental trajectory of the human ability to imagine what others are thinking. It rests on understanding the thoughts and motivations of others even when they are unexpressed.

A frequently employed research paradigm to investigate the developing ability of a child to understand the thoughts of others is called the "false-belief" task.[20] In it, a child might be shown three sequential scenes. In the first scene a boy places a piece of chocolate on the shelf and then leaves the room. In the second the boy's mother enters the room and places the chocolate inside the refrigerator and then leaves the room also. Finally, in the third scene, the boy re-enters the room and looks. After watching these scenes, the child-subject in the study is asked where the boy thinks the chocolate is. To perform this task successfully, the child-subject must hold in mind both the actual location of the object and the earlier location when the boy placed it on the shelf. In addition, the child has to take on the perspective of the boy (theory of the boy's mind) to figure out the answer. Such a cognitive process entails inhibiting knowledge of the actual location and expressing the location believed by the boy.

Until recently, it was thought that children can only perform this task beginning at age four. It turns out that some children as young as fifteen months old turn their gaze to the spot where the object is believed by the boy to be and not at the actual location. Even though they are unable to express this thought in language, they are beginning to acquire a theory of others' thoughts. We believe that the developing ability to imagine the thoughts of others and to anticipate their actions is one of the earliest human precursors of the development of later deep reading skills, and it begins with stories of toads and frogs.

It is this same capacity that will someday allow an older child to imagine how lonely Harry felt growing up before going to Hogwarts, or how curious Lucy felt when discovering the wardrobe as a passage to another world. For young children, as they listen raptly and try to understand the actions of Charlotte or the escapades of Madeleine, they are beginning to learn ever so gradually how to understand the emotions of others when they are experiencing situations both familiar to them and wildly unfamiliar. Literature challenges all of these children to examine what they already know, so as to understand a narrative that often as not takes them beyond the bounds of that very knowledge base. They begin to imagine what it is like to be another person, what it is like to live in another place, what it feels like to be brave or generous or very, very lonely. Such imaginings may be the most important, invisible fruits of literacy whose personal and moral outcomes can never be measured.

What's in a word

Ah, but we get ahead of ourselves. We aren't finished depicting the story of the simple act of reading to your child. The young child who is engaging with print, even if only *eating it* at the start, is not only gaining new concepts about oral language and theory of mind, but also about what *written* language is. The sheer quantity of possible exposures to print in literate homes means that the young child will experience print in multiple ways, particularly what is called *environmental print*, which includes labels on products, print on toys, signs, etc. Just think about all the letters you see in any given day. Young children see those letters, too. There are printed words everywhere around them. But do young children actually learn anything from environmental print? When do they begin to notice shapes and images of often-seen letter patterns and remember them as familiar objects?

Increasing anecdotal evidence suggests that children from twenty months of age on can do just that as they begin to recognize various forms of environmental print. For example, a child of two often recognizes that the car stops (more or less . . .) whenever it approaches the archetypal red stop sign. Another child knows every cereal box label by heart. Another child we both know could distinguish between and among the all-too-various forms of Swiss chocolate and gummi bear wrappers. By the age of three, pre-literate children readily engage in a form of "pre-reading" which involves matching a verbal label to the symbol associated with it. When children see the golden arches, they know that this symbol stands for McDonald's. Further, the child can probably name McDonald's in response to seeing the word on a sign. To be sure, he probably can't identify the first letter as an <M>, or read a word that starts with *m*, and it is unlikely that he can identify the word *McDonalds* if it occurs in a different context. What is happening is a simple paired associate of a visual symbol and a known concept.

Both authors are *very* familiar with a three-year-old, who is not three anymore, who was so keenly interested in cars that he could name the make and model of any car that passed by, including in Germany the once-infamous Trabi. Even on signs, car words like *Mercedes* or *Ford* became instantly associated by him with a particular car with a particular symbol on the trunk and hood. Although he managed to regale many an unsuspecting adult with his seemingly precocious reading ability of almost any car word, he was not reading at all. (Postscript: twenty years have passed, and he reads quite well as he rides to his first job on his sleek, grey Google bus. He still can identify any car on the road faster than any of us.)

The reality is that many young children who are frequently read to seem as if they can "read" the words of their favorite book from start to finish. Even if the book is upside down, as Benjamin Evans, the toddler grandson of our friend Barbara, frequently does in the Boston Public Library—to the utter delight of all passersby! They are reciting from memory the stories they have loved, or they are beginning to make even finer associations with the pictures and pages that belong to those remembered words. Although no self-respecting researcher would ever want to pierce the bubble of a parent's justified pride, these children have not begun to read these precious, dog-eared books. Rather, the children may have begun the fascinating phase of what is known as *logographic* reading. Logographic reading is not absent in the world's writing systems, particularly in their origins. The Chinese writing system, in which a symbol stands for an entire word, remains partly logographic as we discussed in the last chapter. But when a young child engages in this form of symbol identification, he or she is assigning a label to a stimulus in a very similar way. They are not decoding, they are remembering the correct labels, which they can only do within a very particular context.

While probably not a necessary step in the pre-reading stage, there is evidence that children who build a small vocabulary of *logograms* and actively practice that skill gain a helpful scaffold for learning letters. Some research shows that children who can read logograms and other types of environmental print are more likely to be advanced readers between the ages of four and seven.[21] A fascinating study by Victoria Molfese[22] found that low-income four-year-olds who were taught a variety of print concepts—including logos and other environmental print symbols—were more likely to be proficient at reading actual letters six months later.

Why this might be the case lies in two major cognitive leaps that a young child has to achieve in this early pre-stage of learning to read. The first cognitive epiphany—understanding symbolic reference—is no small task, but its origins begin very early and quickly become more and more sophisticated. Imagine for a moment asking a seven-month-old boy if he wants a cookie; next imagine asking this when there is no cookie in the room. The concept implicit in matching a word to a particular object in a space full of objects is hard enough for an infant, but the reality is that by ten to twelve months most of them have learned to do this when the object—particularly, to be sure, a very desirable cookie—is not present.

With environmental print and the many cultural logograms, we are extending this form of cognitive achievement a step further. We are asking children to comprehend that a random visual symbol refers to a seemingly unrelated, typically not physically present, concept. These are all examples of children learning to understand various types of symbols, a necessary precursor to the more sophisticated understanding of the relationship between a single phoneme and the motley lines of a letter symbol meant to represent it.

What's in a letter

It is no small set of intellectual feats that prepares children to learn this relationship, which brings us to the second cognitive epiphany that involves vision and memory, among other important things. To enter the first stages of learning to read, a child must build up a visual inventory of the alphabet's arbitrary letter forms and consolidate them in memory. But there is a trick to be learned in many a writing system that goes counterintuitively to what children have learned up to this point. Before they learn letters, most children have learned that objects in their world are the same whether they are upside down or turned around or inverted in any direction. A chair is a chair, and a cup is a cup from whatever direction you gaze upon it. This is the assumption of *mirror invariance*, an ingenious adaptation in the visual system which allows the brain to understand that an object is the same from every direction.

With letters comes a curve ball. Children must, for all purposes, override their original basic assumption and learn that letters are *not* the same if you turn them in different directions. Children have to learn that flipping a letter can make it an entirely new letter. Flip a <b> around and it is not a funny looking <b>, it is now a <d>. An upside down <M> can become a <W>. This is not simple when you have been operating to that point with a different cognitive rule.

Mirror invariance is standard hardware in the visual system of any individual, young or old, both *before* they learn to read and also *when* they are *not* literate. When individuals become literate, they actually lose their former rapidity in identifying objects which are mirror images of one another. We do not lose the ability entirely, we just take more time performing the identification accurately. This result is true not only for strings of letters, as one would expect, but also for pictures of objects.

Part of the explanation has to do with a qualitative change in the visual attentional systems with regard to the left-right orientation and top-down orientation of letters. With more exposure and practice, children come to the conclusion that orientation is important; and further, that it can help distinguish between the identity of two similar letters. Keep in mind that for many letters, orientation is irrelevant: for example, the lower case letters <i>, <o>, <l>, <t>, or <m>. For another group of letters, the orientation of the letter ensures it is accepted as "correct," but does not create a confusion with another letter: for example, the lower case letters <s<, <f>, <r>, or <z>. We are left with a subset of letters where the orientation of the letter determines the identity of the letter between two candidates: the lower case letters <p>, <q>, <b>, and <d>.

Predictably, these reversible letters create the most confusion for all children and at times have served as a red flag by parents and teachers who are watching for signs of a reading disability. The unfortunate misperception that "dyslexics" can be diagnosed on the basis of letter reversals is fed by the fact that children at risk for a reading disability tend to take longer to master this latter class of more confusing letter forms. There is a fascinating hypothesis why. Neuroscientist Stanislas Dehaene[23] suggests that this phenomenon is not a sign of weakness, but rather of the strength of the right hemisphere visual cortex in dyslexia which insists on seeing "all sides" of the letters.

What's in the visual cortex

Dehaene and his colleague Laurent Cohen and others in the cognitive neurosciences have also found that a very particular part of the brain is involved in connecting the visual processes to letters and words when learning to read at any age and in any language. They refer to this area colloquially as the "Letter box" or *visual word form area* (VWFA), though other neuroscientists refer to it simply in terms of its location in the ventral occipito-temporal cortex. Located a little behind the ear area for most people, it will be discussed more thoroughly in the next chapter when we discuss the expert reading brain. But this area is also important for young children for the recognition of letters and groups of letters, and even words. In children who have not yet learned to read, the Finnish research group led by Heikki Lyytinen has shown that only a few hours of playing a letter-learning game called *Graphogame* causes this area of the brain to become activated.[24] In some children with dyslexia, the lack of activation in this area of the brain can be an identifying feature. Very importantly, this area becomes more responsive when these same children improve their reading abilities. In recent research by Dehaene and colleagues[25] comparing adults with varying abilities in reading, increases in activation in the VWFA were associated with more sophisticated reading skills. Other researchers have found that the VWFA is activated with alphabetic and non-alphabetic languages alike.[26]

One of the most revolutionary findings from Dehaene's group's research[27] involves investigations into the function of the VWFA before literacy is acquired or when someone does not learn how to read. His group has performed fMRI experiments with young children who have not yet learned to read, and also with adults who either never learned to read or became literate later in life. Across groups the VWFA plays an important part in the visual system's ability to make *invariant visual object recognition*. Briefly, this term refers to our ability to quickly identify objects that tend to have very consistent features, like faces. When Dehaene's group showed non-literate subjects a variety of different pictures, the VWFA became activated when the subject saw faces or objects. As the subject became a better reader, the VWFA area no longer showed activation on the left side for faces, but rather on the right side. In other words, when the brain begins to create a circuit in which we store visual information about letters, it appears to reorganize its prior circuitry, particularly for faces. Moreover, his group found that the more facile an individual is at this reorganization, the more likely they are to be a skilled reader.

There are several important implications of this work. First, it is an illustration of how literacy literally rewires the brain. Second, it suggests that some forms of reading impairments may have little or nothing to do with weaknesses in the phonological system, which has been the most hypothesized source of impediment in dyslexia, but rather can arise from difficulties reorganizing the visual recognition system. Finally, it is always encouraging to see that this rewiring for literacy can occur beyond childhood, which we translate into: "you are truly never too old" to learn to read.

What is not in a word, a letter, or the visual cortex for the non-literate person

The latter statement brings us back to the reality faced by the many children and adults who have not become literate. Any study of the cognitive, social, and linguistic differences between children who become literate and those who do not is fraught with multiple difficulties. First, it is extremely difficult to find a population of children with no access to school or with no opportunity to be taught how to read who do not also experience the confounding effects of poverty, malnutrition, instability, or even war. How does one tease apart these dramatic influences on the neurological, social, and cognitive development of the individual from the effects of learning how to read?

Despite these intrinsic problems, a number of important studies have been conducted that were able to isolate and study those variables. Perhaps unsurprising by now, the overall findings of these studies demonstrate that learning how to read adds crucial cognitive and linguistic skills to the repertoire of a developing child. A group of researchers from Florida and Guadalajara compared a group of children between the ages of six and thirteen from the urban areas of Guadalajara and Tijuana, Mexico.[28] Half of the children were literate and attended school, and half were not literate and had never attended school. The children were tested on a range of neuropsychological and linguistic skills, such as spatial skills, memory, attention, vocabulary, calculation skills, and phoneme awareness. One might hypothesize that the literate children would outperform the non-literate children on every educational measure, but that was not the case. The non-literate children outperformed the literate group on a measure of calculation skills, which suggests that some mathematical skills are able to be learned through experiences outside of schools.

The remaining results were the more predictable ones: in every domain outside of calculation, the literate group outperformed the non-literate group. Children who knew how to read were more efficient at performing tasks that assessed memory, spatial abilities, and sound perception. The results of one task of construction ability were nevertheless surprising, since a well-known finding among non-literate aboriginal children shows a clear advantage for spatial memory tasks. This study's children were assessed on a different spatial-related ability to copy a figure using toothpicks. The literate children were faster and more accurate completing their figures. Taken in isolation, it might seem odd that learning to read would change how a child puts together a figure. However, if Dehaene's work concerning the reorganization of the visual system is considered, one could hypothesize that a brain that can rapidly and accurately identify the small features of letters has also become faster and more accurate identifying the small details of other types of figures. This is yet to be replicated, but is thought-provoking.

Far and away the most important results for the goals of this book, however, concerned the dramatic change in the language skills of the tested literate children. On a test of what is called verbal fluency, children were asked to name as many words as they can think of in sixty seconds that either begin with a certain sound (Name as many words as you can think of that start with the /s/ sound); or that belong to a certain category (Name as many *food* words as you can think of). These tests do not measure linguistic sophistication; there are no extra points for the quality of words or for naming more "literary" words. The simple, harsh reality was that children who never learned to read struggled terribly with this task, especially when asked to name words that start with a particular sound.

To be sure, there has been some debate around this study as to whether the *food* category which was chosen would advantage literate individuals over the non-literate. Another common category for this task, for example, is *animals*. Would that have been a better choice? Although it might seem that animals represent a universally easier semantic category across populations, such a thought reveals how unaware we may be of the influence that reading about bears, dinosaurs, lions, or sea lions—animals we would not normally see unless we live near their habitat—has on the range of words that children can recall rapidly. Literacy changes the quality *and* quantity of our everyday experiences with words and, in the process, changes the number and kinds of words the literate person knows well and can retrieve quickly across most common categories. It changes the representations of words in the child's brain.

We want, however, to look for one moment at some of the less studied, positive dimensions of social and cognitive development in a group of pre-literate and non-literate children. Yomi Ogunnaike, a former PhD student of ours and a professor now at the University of Wisconsin-Stevens Point, wrote her dissertation on the implications of the unique cognitive demands placed on three- and four-year-old children growing up in the Yoruba areas of Nigeria,[29] where literacy is not a given. When we say unique, it is without exaggeration. Unlike most Western cultures, Yoruba culture expects very responsible behaviors in young children. For example, pre-school-aged children are expected to help their mother around the home or in small merchant-based businesses, and to "run" errands to stores at ages that would be fodder for visits from the department of social services in Western lands. By contrast, Professor Ogunnaike described not only the special emphases that the Yoruba culture places on responsibility, helpfulness, and expectations around chores for even the youngest children, but also the relationship these responsibilities have on the increased cognitive and social development of the children. Her positive findings of these relationships should give us all pause in our Western-centric views of what childhood should and should not be like.

What Professor Ogunnaike also found, however, reinforced one of the key leitmotifs in our work on global literacy. When the mothers of the children in the study were literate in the home language of Yoruba, there were significantly more educational, print-based materials in the home. Further, these mothers read regularly to their children, something which mothers who were not literate could not do. It is such a simple, seemingly obvious finding that it might have gone overlooked. The reality is that this simple fact of being read to in a literate environment makes all the difference between growing up in a world that expands with every read book, and one that does not; between a developing brain that is beginning to represent all manner of new information about words and letters, and one that does not.

The findings with these literate and non-literate children have been replicated in a number of studies with adults, particularly those measuring the phonemic awareness of literate and non-literate adults. As described in Chapter 2, phoneme awareness provides one half of the foundation for understanding and using an alphabetic system of letters, which at its base requires the reader to assign a particular sound or phoneme to a particular graphic symbol. Several studies comparing non-literate and literate adults underscored the struggle that non-literate adults have in demonstrating any awareness of a particular sound in their language. Some of these tasks might ask a subject to count the sounds in a word (How many sounds are in the word *cat*?), or to leave a particular sound out of a word and tell the examiner what word is left (Say *floor* without the /f/ sound). Some tasks may simply ask the subject to repeat a pseudo-word (Say the word *marp*).

Almost all the studies conducted have found that literate adults outperform non-literate adults on multiple dimensions of language knowledge, but particularly phoneme awareness tasks like the ones just described. These tasks are not just about sound-knowledge; they measure a person's *metalinguistic* awareness, the ability to examine or reflect about some aspect of language. Such a capacity is evident in children who have read for only a short period of time; yet this reflective capacity about words proves difficult time and again for people who have not learned to read.

The first "revolution in the brain"

A series of fascinating studies by neuroscientists Alexandre Castro-Caldas and Alexandra Reis[30] illustrate what they call the "revolution in the brain" that occurs when a person learns a system of letters. In order to study how learning to read changes language processes in the brain, without the confounding factors like other differences in the environment, these researchers investigated a very unusual population sample. They studied siblings who shared the same factors in their home environment and upbringing with one exception—learning to read. In Portugal, a common and traditional practice until fairly recently was that firstborn children did not attend school, but rather helped at home and took care of their younger siblings who *did* learn to read. Castro-Caldas and Reis studied these siblings when they were approximately sixty-five years of age with both males and females represented. Their unusual investigation confirmed what has been found in the more conventional comparisons of literate and non-literate children. Non-literate adults have difficulties with the metalinguistic aspects of language, particularly concerning the sound system. The non-literate siblings were less able to repeat non-words or to identify the initial sounds of their words. Most pertinent to other findings about the ways literacy rewires us, the differences in the literate individuals were reflected in the activation of additional language-based structures of the brain that were not activated in their siblings.

The upshot is that literate persons activate areas when they process language that were not activated before they were literate. Ongoing research by James Booth[31] and Stanislas Dehaene's group indicates that literacy makes new connections between language and visual attention systems that were never there before. For example, Stanislas Dehaene, Laurent Cohen, Jose Morais, and Regine Kolinsky provide the most recent meta-analysis of the changes in behavioral and anatomical regions that occur as a result of literacy. They document changes in three major systems in the reading circuit that will be elaborated in the next chapter: the early visual system; the slightly later activated visual pathway that becomes responsible for representing the "nested levels" of words from letters and letter patterns to whole words; and finally the speech processing areas and their newly formed connections to visual input. Anatomically, the connections between and among these regions become changed with particular changes in the left *arcuate fasciculus*, a bundle of fibers that links many areas involved in speech processes and language comprehension. These authors illustrate that learning to read represents a new, expanded set of networks and a new organization of connections for language itself.

We would like to provide a small, illustrative, anecdotal finding in our own work that has never been published, because the sample of children we studied was too small. With the generous help of our MIT colleague, John Gabrieli, and his team, one of our PhD students at the time, Elizabeth Norton, imaged children with dyslexia before and after they began our RAVE-O reading intervention program. Because they could not read initially, the children were simply asked to *listen* to words that rhymed, while they were in the fMRI magnet at the children's brain imaging lab at MIT. The results still make us happy, despite the small sample of children. Before they learned to read, when the children listened to words that rhyme, they activated typical areas for auditory and language processing. After the intervention, however, not only were those areas activated, but areas in the *visual cortex were also activated*. In other words, even when they only listened to words, the acquisition of reading had made these newly literate children automatically "see" the "heard" words. These familiar words had now become *represented* in their visual networks, which were newly connected to the language areas.

It is another example of how reading "rewires" our brains. It is also an example of the critical importance of *all the exposures* to the sounds and visual patterns of letters and words that children receive. One of the most important lessons in the differences between literate and non-literate environments is that the more exposures children have to all the aspects of language and print we have been discussing, the better "re-presented" this information becomes in the literate child's brain. Every letter, every phoneme, every word "adds" to the elaboration of the developing brain circuit.

Literacy and child's play

Literacy is, however, not only about changes in language and the brain. We would like to bring to the fore a difference in the effect of literacy on children's play, which is, as our colleague George Scarlett beautifully expounds,[32] one of the most important vehicles in children's exploration of their world. Although many developmental researchers have discussed the domain of play and literacy, we want to describe something just a little different about the relationship between print and play. It is based on the observations of the second author during site visits she has made recently in our work in global literacy in places like the slums of Kampala and the villages of India. It begins with the fact that the experiences of a child from birth to three in a literate world differ not just because of socioeconomic forces, but they differ radically because of the exposure to the myriad objects, spaces, signs, and experiences that children learn about in an everyday literate environment.

Most of us never think about it, but the entire *Weltanschauung* of a child in a literate home is dominated by early manifestations of the symbolic world. Before some children are even born, there are baby book showers. (Which we personally think a wonderful concept.) From the first year onward, there is a panoply of alphabet blocks, board books, and letter puzzles scattered about, all of which expose children to the forms of letters, sometimes the names of those letters, and often the *bright colors of childhood* in those letters and books. Everywhere there are vividly colored items and sometimes even specially designated spaces covered with print. The very vibrancy and various shapes of the toys, the books, and the special child-centered places all give expression to the idea that there is a space where children are safe and where they can go to learn about their world and the mysterious, but intriguing symbols it contains. The German philosopher Walter Benjamin wrote several less-known essays about how the colors of childhood play a particular role in the origins of human consciousness,[33] and we believe he could not be more perceptive in his insights.

In stark contrast are the worlds of children raised in environments without toys or books or spaces that are set apart by the colors of an innocent time. These children are found, to be sure, in underdeveloped countries around our world. But we wish to emphasize that they live everywhere, as study after study in the rural US and urban slums in developed countries document.[34] These children are not only missing the special cognitive-affective-social experiences of interacting with the beloved persons around print and books, but they are also missing one of the most beautiful types of play that exist. They are missing the formation of friends that last a lifetime: Curious George, Christopher Robin, Tigger, and Pooh, Charlotte, and Wilbur. They are not only missing the colors and the special vocabulary of books, they are missing the language of *play* and all the friends that accompany it.

Finally, with none of the subtle communicative messages that these colors, spaces, and environmental print convey, they are sometimes missing something more still: the safe haven of childhood. On a recent visit to a preschool in Uganda, the second author was struck by the presence in every classroom of black and white and grey posters with pictures of "Dangerous Objects." Posters of barbed wire and razor blades, not bears and runaway bunnies, dominated the room. While every parent remembers the challenge of teaching their children to avoid electrical outlets and stoves, imagine this challenge in an environment where the notion of children's spaces and toys does not exist, but dangerous objects do and in abundance. The point of this example is not to make a plea for more toys and playgrounds in Kampala, although that would be a desirable outcome. Rather, this example is meant to illustrate in a small way, how the world of language and literacy is created from the very first day of a child's life in a literate home—on the walls, from the ceiling, on the floor, beside the bed, and under the tables—and how different these beginnings are for children who have no exposure to this world.

The simple introduction of letters and books and stories changes the world of childhood. To be sure, it ups the symbolic and cognitive ante, but it simultaneously exposes the children to emotional experiences and narratives they might never otherwise have. And for some children, such experiences are their personal vehicles that transport them away from wherever they are and give them reason to aspire and contribute what they know. Literacy is the one safe haven a child can have in almost any culture. It is a form of play that can happen even when the grounds nearby are littered with dangerous objects. It is a form of play that, as Proust described years ago, can exist like magic "in the midst of solitude" or in the middle of a slum or under the covers with a flashlight.

....

And now, we turn the clock ahead. We want to use the lessons here about the child's developing circuit to examine the reader's own reading brain. The surprises to be found in the development of literacy are not only for kids.

Notes

1. Billy Collins, "On Turning Ten." In *The Art of Drowning* (Pittsburgh, PA: University of Pittsburgh Press, 1995).
2. US Department of Education, Institute of Education Sciences, National Center for Education Statistics, National Assessment of Educational Progress (NAEP), 1992–2009 Reading Assessments.
3. Amanda Ripley, *The Smartest Kids in the World* (New York: Simon & Schuster, 2013).
4. Keith E. Stanovich, "Matthew Effects in Reading: Some Consequences of Individual Differences in the Acquisition of Literacy," *Reading Research Quarterly* 21 (Fall 1986): pp. 360–407. <http://www.keithstanovich.com/Site/Research_on_Reading_files/RRQ86A.pdf>.
5. Jeanne Chall, *Stages of Reading Development* (New York: McGraw-Hill, 1983). Hereafter cited as Chall.
6. Carol Chomsky, "Stages in Language Development and Reading Exposure," *Harvard Educational Review* 42 (1972): pp. 1–33. Hereafter cited as C. Chomsky. <http://www.hepgjournals.org/doi/pdf/10.17763/haer.42.1.h78l676h28331480>.
7. Catherine Snow, Susan Burns, and Peg Griffin (eds), *Preventing Reading Difficulties in Young Children* (Washington, DC: National Academy Press, 1998).
8. Mary Ann Evans, Deborah Shaw, and Michelle Bell, "Home Literacy Activities and their Influence on Early Literacy Skills," *Canadian Journal of Experimental Psychology* 54 (2000): pp. 65–75. <http://dx.doi.org/10.1037/h0087330>.
9. Robert Needlman, Lise E. Fried, Deborah S. Morley, Sunday Taylor, and Barry Zuckerman, "Clinic-based Intervention to Promote Literacy: A Pilot Study," *Educational Intervention* 145 (1991): pp. 881–4. <http://www.reachoutandread.org/FileRepository/Needlman1991.pdf>.
10. Pamela High, Marita Hopmann, Linda LaGasse, and Holly Linn, "Evaluation of a Clinic-based Program to Promote Book Sharing and Bedtime Routines among Low-Income Urban Families with Young Children," *Archives of Pediatric and Adolescent Medicine* 152 (1998): pp. 459–65. <http://www.reachoutandread.org/FileRepository/High1998.pdf>.
11. H. Jonathan Polan and Mary J. Ward, "Role of the Mother's Touch in Failure to Thrive: A Preliminary Investigation," *Journal of American Academy of Child Adolescence and Psychiatry* 33, no. 8 (1994): pp. 1098–105. <http://dx.doi.org/10.1097/00004583-199410000-00005>.
12. Margaret Wise Brown, *Goodnight Moon* (New York: Harper & Brothers, 1947).
13. Edward Kame'enui, Robert C. Dixon, and Doug Carnine, "Issues in the Design of Vocabulary Instruction." In Margaret G. McKeown and Mary Beth Curtis (eds), *The Nature of Vocabulary Acquisition* (Hillsdale, NJ: Erlbaum, 1987), ch. 8.
14. Peter Bryant and Lynette Bradley, *Children's Reading Problems* (Oxford: Blackwell, 1985).
15. Friedrich Max Müller, *Lectures on the Science of Language: Delivered at the Royal Institution of Great Britain in April, May, & June 1861* (Longmans, Green, 1866).
16. A. A. Milne, *Winnie the Pooh* (New York: Penguin, 2009), ch. 1, opening lines.
17. Betty Hart and Todd Risley, *Meaningful Differences in the Everyday Experiences of Young American Children* (Baltimore: Brookes Publishing, 1995; 4th printing, January 2003).

18. William Shakespeare, *The Tempest*, Horace Howard Furness (ed.) (New York: Dover, 1964).
19. Monique Sénéchal, Gene Ouellette, and Donna Rodney, "The Misunderstood Giant: On the Predictive Role of Early Vocabulary to Future Reading." In David K. Dickinson and Susan B. Neuman (eds), *Handbook of Early Literacy Research* vol. 2 (New York: Guilford Press, 2006), ch. 13, pp. 173–82.
20. Kristine H. Onishi and Renee Baillargeon, "Do 15-Month-Old Infants Understand False Beliefs?" *Science* 308, no. 5719 (2005): pp. 255–8. <http://www.sciencemag.org/content/308/5719/255.full>.
21. D. Ray Reutzel, Parker C. Fawson, Janet Young, Timothy G. Morrison, and Brad Wilcox, "Reading Environmental Print: What is the Role of Concepts about Print in Discriminating Young Readers' Responses?" *Reading Psychology* 24 (2003): pp. 123–62. <http://dx.doi.org/10.1080/02702710308232>.
22. Victoria J. Molfese, Arlene A. Modglin, Jennifer L. Beswick, J. D. Neamon, S. A. Berg, C. J. Berg, and A. Molnar, "Letter Knowledge, Phonological Processing, and Print Knowledge: Skill Development in Nonreading Preschool Children," *Journal of Learning Disabilities* 39, no. 4 (2006): pp. 296–305. <http://ldx.sagepub.com/content/39/4/296.full.pdf>.
23. Felipe Pegado, Kimihiro Nakamura, Lucia W. Braga, Paulo Ventura, Gilberto Nunes Filho, Christophe Pallier, Antoinette Jobert, José Morais, Laurent Cohen, Régine Kolinsky, and Stanislas Dehaene, "Literacy Breaks Mirror Invariance for Visual Stimuli: A Behavioral Study with Adult Illiterates," *Journal of Experimental Psychology: General* 143, no. 2 (2014): pp. 887–94. <http://dx.doi.org/10.1037/a0033198>. Hereafter cited as Dehaene et al. 2014.
24. Silvia Brema, Silvia Bacha, Karin Kucian, Janne V. Kujalaa, Tomi K. Guttorma, Ernst Martinc, Heikki Lyytinen, Daniel Brandeis, and Ulla Richardson, "Brain Sensitivity to Print Emerges When Children Learn Letter–Speech Sound Correspondences," *Proceedings of the National Academy of Sciences USA* 107, no. 17 (2010): pp. 7939–44. <http://www.pnas.org/content/107/17/7939.full.pdf+html>.
25. Stanislas Dehaene, Felipe Pegado, Lucia W. Braga, Paulo Ventura, Gilberto Nunes Filho, Antoinette Jobert, Ghislaine Dehaene-Lambertz, Régine Kolinsky, José Morais, Laurent Cohen, et al., "How Learning to Read Changes the Cortical Networks for Vision and Language," *Science* 330, no. 6009 (2010): pp. 1359–64. <http://www.sciencemag.org/content/330/6009/1359.full>.
26. Charles A. Perfetti, Ying Liu, Julie Fiez, Jessica Nelson, Donald J. Bolger, and Li-Hai Tan, "Reading in Two Writing Systems: Accommodation and Assimilation in the Brain's Reading Network," *Bilingualism: Language and Cognition* 10, no. 2 (2007) pp: 131–46. <http://journals.cambridge.org/abstract_S1366728907002891>.
27. Dehaene et al., 2014.
28. Esmeralda Matute, Teresita Montiel, Noemí Pinto, Monica Rosselli, Alfredo Ardila, and Daniel Zarabozo, "Comparing Cognitive Performance in Illiterate and Literate Children," *International Review of Education* 58 (2012): pp. 109–27. doi:10.1007/s11159-012-9273-9.
29. Yomi Ogunnaike, "Yoruba Toddlers: Relating Cognitive Performance to Family Sociodemographics and Mediating Factors in the Child's Environment" (Tufts University, ProQuest, UMI Dissertations Publishing, 1997).

30. Alexandre Castro-Caldas and Alexandra Reis, "The Knowledge of Orthography Is a Revolution in the Brain," *Reading and Writing: An Interdisciplinary Journal* 16 (2003): pp. 81–93. doi:10.1023/A:1021798106794.
31. Nadia E. Cone, Douglas D. Burman, Tali Bitan, Donald J. Bolger, and James R. Booth, "Developmental Changes in Brain Regions Involved in Phonological and Orthographic Processing," *Neuroimage* 41, no. 2 (2008): pp. 623–35. doi:10.1016/j.neuroimage.2008.02.055. Dehaene, 2015.
32. W. George Scarlett, Sophie C. Nadeau, Dorothy Salonius-Pasternak, and Iris Chin Ponte, *Children's Play* (Thousand Oaks, CA: Sage Publications Inc., 2005).
33. Walter Benjamin, *Selected Writings. Volume 1* (Cambridge, MA: Harvard University Press, 1996).
34. Andy Isaacson, "Are Tablets the Way out of Child Illiteracy?" *Smithsonian* (September 24, 2014). Hereafter cited as Smithsonian. <http://www.smithsonianmag.com/innovation/are-tablets-way-out-child-illiteracy-180952826/?no-ist>.

4
A Neuroscientist's Tale of Words

> There is then, first, the name, second, the definition, third, the representation, and fourth, knowledge.... and understanding and true belief about these things...
>
> Of these things understanding comes closest in kinship and likeness to the fifth...[1]
>
> Plato, *Seventh Letter*

> And as imagination bodies forth
> the form of things unknown,
> the poet's pen turns them to shapes and gives to airy nothing
> A local habitation and a name[2]
>
> Shakespeare, *A Midsummer Night's Dream*

> People sometimes say that language is a "mirror of thought" or a "window into human nature"...language is more like a collection of small and oddly shaped peepholes with distorting lenses. If we squint through them all the right way, we can assemble the various perspectives into a sense of the larger schema behind them. And that's what we need linguistics for.[3]
>
> Ray Jackendoff, *A User's Guide to Thought and Meaning*

Philosopher, poet, linguist. From three different perspectives, Plato, Shakespeare, and Jackendoff help us understand the varied ways that words give shape and substance to our thoughts and also give us glimpses of the never-quite-crossed spaces between word and thought. The written word—both when we read it and sometimes even more clearly when we write it—brings a subtle form of *consciousness* to this smallest of gaps. This is because reading involves an ingenious cycle of bringing to bear what we know to what we read; grasping new meanings from the convergence of the two, but being aware of something outside them; expanding whatever we now know; and deploying this newly increased knowledge to whatever we read in the next word, sentence, or text. Reading is based on both this constantly interacting knowledge about words and also on the unarticulated thoughts behind them that beckon us, if we let them.

As David Constantine writes in his book, *Poetry*, "writing and reading are kindred acts. In both a realization takes place. Both are knowledge in the making."[4] In this last of my "primer" tales, I wish to explore what goes into reading's very particular form of "knowledge in the making" in a way that may be unusual for both reader and author. There are few human beings who have more closely examined the contribution of words to knowledge-making than Plato. I wish, therefore, to leave the comfort zone of my more typical ways of speaking about how the brain processes language and use some of Plato's philosophical efforts to think about words and thoughts as my foundation. My goal, not unlike the process of reading itself, is to use Plato's prescient knowledge about words as the basis for adding new knowledge about the stunning new ways that written words are studied today through the cognitive neurosciences. In the process we will look at the many, convoluted hiding places that words inhabit across multiple regions of the brain: the cerebral loci of Shakespeare's "local habitation." We will also, it is my hope, understand more fully both the beautiful complexity of the reading act, and what it takes for each person to become fully literate.

To begin, in the middle of the *Seventh Letter*, Plato describes four aspects of how we come to know a thing through words, and then, he reflects on the ultimate inadequacy of words to express the essence of our thoughts, the fifth aspect of knowing that goes beyond words. Whether or not Plato or one of his devoted students wrote this letter or part of this letter may never be known.[5] More certain is the way this letter organizes in one place Plato's multiple descriptions about how we know a thing through our words and thoughts. With neither an image of the reading brain nor a linguist's analysis of what we do when we speak or read a word, Plato emphasized what amounts then and now to a fair accounting of what a word embodies and what it does not.

With some linguistic license, I have given a particular organization to the first four of these dimensions of the word: *image or representation, name, definition—meaning and function, knowledge*. I do so because these first four aspects represent a remarkable approximation of the basic processes the brain deploys whenever it encounters a written word. The fifth aspect goes outside what present knowledge of the brain can tell us, but is no less important for it, and will reappear in the discussion of deep reading in the next chapter. In this chapter we begin with a very brief outline of Plato's four dimensions, followed by a more in-depth physiological treatment of the first three. This will be a neuroscientist's tale of Plato's words, with a small surprise thrown into the mix. In Chapter 5 we connect this collective information to the reader's background knowledge, as the platform from which to view the profoundly important *deep reading* processes at the heart of reading. Together these two chapters illumine how Plato's view of words provides an unexpected view of the reading brain in action.

Overview

To begin from a physiological level, when we first turn to read a *single word*, we move our critical attentional systems from whatever went before, to process the visual *form or representation* of the word. Plato refers to the internal image (*eidolon*) which we create to represent a thing; something akin to this occurs when we represent letters and words in the visual system of the reading circuit, in the area referred to as the *visual word form area* (VWFA).

The visual representation quickly activates all manner of input that will eventually become a name (*onoma*), as we retrieve the sounds or phonemes and meanings that correspond to the visual system's information. This fusion of image, sound, and name is almost automatically being connected to the vast array of collective *meanings and functions* that we store about words (e.g. semantic, syntactic, and morphological) that Plato referred to as *definition*. The now-known name activates the sum of our knowledge (*episteme*)—that which is shared with our world and that which is unique to us. More specifically, during this dynamic, synthetic moment the word has become a snowball of input from perceptual, cognitive, motoric, and linguistic processes, mixed with both our uniquely personal memory store of associated events and feelings and also the more commonly shared roots of meanings in the word and the "roles" this word usually plays. Along the way—across all the labyrinthine neuronal networks called upon in the word's journey—it does something more still: it approaches and evokes in us what Plato thought of as the fifth dimension. This is the essential quality of *being* or conceptual schema behind *onoma*, even if the word will never itself reach it.

Such is the way of words, whether for Socrates, who thought that the spoken word was alive in dialogue with others, but not to be written down; for Plato, who wrote Socrates' words down to preserve them; for Ray Jackendoff, who directs our attention to the thoughts evoked by our words; or for us, who live our lives largely oblivious to the whole churning world that lies below the surface of our spoken and our written words. It is my special task in this chapter and the next to try to bring to life some of what lies below the surface of our brain when we read a single word, or—the still more amazing feat—a line or passage of words that can be linked by our brains to staggering numbers of possible thoughts.

Tales of words—structural, temporal, and physiological

Let us begin with... uncertainty! I intentionally surprised your expectations or *predictions* of what I might say next. The reality is that much mystery remains about how the brain reads words, particularly about how *important and uncannily accurate our predictions* are about whatever we are reading. We are constantly predicting what might appear next and re-evaluating our predictions from millisecond to millisecond when we read almost anything. The role that these predictions play in reading is taking center stage in more recent accounts in the neuroscience research, and will be a leitmotif in these chapters.

But first a good word about "uncertainty." Each time I approach the task of describing the reading brain, I learn something heretofore unknown or less known. I also encounter descriptions that need to be altered because new evidence and new ways of thinking replace older conceptualizations. A thoughtful caution mixed with anticipation, therefore, is best used in any examination of the reading brain for some time to come. Not only are our various means of investigation— for example, increasingly varied forms of neuroimaging—becoming ever more precise and sensitive, but so also is our understanding of how structures and their neurons work together to perform a function. Thus, within descriptions of any of the multiple processes we use when we read, the reader will note that I largely eschew descriptions of either a "right or left hemisphere task" or the idea that a given function is "located" in a single structure. Rather, each process that is incorporated in the reading circuit—like phonology or semantics—inhabits entire *neuronal networks*, that, often as not, involve multiple and distant regions in one or both hemispheres across multiple layers of the brain.

Indeed, whole new directions in our knowledge are based not only on understanding the topography of these networks, but also on how these networks come to be connected and coordinated *in time* across large distances in the brain. For example, Stanford neuroscientist Brian Wandell and his colleague Jason Yeatman[6] are investigating how specific white matter fiber bundles (encompassing millions of neurons) connect the major visual, cognitive, and language regions in the development of the reading macrocircuits. Similarly, German neuroscientist Angela Friederici's team studies how large white matter pathways form the very basis of the syntactic network that gives structure to our language.[7] Other researchers, using electrophysiological methods, study how the various components within these macrocircuits operate from millisecond to millisecond.

Furthermore, and differing from my own descriptions of the reading brain a few years ago, some parts of the neuronal networks appear to be multipurpose and used for other processes as well. Michael Anderson[8] uses the term *neural reuse* to describe how neurons—even those that we have believed to be the principal region underlying one set of functions—can sometimes underlie other functions as well, depending on the task that is required of them. Anderson describes how a single, individual neuron can function in different ways, when required to do so by different higher-level networks of cells. He uses the example of the starburst amacrine cell in the retina to illustrate how this colorfully named neuron can be used for either motion perception or eye movements, depending on which network is being activated for the task. Such a view of our intensely interactive brain in both its strong and weak versions is changing how we interpret (and make sense of) years of sometimes contradicting findings based on more localized conceptualizations of brain structure–function relationships.

In similar vein, we are entering an exciting moment in cognitive neuroscience research on reading and language, as findings from *convergent* research approaches (e.g. in which multiple imaging methods are used) increase the precision of our ability to track the word within the particular structural parts of the reading brain macrocircuit in *time*. My Tufts colleague Gina Kuperberg and her team[9] have begun to use an elegantly combined set of imaging methods, including fMRI—which gives highly specific, neuroanatomical, *structural* information—alongside ERPs and MEG, which give far more precise, *temporal* information, in order to study *how and when* different aspects of the semantic system function when we read or speak. Whenever possible, therefore, I will include findings from converging research approaches in my descriptions of the components of the reading circuitry. Nevertheless, both author and reader must be content with what continues to be a still-emerging snapshot of the reading brain. As neuroscientist Michael Gazzaniga[10] stated recently, we will soon have an entirely new vocabulary for describing cognitive activities in space and time, at which point this chapter's descriptions will need their next iteration.

Until then, however, there is much to learn as a foundation for that time, beginning with several essential design principles that are the basis for our ability to create a macrocircuit[11] for processing written language. This new global reading circuit is different from the circuit for oral language, or from any of the basic circuits our species possesses, like vision and cognition, but it couldn't exist without them. Indeed, it is formed from their networks.

A few basic design principles that allowed us to read

> It seems somehow disconcerting to be told that your life, all your hopes, triumphs, and aspirations simply arise from the activity of neurons in your brain. But far from being humiliating, this idea is ennobling.[12]
>
> V. S. Ramachandran, *Phantoms in the Brain*

Our brain has been more or less the same for thousands of years with genetically hardwired circuits and their component structures that are the basis for all our essential functions. From vision and hearing to language and cognition, our basic functions have been unfolding in the same predetermined way for all these years, in every continent on our earth. This is because our genes dictate the formation of relatively universal circuits that are the same across time, culture, and geography. What is not universal are the ways these basic circuits can become connected in different ways in individual brains and the varied ways they can change to accommodate new learning in different environments and cultures. One of the single most significant, indeed game-changing advantages of the *Homo sapiens* brain is that our brain has the capacity to connect itself in new ways *within* those original, genetically dictated circuits and, very importantly, *across* them. We are the connection-makers.

It begins with an extraordinary ace in the brain's design. At the heart of our new capacities is *neuroplasticity*. This feature in our design is the basis for our ability to create new forms of connectivity across previously unconnected structures in the brain, which allows us to go beyond our original repertoire of basic functions. This is what enables us to learn completely new functions—like the cultural inventions numeracy and literacy—that have no genetically predetermined program for their development.

In both of these cases, the human brain learned to connect some of its most basic structures and processes in new circuits that became, over only several millenia, unparalleled in their neural complexity. From the identification of simple marks designating the number of goats or sheep or wine vessels has emerged our capacity to measure the mass of the infinitesimally small Higgs-Boson particle with its possible contributions stretching back to the start of the universe. From the creation of the first symbol on a cave wall or on a rock has emerged our ability to read Aristotle's *Nicomachean Ethics*, Aquinas's *Summa Theologica*, and Virginia Woolf's book that has much to offer about reading, *To the Lighthouse*. An understanding of how a reading brain circuit could emerge with no genes specific only to it, and, therefore, no single ideal version of itself, provides a valuable framework for understanding how we humans learn any new function. Most importantly for our goals here, an understanding of the present reading circuit prepares us for questions about its next, possible iterations that follow in the rest of the book.

Connectivity and neuroplasticity

The emergence of a reading circuit represents one of the best examples of the brain's increasingly sophisticated connectivity. Cross-linguistic data provide an unusual but appropriate introduction for any discussion of the reading brain's connectivity because they illustrate par excellence a core assumption in this book: there is no one, universal reading brain circuit. There are, in fact, already quite a few, and (in another bit of forecasting) there will be more.

Thus it is that the circuit for an English-alphabet-reading brain has both shared components and some different component parts from non-alphabetic orthographies, and even from some other alphabetic ones.[13] Charles Perfetti and his colleagues Donald Bolger and Walter Schneider[14] created the first meta-analysis of forty-three brain imaging studies of readers across different writing systems: in Western alphabetic languages (that share a Roman alphabet like English, Finnish, Italian), in Japanese Kana and Kanji, and in Chinese. By configuring all the available data, they uncovered the presence of three main anatomical regions present across all studied languages.

The three large, convergent regions (all of which we will later discuss in detail) include the visual areas in the occipital lobes and in the occipito-temporal junction; language-related regions of the temporal-parietal lobes; and the speech, language, executive, and motoric areas of the frontal lobes. Regardless of orthographic features, these general areas were activated across all languages studied. And indeed, as Ken Pugh and his colleagues[15] depicted some time ago, these three, very large areas comprise what has long been considered a very basic, global neuroanatomical model of reading, which, along with the cerebellum, has become a foundation for the elaborations and refinements of the last fifteen years that will be sketched here.

The specific pattern of activation within these general areas and indeed the temporal sequence of this activation, however, do differ, and in fascinating ways for different orthographies. Almost as one might predict, the more logographic Chinese and Chinese-derived Japanese Kanji scripts show greater recruitment of specific occipital (visual) and temporal areas across both right and left hemispheres that are necessary in dealing with the complex visual and spatial characteristics of Chinese-based characters and word-form processing. When one considers that the typical Chinese reader is reading at least 4,000–5,000 characters by the middle grades, this only makes sense.

By contrast, the alphabetic systems require far fewer characters, and therefore, less cortical space in visual areas, and particularly less use of one set of networks in the right hemisphere temporal-parietal areas activated in Chinese systems, areas likely involved in linking meaning and image. On the other hand, in alphabet-reading brains, the more time-consuming phonological skills require more cortical areas involved in these sound-related processes. Illustrating how sensitive the circuits are to the internal characteristics of the languages, there are also differences found within alphabetic systems, based on how regular (shallow) or irregular (deep) the orthography of the language is. The more regular orthographies like German, Italian, and Finnish rely more on activation of phonological-related areas than do the less regular English and French orthographies.[16] New research by Swiss neurologist Jean-Marie Annoni and his team has begun to refine this conclusion by showing that the latter, less regular orthographies also may require more activation by visual and attentional networks.[17]

As Perfetti and his colleagues are the first to underscore, the regions discussed are not meant to be exhaustive, but they illumine three principles: first, there is no one ideal reading circuit; second, all reading circuits share some basic, common structures; and third, more subtle differences in circuits reflect the emphases in different orthographies. It is a set of principles that we will return to in a discussion of the subtle or not so subtle differences I hypothesize for the effects of different mediums.

The fact that over time the species has developed various circuits, however, does not explain how any of these circuits emerged from seemingly nothing. For that we turn to several principles in the brain's design that were briefly touched upon earlier and that have been leitmotifs of my work for the last decade. First, there are no genes that are specific to a reading circuit. Rather, the neuroplasticity in the brain's design allows it both to connect its older structures in new ways to make the reading circuit, and also to repurpose the neuronal networks within these original components to carry out new functions.

In the case of the invention of literacy, the earliest examples of symbolic writing systems like Egyptian hieroglyphs and Sumerian characters required connecting very specific, relatively circumscribed regions whose neurons were and indeed still are used in vision and language and thought. Over time, as writing systems became increasingly abstract, more and more neuronal networks in various regions needed to be incorporated. At a macro level, the present reading brain represents an evolving elaboration of the older structures and networks devoted to more basic human functions from attention and memory to vision, cognition, language, motor, and emotion. The more complex the material, the more processes within these functions become recruited. The circuit for reading *Moby Dick* or *Daniel Deronda* needs to be far more elaborated than the circuit used for the first basic hieroglyphs five millennia ago for conveying the number of wine jars, although the latter will always remain one of the stunning achievements in human history. What future circuits will look like will depend on the principles discussed here, and several factors to be discussed later, but first a review of a few basic principles about how the first brain circuits could ever form in the first place.

It is always a pleasure when a fellow scholar finds the apt term or metaphor to describe something otherwise onerously difficult to explain, like how neuronal populations learn to work together for a new function. So it is with cognitive neuroscientists Stanislas Dehaene and Laurent Cohen's use of the term *neuronal recycling*. They use this term to describe how, in the formation of a new cultural invention, the brain reuses regions that were originally dedicated to skills that are cognitively or perceptually related to the new one. In their words neuronal recycling allows humans to "transform an 'ancient function'... into a novel function of a culture."[18]

Dehaene's work in both numeracy and literacy provides pertinent examples of such novel cultural functions. With regard to our ability to perform arithmetical operations, Dehaene has shown how human beings have recycled brain regions that our primate relatives activate for basic numeracy skills. In the presence of two bowls of either six or eight pieces of fruit, it should never be doubted which bowl a chimpanzee will choose. Dehaene and his group have studied the areas used by primates for activities involving numeracy, and how some of these areas become repurposed in *Homo sapiens* brains for higher mathematical skills.

In similar vein, Dehaene uses the combination of his concept of neuronal recycling, with its related concept of a *neuronal niche*, to illumine and delimit several aspects of neuroplasticity underlying literacy's emergence. Similar to my own starting point some years ago, Dehaene's conceptualization begins with the reading brain's ability to use its older networks for a new function, but he makes an extremely important caveat that expands previous views, including my own. According to this view, our brain's original parts possess very particular parameters on what they can and cannot do. These parameters, in turn, dictate what will be easily acquired or not in the acquisition of all new skills. In other words, nature and nurture work very closely together when a new set of skills is developed. There can be no new skill without learning, to be sure, but learning doesn't happen willy-nilly; rather, it is constrained by the range of capacities of the neurons in the original region.

Within this view, Dehaene shows how the principle of neuroplasticity in the reading circuitry emerges within fairly strict limits. In the process he also shows why reading circuits as different as the Chinese and English examples still share more similar regions than different ones. The constraints of nature govern what can be nurtured. In other words, our reading brains differ, but only by so much. A prime example of Dehaene and Cohen's constrained recycling principle can readily be seen in one of the major components in the reading circuit, vision. Whatever the language used, the visual system is able to acquire speed-of-light recognition capacities, fundamental for identifying characters or letters and letter patterns that are the basis for reading.

The "features" of the letters themselves play their own role in this story. Consider once more our species' earliest writing by the Egyptians and the Sumerians. In both of these writing systems, the earliest known characters looked very much like objects in nature. According to the basic premise of the neuronal recycling hypothesis, this resemblance is anything but coincidental. Rather, the features in the earliest characters and indeed the letters in most writing systems today are comprised of visual features that are the natural province of visual regions already "pre-dedicated" to the rapid recognition of similar visual features in objects in nature and faces.[19] In other words, those neurons whose primary function is to identify fine features in nature, faces, and objects are the first to be called upon to identify the fine features of letters. These neurons follow rules set up by nature and continue to conform to limits set long before.

A Neuroscientist's Tale of Words

As my Tufts colleague, philosopher Dan Dennett[20] might respond here, *what went before* is evolutionarily important to understand. The ability almost immediately to identify subtle visual differences in an animal's tracks on the ground as prey or predator and the ability to distinguish the small distinctions between edible and poisonous plants and berries made all the difference to many of our hominid and primate ancestors. The key shared feature in both our ancestors' survival and our present ability to read fluently is speed or timing. Only if recognition can be accomplished in milliseconds could our ancestors run for cover in order to survive, and only in this way can the flash of letters to the retina activate a particular set of neurons in our visual cortex fast enough to be connected to the rest of the global reading circuit across the whole brain.

The importance of speed cannot be overestimated. Its study represents a critical plank in research in cognitive neuroscience, particularly in electrophysiological methods like ERP (Evoked Response Potential) methods that illumine the precise time-course of neural activity for a given function. Phil Holcomb and his team at Tufts University have applied these methods to understanding *what we do when* during the reading act. In a beautiful review, called "Watching the word go by," he and Jonathan Grainger illumine how many of the tasks of the reading circuit—from early visual to later semantic processes—are accomplished by 300 to 500 milliseconds.[21] But now to a more in-depth look into how the brain is able to use only a hundred plus milliseconds to identify letters.

Retinotopic and tonotopic organization principles

To explain this capacity for instantaneous recognition, we turn to two more design principles: *retinotopic* organization and the automaticity made possible by *working groups* of cells, or cell assemblies. Retinotopic organization involves an ingenious design principle in which individual cells in a sensory organ like the retina correspond to particular groups of cells in the primary visual areas and other vision-related areas (there is an analogous tonotopic organization for the ear and auditory areas). This highly organized system is the basis for our species being able to respond at breakneck speeds when we see and then recognize anything from a face to woolly mammoth tracks to the letters on this page. This can happen almost instantly because there are neuronal groups in the retina that correspond to working groups in the visual areas whose basic tasks are to detect features and categories like color, motion, objects, faces. Over the last twenty-five years, as the work of Stanford colleague Brian Wandell and his colleagues[22] attests and contributes to, we have been approaching the still-elusive goal of a comprehensive retinotopic map of the entire visual cortex.

In part thanks to their research and to the massive research on vision over the last two to three decades, we know a great deal about how the visual cortex is organized, which helps us understand how cognitive functions like reading can attain such rapid rates. Within the occipital lobes, there is a macro-level "division of labor" whereby some areas are devoted to primary perceptual input like color and motion and other areas are dedicated to visual processing at more complex levels. Thus, simple visual information such as shape and size is processed in the primary areas, and more complex information like letter and word pattern information is processed further by neurons able to detect more highly specific types of visual information.

Exactly how these cells are organized in terms of a hierarchy of specialization is a matter of continued discussion. As an example of one model, Dehaene and others suggest that the finer the features required of the cells, the more those cells are found towards the outer regions of the visual cortex; and the larger or coarser-grained features are identified by neuronal groups closer to the brain's midline. Thus large patterns for things like buildings would be closer to the midline, while face recognition cells would be closer to outer areas used for smaller object recognition. Interestingly, the "new" category of letters appears to fall somewhere in between faces and small objects like tools.

That said, just as Dehaene and Anderson emphasized, we need to keep the same flexibility about "categories" that these neuronal areas *themselves* exhibit, with some neuronal groups for face and object recognition also activated for letters. It is important, therefore, to avoid thinking that Neuron X performs one and only one function. The reality is usually more complex with some cells activated for more than one neighboring function. The next principle concerns how these cells learn to work together, and for that design principle we turn the clock back a bit to the 1950s and then forward to the present.

Working groups / cell assemblies

In the middle of the last century Canadian psychologist Donald Hebb provided an extremely useful platform for understanding how cells learn to work or fire together. Although our understanding has become far more elaborated in the six decades since Hebb wrote *Organization of Behavior*,[23] the basic outline remains intact. When Cell A excites Cell B persistently over time, there is a change in the synapse between them that is strengthened (or in some cases depressed/inhibited) through a synaptic memory trace. Cell A's efficiency in exciting Cell B is increased every time they activate in unison, and over time they will begin to function as a dedicated unit.

Multiply this basic concept by thousands upon thousands, and you have the formation of untold numbers of working groups of cells that can now fire as highly programmed units whenever activated. The most famous Hebbian phrase that every undergraduate learns about this process is that "the cells that fire together, wire together," and it is as good a way of thinking at a macro-organizational level in the reading circuit, as at the level of single visual Cells A and B.

The visual cortex alone represents an entire repository of connected working groups of cells, each of which corresponds to various levels of organization and contributes to identification and recognition within 150 to 200 milliseconds. The auditory cortex follows similar principles for sound identification, and working groups in large areas within the temporal and parietal lobes perform similarly at the word level, but with later temporal windows. The only way any of this complex organization could ever work, however, goes back to Hebb. Working groups of cells must learn to become units that can fire almost automatically in time in their given spatial habitats, so as to send their information *back and forth* both to be connected within their own relatively small part of the cortex and also to connect to other component processes in the global reading circuit and to receive their input to refine their own.

To return the clock to current research, MIT neuroscientist Earl Miller hypothesizes that the rhythmic synchronicity in the brain's wave patterns (i.e. oscillations) may be what helps to coordinate the neural activity across the very distant regions of the attentional networks essential in reading.[24] In other words, our essential cognitive functions are not only dictated by where neural networks occur, but also by the very particular firing pattern that these networks learn and which binds them all together not just locally, but temporally across large distances in the brain.

Understanding the importance of space and time in the underlying processes of reading underscores that the act of reading text is anything but a straightforward, feed-forward process. If only it were all linear, we could understand reading far more easily; but then we wouldn't have the beautiful complexity that enables us all to read this sentence without missing a beat or a boat: "I desperately searched for the crimson bow and knew immediately it was your boat."

Most of you had to make a quick garden-path move to retrieve the correct pronunciation of *bow* after you reached the word *boat*, which clued you into its less frequent meaning. Nevertheless, you were actually faster than you might have been, because I "primed" you beforehand when I wrote "beat or *boat*." No simple principle of linearity will ever describe the temporal and spatial chiaroscuro that is the reading brain at its "back and forth" work on this and on many sentences. Thus even within the most basic discussion of the principle of cell assemblies, we have to remember that Cell B can also influence Cell A and indeed that whole networks in entirely different regions project feed-forward and feedback input. These interactions are the key to how we can disambiguate words like *bow*, by the interactions between our *recognition* and *prediction* processes.

In fact, the great majority of our words are primed or facilitated for us before we even see them by whatever we read before. All of this complexity doesn't mean that for many of our most frequently seen words, there isn't a much simpler and more direct plan of attack, particularly for single words. But it does mean that as basic recognition is needed for words in whole sentences, reading presses upon its working groups some of the most intensely *dynamic and interactive* types of operations that process in parallel fashion from across hemispheres and lobes until final identification and comprehension are completed.

In brief summary, the major goal in discussing these design principles is to begin to appreciate how the reading circuit rests on the smooth, rapid-fire, parallel processing of tiny groups of neurons that had to learn both whole new functions and also how to fire together within and across many initially unrelated regions of the brain. Millions of cells, therefore, have to work together to allow you to identify the visual representation of the word *bear* in less than 200 milliseconds; to know its name's sounds, meanings, syntactic functions, and associations within another 200 to 300 milliseconds; and... not to forget... to add contextual and background knowledge and no small amount of affect when you have to read the word in a sentence, like "Reading is a bear."

With these very basic principles as background, we will now use Plato's timeless view of words as a scaffolding to probe more deeply into the "particulars" of the reading brain circuitry. In so doing, we will better understand how great a leap lies between the literate and the non-literate brain, and what elaborate circuitry is necessary for the development of the *literary mind*. As we have just seen in macro-view, the connections that form the reading circuitry include massive numbers of networks from across the brain—from the brainstem and the cerebellum at the base of the brain, through the midbrain and up through both subcortical levels to the cerebral cortex. Such an expansion of connections serves not only reading, but the *having of whole new thoughts*. An understanding of the literate brain, therefore, prepares us to think both about non-literacy and about things literary in far more appreciative ways.

Plato, Socrates, and who taught whom

Just in case a few of you might have forgotten the lineage of our three most famous Greek philosophers: Socrates taught Plato, and Plato taught Aristotle. What few people ever think about or indeed ever know is that Socrates had a teacher as well, who was one of the most mysterious, little-known figures of all time: a female philosopher named Diotima. Most intriguingly, according to Plato's account, Socrates credits Diotima, the "female maiden from Manitea," as the original source of the *Socratic* method!

For many years I have imagined conversations with Socrates about how prescient he was in his concerns about the threats to memory and internal knowledge that the acquisition of literacy posed, not only to Phaedrus, to loyal Antisthenes, and to the rest of his pupils in ancient Greece, but also to the youth of the twenty-first century. I imagined his astonishment at the idea that someone who lived and wrote two and a half millennia later would "read" and agree with him about his worries for the young that will be introduced in Chapter 6. But one of the questions I would most like to have asked Socrates is about Diotima and her teaching. I will not comment on the obvious issues contained in history's naming her dialogical method after her male pupil. What I would like to know is how Diotima, who might well have been non-literate, contributed to Socrates' largely negative and Plato's ambivalent thoughts about written words. Among other questions, I wish it were possible to know whether Diotima's potential lack of exposure to literacy was the source of Socrates' determined eschewing of its use.

Certainly, Plato's ambivalence shines both through his use of writing to preserve Socrates' concerns, and through his own barely disguised worries: "That is why no intelligent man will ever dare to commit his thoughts to words, still less to words that cannot be changed, as is the case with what is expressed in written characters."[25] (One can only wish that our youth on Facebook showed similar worries.) Regardless, however, of what Diotima, Socrates, or Plato might have thought about literacy, their thoughts about *words* guide this chapter in ways that I hope would give them and the reader some satisfaction and, perhaps, a surprise or two.

Within that context, therefore, I ask the reader for a little "suspension of disbelief" for what I wish to do next. I cannot name a method of teaching after Diotima, but I can name my reading brain after her. Thus in the rest of this chapter, you will see an artistic rendering of *Diotima's brain* as the basis for building a literate brain from Diotima's probably non-literate one. I have asked my former student, and well-known cerebellum researcher at American University, Catherine Stoodley, to illustrate the beauty and the complexity of some parts of the reading circuit for this chapter and the next, as she has done for me before. I asked her to imagine and draw several views of Diotima's imagined brain to illustrate Plato's different dimensions of words. Because Catherine is first a neuroscientist, second a very talented artist, and third a wonderfully whimsical mother, she decided to draw a view of the brain of this philosophical "grandmother" as if it were ten feet high. See her first drawing of Diotima's brain (Figure 4.1) with a few of Plato's more famous readers looking on to give visual perspective. She and I are quite curious whether you can guess who these figures are, for they will have cameo appearances in each of the figures that follow. To give you one recursive set of hints along with a bit of comic relief, the oldest figure's work became part of the foundation for Western philosophy largely through the efforts of the depicted saintly monk, whose thirteenth-century emphasis on human reason was also a hallmark of this nineteenth-century novelist, whom everyone believed to be a male, till they (and Queen Victoria) learned she was not.[26]

Eidolon—imaging the word through processes of attention and vision

Attention

The circuitry begins in Diotima's brain, as in everyone's, with attention. Several forms of attention are activated when we attend to anything. Reading a word (singly or in text) requires the deployment of different attentional systems that change with the reader's expertise, the specific task, and the characteristics of the medium. Let me give you an example. Consider the term, *Periventricular nodular heterotopia*. I remember the very first time I ever saw it. It was in the middle of a letter from Boston neurologist Bernard Chang many years ago, in which he described a rare seizure disorder that was characterized by only one shared behavior across all his patients with it: dysfluent reading. I remember seeing this word in the letter and stopping everything I was accustomed to doing when I read. I had not seen the term before; I did not know how to pronounce it; and I had no clue at first glance what it meant. With suddenly laser-beamed attention, I moved all my attention to focus on this term; I inhibited every other aspect of my normal reading; and I concentrated on it till I saw all the cues to its meaning within its very regular morphemes.

With that newly attended information, I was able to pronounce the term easily, and figure out, albeit incorrectly at first, what it meant. I thought the ventricles must refer to the heart, when, in fact, they refer to the brain's ventricles, which I should have deduced in any letter from a neurologist. But the point here is a different one. I literally stopped my normally fluent reading to attend to the process of reading this unknown word, and in the process laid bare how little explicit attention I usually give to the multiple, implicit attentional processes that all of us employ every time we read.

Figure 4.1. Diotima's brain

The first step actually involves not one, but three aspects of attention that prepare or *orient* us for all that follows and that are very similar to what I did when I had to stop everything and attend to periventricular nodular heterotopia (hereafter: PVN). First, we must *disengage* our attention from whatever went before and *inhibit* whatever information was just in our visual or auditory processing from the previous word, so that we can *move forward*. This disengagement process involves a posterior part of our parietal lobes (see Diotima's brain). Next we need to move our attention to the word that confronts us, so that our typically precise and regimented eye movements stop to concentrate on this visual information. An area within our midbrain called the *superior colliculi* helps regulate the typical eye movements (called saccades) that we usually use to sweep the words on a page.

Third, we need to *spotlight* or focus our attention on whatever the visual stimulus is, in this case PVN. Miller and Buschman[27] demonstrate how the bottom-up stimuli that attract our attention (e.g. the quick flash of a moving object) move from the parietal areas to the frontal areas, while our more cognitive-controlled forms of attention move from the frontal areas to the varied regions of the visual cortex. This latter kind of attention requires the precise coordination of our frontal cortex and of our *thalamus*, which lies below the cortical surface of our brain in the second layer of the brain (diencephalon) and acts as a kind of coordinating switchboard for different layers of the brain. Together, this first set of attentional processes comprises what is referred to as the *orienting system of attention*. And that is what I did when I first encountered PVN; I oriented my attentional focus.

The orienting attention system literally sets us up to read, by preparing us for the next forms of attention. In other words, the first attentional system performs the "Moses role": it prepares the way, but never enters the place itself. The next functions of attention move to the promised word by setting in motion all the things we need to do to read the word and to keep available whatever information we need in our working memory. Dehaene and Jean-Pierre Changeux describe how these latter aspects of attention work together with multiple aspects of cognition in our frontal lobes as a *global neuronal workspace*[28] for varied human activities. In reading, this cortical workspace allows the reader to assemble, evaluate, and synthesize all that is occurring across the rest of the brain. We will return many times to the powerful roles played by the frontal lobes, particularly the large prefrontal regions (that lie immediately behind the forehead), in setting up, monitoring, and integrating information from across the brain when we attend to a written word. The specifics of the particular reading task dictate what is used where and when.

The "when" is barely calculable by us. The multiple attentional preparations operate with such rapidity that we are rarely, if ever, aware of them, except when they don't function well, as with individuals who struggle with attentional disorders, or when we are confronted with words that give pause like PVN or terms like *onomatopoeia* or *anastomosis* that momentarily confound psychologists but sail by for people in literature.

Vision

After the early attentional systems set the processes in motion, the complex visual system makes its contributions. Different groups of neurons relay information on specific categories of visual information (e.g. color and motion). Rendering retinotopic organization artistically is no mean feat, particularly since highly specific groups of cells in the retina transmit information to their corresponding working groups in the visual cortex, which is the neuronal equivalent of miles away. Getting there requires a journey and a half, which is shown in Cat's drawing of the visual pathways from Diotima's eye to her occipital lobes.

Seen in Figure 4.2, you will notice Aristotle's rather keen attention to how information in the visual pathways moves. After the visual information is perceived by specific cells in the retina, it proceeds along the optic nerve tract to the optic chiasm, where there is a split between some signals going to the occipital lobes in the right hemisphere and others to the left hemisphere. Along their respective routes there is a string of critical pit stops: at the thalamus (where an area called the *lateral geniculate nuclei* integrates visual information), through the long, beautifully constructed fiber tracts of the *optic radiation* areas, and finally within the very specific fourth layer of the *primary visual cortex* in the occipital lobes.

After the retina's information arrives at the occipital lobes, it goes, as noted, to a very specific location: the fourth layer of the visual areas

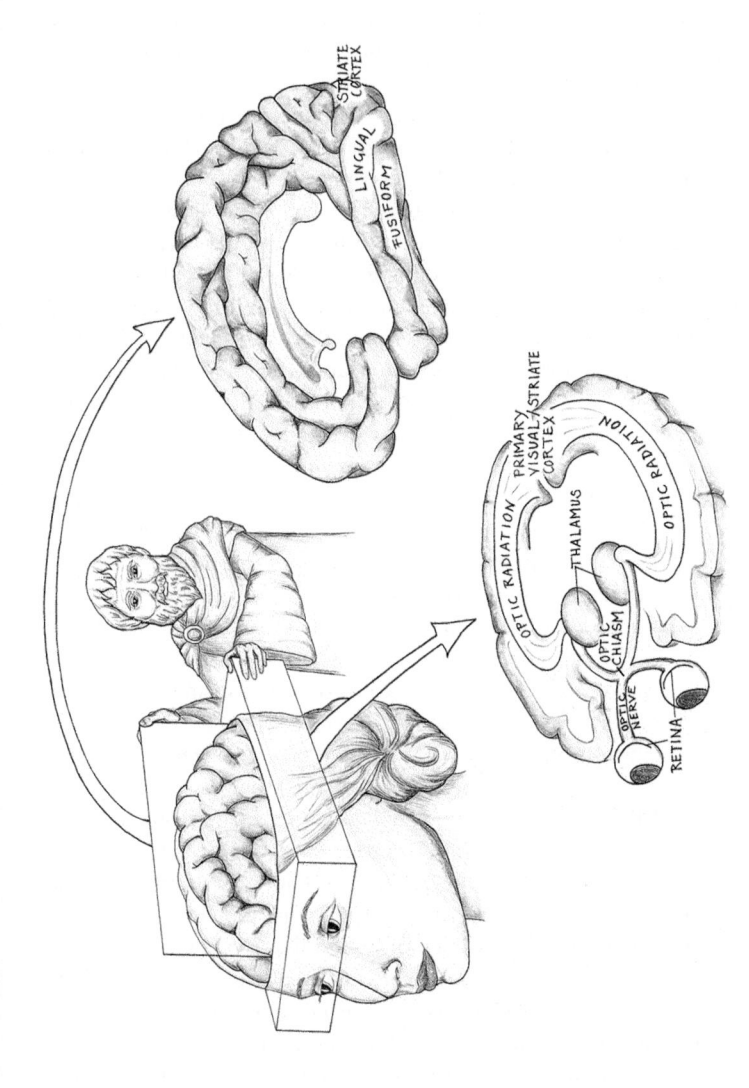

Figure 4.2. Diotima's visual system

called the *striate cortex* (Latin word for *stripe*). If you can ever look with the naked eye at this posterior part of the brain's occipital lobes where the nerve fibers come in from the retina, you will be able to see a stripe. This is caused by the pattern made from white, myelinated cells coming in from the thalamus and meeting short, grey, unmyelinated cells in the visual areas. Their neatly organized arrangement in the visual cortex of grey cell, white cell, grey cell, white cell, etc., forms a stripe to the naked eye. Indeed, everything is astonishingly organized in the six layers of the striate cortex. Adjacent to the striate cortex are the *extrastriate* regions, that function in more complex visual pattern information processing. We only wish that Aristotle could have had this information in his still fascinating discussions of perception and thought. I have no doubt that he would be intrigued by the very idea that visual information becomes transformed in such a way that it aids recognition of the next visual information. It is yet another aspect of how visual processes involve prediction, which, in turn, aids more rapid recognition.

As Brian Wandell[29] in his mapping of the visual system underscores, the first principle here is that specialization of function begins in the retina. The second is that the retina projects to corresponding areas or zones of specialization in visual regions, which themselves provide feedback signals that influence how the next incoming information is processed. After the primary visual cortex receives its incoming information, it sends the information on for further processing to neuronal groups specializing in particular areas.

This highly interactive second principle of specialization of function helps contextualize earlier work by neuroscientists Martha Farah and Thad Polk. They have long studied patients who sustained very specific damage to the extrastriate cortex that renders them no longer able to read, a condition called *acquired alexia*. (Note: this is very different from developmental dyslexia where the child has difficulty learning to read.) Farah and Polk's work demonstrated that there are specialized visual areas used for the "*rapid encoding* of multiple shapes." Further, they stated that letters comprise a "specialization within a specialization"[30] within this area. Farah, Polk, and their group found that there are different neural substrates for letters and numbers—with one fascinating exception: Canadian postal workers. The brains of these postal workers do not show the same specialization differentiating letters and numbers, because they are daily required to process letters and numbers together in Canada's postal codes (e.g. the postal code for our Toronto friend Maureen Lovett is M5G 1X8). It is a pity that postal workers from London were not included, with the city's 812 equally mixed, letter-number postal codes. (We already know that London taxi drivers with their superior spatial navigation skills have larger posterior hippocampi than the rest of us. London postal workers should have their own claim to areas of cortical superiority.)

Thus, whatever we see with our eyes is matched with correlative working groups of "first responder" cells that make the original match that cascades into ever more sophisticated levels of processing in other visual areas.[31] In one of the now classic, pioneering studies of how the levels of identifying written words are processed in the brain, Washington University neuroscientists Marcus Raichle and Steve Petersen[32] showed that when subjects just looked at a visual symbol, they activated both the striate, primary visual cortex and some extrastriate areas. When they read a permissible word like *brain*, specific parts (lateral and medial) of extrastriate cortex appeared activated. If the subjects were confronted with obviously false fonts or illegal letter strings (e.g. *rbnai*), their extrastriate regions were not activated. The most interesting condition involved "tricking" the visual areas with nonsense words that follow English spelling rules (e.g. *biran*), *and* that might remind their subjects of dead poets: in this case, the same extrastriate regions were once again activated, along with what are called the *fusiform and lingual gyri*, directly below the cortical layer. (I hope you realize that I used a little poetic license with my examples here: Petersen and Raichle et al.'s design never included the "dead poets" condition!) What their research began, however, was the study of the different levels of visual processing that occur in the initial identification or precursors of reading. It is a beautiful illustration both of how highly trained the visual cortex becomes in its knowledge of its own acquired writing system, and also of how important multiple exposures to letters and letter patterns are for young readers so that they form high-quality representations of these letters.

Since their landmark study, many of the original findings—that were based at the time on one of the first forms of imaging, PET scans—have been elaborated, refined, and clarified with more precise forms of imaging. For example, fMRI methods today dramatically increase our ability to image underlying structures. Nevertheless, these methods remain too sluggish to capture *when* an activity occurs. ERP and MEG methods offer the converse: they can pinpoint when an activity happens, even though the structural resolution is inferior to fMRI. As mentioned at the outset, an exciting innovation by current researchers is the ability to use converging information from both types of methods, so as to bring both structural and temporal precision to the evolving knowledge base for the reading circuitry.

One of the more prominent additions to our evolving picture of reading's early identification processes involves an area that has gained as close to "notoriety" as a cortical region can get. Found at the juncture of the occipital and temporal lobes (see Figure 4.1), there is a region that you may recall from past chapters as activated across all known writing systems during the identification of letters/characters. Part of what Perfetti and his colleagues included in their three "universally shared" regions, this area has been the subject of special study by Dehaene, Bruce McCandliss, and their colleagues who colorfully refer to it as the "*letterbox*" or the VWFA.[33]

As briefly alluded to earlier, this group of researchers posit a particular hierarchical organization of the VWFA in which discrete groups of neurons become repurposed for discrete aspects of letter and word identification. According to this view, the hierarchy follows principles of increasing abstraction, with neurons for letters to be found in the posterior or rearmost areas of the VWFA, followed by letter chunks like morphemes (without meaning attached yet), ending with whole words represented in the most anterior regions. Brian Wandell contextualizes this conceptualization of a hierarchical organization as one of several possible arrangements.

To be sure, not all researchers share this term or this view of a specified letterbox function. Ken Pugh and his research group at Haskins Laboratory, for example, prefer to describe this area, like Wandell, in more topographic terms, as the ventral occipital-temporal (vOT) juncture. From a very different perspective, British researchers Cathy Price and Joseph Devlin argue for a much broadened, "polymodal" view of this region so as to include other functions like object naming and various word-retrieval processes.[34] The controversy that exists around nomenclature and the functions for this key reading region—a region that appears to be universally shared across different languages' reading circuits—brings us to repeat an important cautionary statement that must be the conceptual denominator of any description of the reading brain during this moment in time. Our knowledge about the complex, reading brain's circuitry continues to evolve along with our ever increasing knowledge about the regions and functions that subserve it. It is the case that new insights will inevitably cause researchers to eat many words once loved or disdained, as I have done and will do. This is part and parcel of any relatively new field of research like cognitive neuroscience.

To summarize, if you think of vision as a microcosm of how the whole brain works, this visual journey eventually uses input for identifying the word from all five layers of the brain; attains astonishing rapidity through specialization of function; and propels the rapidity of later processes through a dynamic, feed-forward, feed-back check and balance system provided by both new and previous input about what was just seen and understood. The latter interactions appear to occur potentially before the whole of the visual cortex is fully activated.

This initial identification of the visual form or image of a single word is, as you know already, only the start of things. Close on the heels of this identification comes the near-to-simultaneous parallel processing of multiple cortical and subcortical pathways that connect visual information to all related language, cognitive, affective, and articulatory input. The connections to these associated pieces of information confront us with an even more typical level of processing written words in *text*.

To this point, we have been largely discussing what transpires for a single word to be identified. The beauty of the reading brain emerges whole-cloth when the complexity of sentences with all their cognitive richness is involved, and when the information from previous words works, in Gina Kuperberg's apposite term, "*proactively*"[35] to make some words more likely to be activated or recognized than others. The notion that we are predicting what we will read based on what we know and what we have just read updates any previous, however unintended, impression of a tidy sequence of events in the visual descriptions. To appreciate the multiple contributions that are interacting almost as soon as the last of the visual areas go to work (if not sooner) requires that we understand the range of processes underlying Plato's other dimensions in a word, beginning with what goes into a name. Thus I am asking the reader to think nonlinearly, even as I am forced to write in linear fashion.

Onoma—retrieving the name of the word

> ...the stones remain less real to those who cannot
> name them, or read the mute syllables graven in silica.
> ...To name is to know and remember.[36]
>
> Dana Gioia, "Words"

What Ray Jackendoff memorably described as "a collection of small and oddly shaped peepholes with distorting lenses"[37] refers to the many varied types of information we store about words: from their often multiple meanings and different syntactic roles, to the very particular "life" that some words inhabit for us inside our long-term memories. It is, however, one thing to know that the various dimensions of words are influencing each other in dynamic interactions (see the work of Kurt Fischer), it is another to conceptualize how it all happens. This is particularly the case for the ways our visual, phonological, semantic, and syntactic sources of information all contribute to retrieving the name or label of the written word and connecting this label to what we know. Previous knowledge about the meaning of the word speeds up the retrieval of its name when it is read, and, due to our proactive processing system, knowing the context for the word speeds up both recognition and the retrieval of its name.

The reality is that the retrieval of a word's name is one of the most complicated acts within the overlapping oral and written language circuits. Years ago, in full disclosure, I wrote an entire dissertation on the topic of word-retrieval and how it incorporates input from a massive number of perceptual, linguistic, cognitive, and affective processes. It is this very complexity that makes the retrieval of a word exquisitely sensitive to many factors and vulnerable to loss. This is why naming problems (called *dysnomia*) accompany all forms of aphasia, as well as, to be sure, the aging process. When the poet Dana Gioia writes that "to name is to know and remember," there is every form of linguistic, physiological, and existential reality beneath his words, particularly within the varied linguistic systems. In this section we will discuss the input from the phonological or sound-based systems on the word's retrieval, and in the next section will focus on input from the meaning-based and syntactic systems.

Do you remember Emily Dickinson's memorable lines quoted earlier: "The brain is just the weight of God.... For Heft them Pound for Pound, and they will differ if they do, like Syllable from Sound"? I often quote this poem about the brain by our beloved poet from New England, because there are many reverential thoughts to be inferred, particularly about the relationship between human beings and divine nature. Within the more modest goals of this book, I wish to emphasize only one of Miss Dickinson's insights here, albeit unintended: our brain's ability to differentiate sounds from syllables, with some working groups of neurons responsible for each of these categories.

For, just as we humans are endowed with a genetically provided retinotopic organization, we also have an analogous tonotopic organization, which functions along similar lines for the different units of sounds within our language. For example, each type of sound activates specific working groups of cells, with different levels of response contributing to the identification of a single sound or the sounds within a word or a sentence. Thus, simple sounds like pure tones are processed in a primary input area, called Heschl's gyrus, while the more complex processing of phonemes and larger speech patterns occurs in other temporal-parietal areas and in widely distributed neural networks across the brain.[38]

In Chapter 2, we briefly discussed how essential phonemes are for oral language. They are equally critical for written language. Reading acquisition depends at its core on the brain's initial ability to integrate information about the letter or grapheme with information about the sound or phoneme. Unless the phonemes of the language are fully represented in their respective regions, there can be no Grapheme/Phoneme Correspondence (GPC) rules to apply. There will be no decoding. There will be no reading or literacy. There will be no literary mind. The fundamental blocks of reading depend upon the brain's capacity to set up cell assemblies for high-quality representations of both letters and phonemes.

Not that long ago, our understanding of speech and language was based heavily on a fairly localized view in which two structural areas in the left hemisphere—Broca's area in the frontal lobe and Wernicke's area in the temporal lobe and the connective fiber bundles between them (*arcuate fasciculus*)—dominated our understanding of many language functions. Within this view, the upper, more anterior part of the temporal lobes, Wernicke's area, was thought largely responsible for the more complex types of information that enable us to *comprehend* linguistic sounds and words, while Broca's area was thought of as the center of *speech production* processes.

Our present conceptualizations involve a far more differentiated understanding of these two complex areas and how they are connected within extensive cortical and subcortical networks in and under frontal, prefrontal, and bilateral temporal-parietal areas. Further, there are new emphases on how some pivotal areas serve as "hubs" for connecting the widely distributed information they are receiving, processing, and forwarding. A *hub,* as neuroscientist Olaf Sporns describes, refers to an area that integrates the varied subsystems involved in a cognitive function.[39] If you look at Figure 4.3, you can see George Eliot looking very appropriately at the multiplicity of hubs that all contribute to language: including not only Wernicke's area in the left posterior superior/middle temporal cortex and Broca's area in the left inferior frontal cortex, but also the left anterior superior/middle temporal cortex,[40] along with the VWFA. This figure shows at a glance how auditory and phonological and other language processes include regions stretching across the cortex.

Processing of sound is hardly restricted to the cortical and subcortical layers of our brain. As this book's neuroscientist-artist Cat Stoodley[41] knows better than almost any of us, the right cerebellum is extensively involved in both the processing and time-locked coordination of phonemes, as well as of semantic-linked input, discussed in the next section. There are other areas: for example at the top of the brainstem is the midbrain (that is, the third or mesencephalon layer). It contains, among other interesting things, two sets of hill-like structures (hence their Latin names, *superior colliculi* and *inferior colliculi*) which are integral to coordinating visual and phonological processes used in reading. The structural proximity for these two functions is one of several examples of the elegance in design that likely contributes to the efficiency necessary when many regions of the brain must be integrated rapidly for reading to occur.

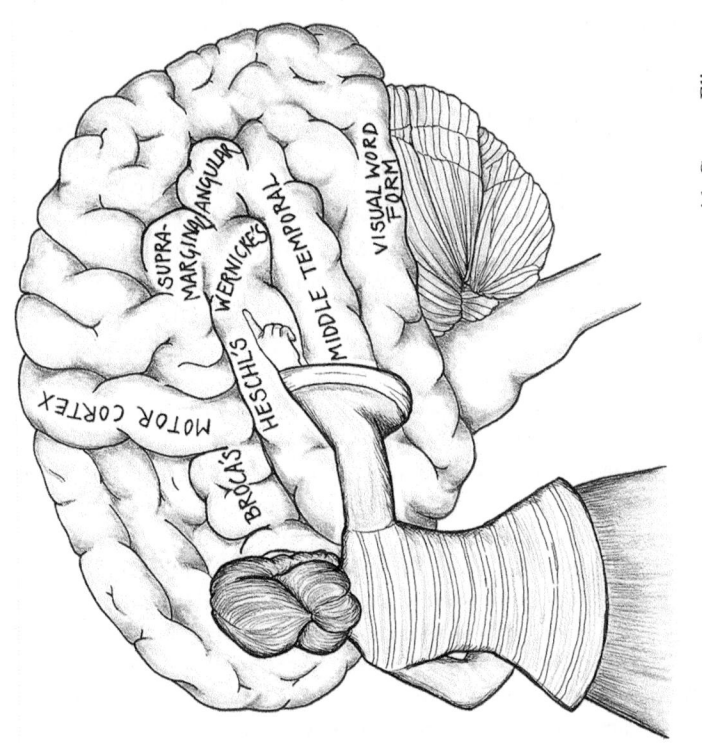

Figure 4.3. Phonological and semantic processes with George Eliot

Finding the name

One might predict that a description of what happens when we retrieve written words would involve not just activating the phonemes, but also activating areas responsible for articulating the phonemes (e.g. lips, teeth, larynx, tongue, etc.) on the motor strip adjacent to Broca's area. Indeed, that happens, particularly at the end of the reading act if we are reading aloud. But perhaps one of the more unanticipated surprises in the reading brain is how involved the motor cortex is when we read not only aloud, but also silently when we read with care.

What comes with a fresh startle every time I read it are the results from research groups as disparate as Pulvermüller[42] who studies "action verbs"; Raymond Mar[43] who studies "embodied comprehension" in the brain; and Natalie Phillips[44] who studies Jane Austen! All of them are finding that when we read with care (particularly something previously unknown to us), the motoric areas also activate as we read words that elicit motion (like *run*) or sensations (like *touch*).

More specifically, literature scholar Phillips joined forces with a group of Stanford neuroscientists to study what is activated when English literature majors read either superficially or in what Philips and many others before her refer to as *"close reading"*: that is, in carefully attended, systematic fashion.[45] In contrast to what they did when merely reading at a surface level, when the students read the same text with close attention, their motor strip became intensely activated in parallel with the actions of the characters in the novel they were reading. This is because when we read certain words, neurons in our frontal lobes' motoric regions simulate the activity of these words. Neuroscientist Pulvermüller, for example, found that our "action verbs" mapped into particular parts of the motor strip, so that *kiss* activated areas for the mouth, while *kick* activated areas for the leg and foot.

Equally provocative and supportive, Raymond Mar's group studies how differences in the types of writing (e.g. action-based; visually vivid; emotionally charged; fictional vs non-fictional) require different types of cognitive, linguistic, perceptual, affective, and motoric responses, which, in turn, activate different regions and networks. Suffice to say that when we read the actions of our characters—like Pip fleeing from Joe in *Great Expectations*—we run too. Similarly, when we read how Daisy felt the soft cashmere of Gatsby's seemingly never-ending piles of sweaters, we feel them too. The corresponding neuronal groups for the muscles in our motoric system and for tactile perception in our somatosensory cortex activate when we read action and sensorially laden words. In other words, we flee, we see, we feel right along with the characters we read. I think George Eliot would be singularly impressed by the idea that we humans are quite literally acting out physiologically what we read.

Meanings—connecting semantic and syntactic systems

> Each word inheres in a labyrinth of branching interverbal relationships going back...to (the reality) that all words were originally metaphors.[46]
>
> J. Hillis Miller, *Ariadne's Thread*

Written decades ago, Miller's evocative description of the word presages the concept of underlying linguistic networks, complete with conceptual associations, polysemous meanings, contextual influences, evoked images, complex syntactic functions, as well as allusions and figurative thought. Indeed, the semantic, syntactic, and morphological aspects of language, as discussed in Chapter 2, embody whole, labyrinthine networks of regions that are responsible for giving us what goes into the extensive knowledge we possess about every word. Miller's description of the labyrinth inhabited by words could not be more true neuroanatomically, or linguistically, where it is often referred to as a *semantic relatedness network* (or sometimes simply *semantic neighborhood*). In the following two subsections, I hope to provide a single, brief glimpse of the multifaceted nature of our semantic and syntactic networks and how our brain processes the many layers of meaning we enter when we "see a world" within a word.

Semantic contributions to the meaning of a word

> To see a world in a grain of sand, and heaven in a flower[47]
>
> William Blake, "Auguries of Innocence"

I think both William Blake and George Eliot would have loved the very idea of the semantic "network." It gives concrete substance to how a word, like a single "grain of sand," contains a world or sphere that has a physical reality—in this case, within the brain's hidden convolutions—and a less tangible one. Nevertheless, given his epoch's inventive but inaccurate view of the brain (think Franz Joseph Gall), Blake might be overwhelmed with what we now know about how much of the brain is involved when we search for a single word's meaning.

This book's readers will not. Semantic representations are widely distributed across the entire cortex, with extensive activation in particular in three now familiar general regions: frontal lobes, tempo-parietal regions, and the right cerebellum. Many of these areas neighbor regions subserving phonological processes, or, as in the angular gyrus—which lies at the juncture of the temporal and parietal lobes—are relatively indistinguishable from each other within this area.

In an effort some time ago to bring clarity to the overlapping structures and functions in Broca's area, my colleagues John Gabrieli at MIT and Russ Poldrack[48] at Stanford suggested that the anterior portion of Broca's area may be more occupied with direct semantic content, while the posterior regions may be more involved in the access and retrieval of this information in its phonological forms. This close-but-separate arrangement is akin to the way Broca's area is situated conveniently near the areas in the motor cortex responsible for the lips, tongue, mouth, and larynx. Just as we saw before, proximity increases efficiency in both oral and written language.

There are, however, differences between the word's sound and meaning systems that broaden our understanding. For example, one large difference between phonological and semantic areas concerns the relatively greater distribution of semantic operations found bilaterally, as opposed to the more straightforward left hemisphere distribution used in phonological processing. The precision needed by phonological processes is well-suited both to the particular regions and to the types of neurons more prevalent in left hemisphere structures.

By the same token, the great breadth of semantic functions—from imagability, to contextual associations, to polysemy (the beautifully sonorous-sounding function that refers to multiple meanings)—is well suited to a broader range of bilateral regions that include right hemisphere, temporal-parietal areas. As Daniel Levitin[49] described, many right hemisphere neurons are "more broadly tuned, with longer branches and more dendritic spines," all of which are conducive for integrating input from larger expanses across the cortex. In other words, the physiology of the regions and even the types of neurons in these regions reflect the multiplicity of characteristics in the semantic process and the wide distribution this involves. More specifically, the broad bandwidth of semantic processes is well served by a set of bi-hemispheric and right cerebellar networks that undergird both the precision needed for the retrieval of meanings, and also the multiple forms of creative associations that meaning elicits in us.

Gina Kuperberg conducts groundbreaking research on regions subserving different semantic functions. She and her colleagues are finding intriguing evidence for a "hub" in the more anterior parts of the upper temporal lobe areas called the *superior temporal gyrus*. Kuperberg's group[50] showed that activity in this semantic hub links words with widely distributed semantic information. This involves rapid connections from what we have read immediately before to what we know from the text's context. The result is referred to as *semantic facilitation*, where we are, to reuse Kuperberg's term, *proactively* readied to understand the present text on the basis of what went before.

Through her cutting-edge uses of three different forms of brain imaging—fMRI, MEG, and ERP—she and her colleagues are able to capture *both* the neuroanatomical portrait of the structural networks underlying semantic processes (through fMRI) *and* their temporal sequence within a very precise window of time (through MEG and ERPs). It now appears that the *first* processes involved in the extraction of meaning occur between 350 and 450 milliseconds (the N400 in the electrophysiological literature): that is, the time right *after* the visual and phonological aspects of a word are activated, and right *before later* types of semantic processes. As alluded to earlier, the N400 represents a kind of window on the brain's timetable for performing various activities. It has been studied comprehensively, because it is the moment when meaning is bestowed on all that went before, whether in the processing of a word or, outside the language domain, in the recognition of a face. Marta Kutas, who has contributed some of the seminal work on the N400, describes it as an "electrical snapshot of the intersection of a feedforward flow of stimulus-driven activity with the ... dynamically active neural landscape that is semantic memory."[51] In other words, everything we have just processed converges with what we know in our memory, and is changed during this small window of time. If our predictions are met, we move forward; if we make prediction "errors," extra milliseconds are needed to analyze exactly what we have, literally, in front of us.

For example, think back to the "garden path" loop you made when discovering *bow* referred to a boat, rather than to a gift-wrapped package. When you encountered this prediction error, you experienced how later semantic, contextual information (i.e. when you read *boat*) influenced your pronunciation *after* its visual presentation and *after* the first, but *not last piece of* phonological input. Mark Seidenberg and his colleagues[52] study the various pathways involved when we read, and emphasize how this later semantic information is linked back to phonological information, with a special role played by the left angular gyrus in this later back and forth processing.

A great deal happens during the extra milliseconds of later processing when revision is needed in reading. Typically, we are busily mapping our critical predictions within a very narrow time window. However, if our predictions prove false when we encounter later semantic-contextual information (as in the *bow* example), we must expend more time to correct our error (usually between 500 and 800 milliseconds). This is not necessarily a negative aspect in reading. Rather, this time can serve to reappraise and expand our former thoughts, which can, in turn, enhance our overall comprehension.

Just not too much time. As Kuperberg suggests, we learn to map our predictions through input from multiple levels of representations, so that we can make these adjustments without undue loss of efficiency. Kuperberg and her colleagues describe a simple, but fascinating example of the semantic system's dynamic learning in oral discourse when we realize a speaker is not fluent in English.[53] We literally learn to adjust our predictions on the spot. In other words, our semantic processes are anything but temporally static and, in Kuperberg's words, help us "to learn to expect the unexpected," one of the most essential aspects to deeper forms of listening and reading.

These slightly later activated semantic functions involve their own set of neural networks, including the middle part of the frontal lobe of the left hemisphere, and, as Seidenberg's research buttresses, the angular gyrus, most likely in both left and right hemispheres. We have known for some time about the role of the left angular gyrus in connecting various forms of input necessary for reading, thanks to the pioneering work of nineteenth-century neurologist Jules Dejerine, twentieth-century neurologist (and revered teacher) Norman Geschwind,[54] and John Gabrieli's research group at MIT.[55]

These more recent findings point to a higher, meta-associative level in semantic processing that is critical to the formation not only of a literate person, but also, I believe, of the literary mind. As the emerging work on semantic processing demonstrates, it is not only our ability to bring to the fore the meaning of what we read in any given moment, but also the essential ability to *use the context of what we have already read to predict what we will read* that helps us to understand the rich, layered meanings in text and to read and think ever more efficiently and deeply.

The converse is equally important. If we do not possess this bank of semantic knowledge and know how to use it, our reading will be proportionately impoverished. Think of two children Susanna and Solomon who come from very different backgrounds. This will influence everything they hear or read. We will return to elaborate upon this point in the next chapter when we discuss the role of background knowledge in the deep reading processes.

Syntactic contributions to understanding the word

It is fitting that the last dimension of words to be discussed in this chapter began the last century's renaissance of research into language through Chomsky's work on syntax. Over the last decade or so, an increasing group of cognitive neuroscientists has sought to understand the elaborated circuitry needed to process the syntactic rules and relationships among words in text—like recursion, word order, and clausal relations discussed in Chapter 2—and what happens when such rules are lost, as in various forms of aphasia, other language disorders, and the aging process. In one well-known direction within this research, neuroscientist Angela Friederici[56] and her colleagues at the Max Planck Institute in Dresden use the study of both typical adults and patients with different lesions from aphasia to help specify what is or is not occurring during syntactic processing. Friederici and her colleagues have been studying two major syntactic pathways within the language's macrocircuit: first, the dorsal pathway where the posterior parts of Broca's area and the posterior parts of the superior temporal gyrus are connected by the bundle of fibers in the arcuate fasciculus. (Recall these regions represented the principal structures in our earlier conceptualizations of language.) The other, ventral syntactic pathway involves connections between the posterior superior temporal gyrus and the angular gyrus for higher sentence-level processing.

Some recent work on syntactic functions does not restrict syntax to these pathways, but rather underscores the wide-ranging distribution of regions involved, not unlike the other linguistic functions, but with some differences. Like the phonological systems, syntactic processing appears to draw more heavily on left hemisphere connections with other language processes, rather than the right hemisphere. More surprising about syntax, however, are some very recent, thought-provoking studies of patients with syntactic deficits and of syntactic functioning in the elderly. These groups of individuals appear to employ more right hemisphere involvement than previous research showed. Indeed some researchers have begun to suggest that the new data on syntactic function point to a "phylogenetically older, bi-hemispheric system for language" that underlies modern human language.[57]

Although these thought-provoking speculations will need more supportive data, a central issue in current research on syntax involves the intrinsic difficulty in completely disentangling syntactic from semantic processing (whether or not pathology or age is involved). There are very great differences between "The flying dinosaur ate the baffled Maui tourist" vs "The baffled Maui tourist ate the flying dinosaur," even though all the words are the same. On the other hand, "The baffled flying dinosaur was eaten by the Maui tourist" *is* the same as "The Maui tourist ate the baffled flying dinosaur," even though the words are different. The ongoing research in syntax and semantics highlights the importance of looking at any one process like syntax within the context of the tight, almost automatic, interlocking reciprocal interactions between the various levels of syntactic and semantic representations. To summarize here, it is these rapid interactions among the varied representations that enable us to read and think in ever more sophisticated ways. Words need a structure to reflect our thoughts; structures need words to give them meaning.

There are, to be sure, other perspectives on syntax that describe how syntax scaffolds our thoughts. Towards that end, I would like to move from more neuroanatomical descriptions of language processes to more philosophical ones that have structured this chapter's beginning, middle, and end. For example, in *Reading and the Reader* Philip Davis writes that "syntax fills out" our thoughts, gives them "visible habitation on the page through the act of sentence construction."[58] Such a perspective returns us to the philosopher, playwright, and linguist who began this chapter's exploration of the relationship between words and thought. To Davis a primary function of syntax in literature is to help the reader "create an apparatus of thinking that can have and bear the thoughts." Like Jackendoff, who directs us to the thoughts that lie on the other side of words, like Shakespeare who speaks about the "habitat" for words, Davis suggests that it is syntax that allows these thoughts to have a place, to have an "apparatus" that will elicit in us, the readers, even what the words on the page themselves do not or cannot convey.

What would be essential to emphasize at this juncture is that the grammatical apparatus itself changes. Syntax changes, with development, with use, and, I will argue later, with medium. As Carol Chomsky documented earlier, the syntactic knowledge of children grows over time and with exposure to more sophisticated types of reading. And, to make a rather pronounced synaptic leap from research to reader, the current readers' comfort with various forms of syntactic complexity is changing with the use of mediums that advantage shorter types of text which, in turn, encourage simpler syntactic forms. The importance of this set of facts is multilayered: the development of syntactic knowledge undergirds (both neuronally and cognitively) our increasing ability to read ever more complex text, which reflects and allows us to "have and bear" ever more complex thoughts. It is one of the less discussed and, therefore, all the more critical issues we will return to in Chapters 5 and 6.

....

After all this chapter's emphases on neuroscience-based research about words, it would be easy for the reader to lose track of the first assumption about reading and literacy in this book's introduction: "Literacy propels the ever deepening expansion of thought, as whatever is read becomes integrated with what is known, felt, inferred, hoped, and imagined by the reader." This chapter's repurposing of the first three dimensions of Plato's approach to words highlighted the cognitive and physiological underpinnings of visual, sound-, meaning-, and syntactic-based language functions within the reading brain circuitry.

There remain many unresolved questions. Over the last three to four decades, some of the most central questions for researchers of reading have concerned the various "routes" we use among these processes within the reading brain circuit when we read. For example, what pathways do we pursue when reading different kinds of words, like those that are regular and transparent in their spelling (like *bat*); those that are irregular or opaque (like *yacht*) that are products of history and convention; and those many words that fall in between? The work of Mark Seidenberg[59] and his colleagues reflects many of the changes in the methods used to model how we read different words from early computational models through later neural network models. More recently, he has helped to move our conceptualizations beyond what were once thought as dual routes for the reading of regular and irregular words into conceptualizations that take into account the varied characteristics of words—that go well beyond their orthographic features. These still emerging views include multiple pathways involving complex interactions among varied cognitive and linguistic regions. These newer conceptualizations reflect both the characteristics a particular word might require and our growing understanding of the reading brain. As Dehaene emphasized a few years ago, "it is impossible to model reading without a thorough analysis of the brain's architecture, which relies on multiple parallel and partially redundant pathways."[60]

We are not there yet, but we are closer than at any time. Surely Sir Edmund Huey would be as pleased as Aristotle and George Eliot to observe our progress. I love to quote this one passage for those many who have never read his beautiful book on reading at the beginning of the twentieth century:

> And so to completely analyze what we do when we read would almost be the acme of a psychologist's achievement, for it would be to describe very many of the most intricate workings of the human mind, as well as to unravel the tangled story of the most remarkable specific performance that civilization has learned in all its history.[61]

For the readers of this book there remains a different sphere of knowledge about the reading act that we have yet to "unravel": the uniquely personal contributions elicited by the word within the readers themselves. Plato's fourth dimension, *episteme*, represents this *internal platform of knowledge*. Nothing is more important for an understanding of both the literate individual and the literary mind than this internal knowledge, save the transformative cognitive and affective processes that spring from it. This is the stuff of *deep reading*, and the topic of the next chapter's exploration of what comprises the deep reading brain.

Notes

1. Plato, *Phaedrus and the Seventh and Eighth Letters*, trans. Walter Hamilton (New York: Penguin, 1973), p. 138. Hereafter cited as Plato.
2. William Shakespeare, *A Midsummer Night's Dream* (New York: Simon & Schuster, 1973).
3. Ray Jackendoff, *A User's Guide to Thought and Meaning* (New York: Oxford University Press, 2012), p. 67.
4. David Constantine, *Poetry: The Literary Agenda* (Oxford: Oxford University Press, 2014), p. 7.
5. Leon Edelstein, *Plato's Seventh Letter* (Leiden: E. J. Brill, 1966).
6. Brian Wandell and Jason Yeatman, "Biological Development of Reading Circuits," *Current Opinion in Neurobiology* 23, no. 2 (2013): pp. 261–8. <http://dx.doi.org/10.1016/j.conb.2012.12.005>.
7. Angela D. Friederici and Sarah M. E. Gierhan, "The Language Network," *Current Opinion in Neurobiology* 23, no. 2 (2013): pp. 250–4. <http://doi.org/10.1016/j.conb.2012.10.002>.
8. Michael Anderson, *After Phrenology: Neural Reuse and the Interactive Brain* (Cambridge, MA: MIT Press, 2014).
9. Ellen F. Lau, Alexandre Gramfort, Matti S. Hämäläinen, and Gina R. Kuperberg, "Automatic Semantic Facilitation in Anterior Temporal Cortex Revealed through Multimodal Neuroimaging," *Journal of Neuroscience* 33, no. 43 (2013): pp. 17174–81. <http://doi.org/10.1523/JNEUROSCI.1018-13.2013>. Hereafter cited as Lau and Kuperberg.
10. Michael Gazzaniga, interview on National Public Radio, March 2015.
11. Steve Petersen and Wolf Singer, "Macrocircuits," *Current Opinions in Neurobiology* 23, no. 2 (2013): pp. 159–61. doi:10.1016/j.conb.2012.11.009.
12. V. S. Ramachandran and Sandra Blakeslee, *Phantoms in the Brain* (New York: HarperCollins, 1998), p. 256.
13. Eraldo Paulesu et al., "A Cultural Effect on Brain Function," *Nature Neuroscience* 3, no. 1 (2000): pp. 91–6. <http://doi.org/10.1038/71163>. Hereafter cited as Paulesu.
14. Donald Bolger, Walter Schneider, and Charles Perfetti, "Cross-Cultural Effects on the Brain Revisited: Universal Structures plus Writing System Variation," *Human Brain Mapping* 25, no. 1 (2005): pp. 92–104. doi: 10.1002/hbm.20124.

15. Kenneth R. Pugh, W. Einar Mencl, Annette R. Jenner, Leonard Katz, Stephen J. Frost, Jun Ren Lee, Sally E. Shaywitz, and Bennett A. Shaywitz, "Functional Neuroimaging Studies of Reading and Reading Disability (Developmental Dyslexia)," *Mental Retardation and Developmental Disabilities Research Review* 6, no. 1 (2000): pp. 207–13. doi:10.1002/1098-2779(2000)6:3<207::AID-MRDD8>3.0.CO;2-P.
16. Paulesu.
17. Karin A. Buetler, Diego de León Rodríguez, Marina Laganaro, René Müri, Lucas Spierer, and Jean-Marie Annoni, "Language Context Modulates Reading Route: An Electrical Neuroimaging Study," *Frontiers in Human Neuroscience* 8, no. 1 (2014): pp. 1–16. doi: 10.3389/fnhum.2014.00083.
18. Dehaene, p. 147.
19. Mark A. Changizi and Shinsuke Shimojo, "Character Complexity and Redundancy in Writing Systems over Human History," *Proceedings of the Royal Society B: Biological Sciences* 272, no. 1560 (2005): pp. 267–75. doi:10.1098/rspb.2004.2942.
20. Daniel Dennett, *Intuition Pumps and Other Tools for Thinking* (New York: W. W. Norton Co., 2013).
21. Philip Holcomb and Jonathan Grainger, "Watching the Word Go By: On the Time-Course of Component Processes in Visual Word Recognition," *Language and Linguistics Compass* 3, no. 1 (2009): pp. 128–56. doi:10.1111/j.1749-818X.2008.00121.x.
22. Brian Wandell, "The Neurobiological Basis of Seeing Words," *Annals of the New York Academy of Sciences* 1224 (2011): pp. 63–80. Hereafter cited as Wandell. doi:10.1111/j.1749-6632.2010.05954.x.
23. Donald Hebb, *The Organization of Behavior: A Neuropsychological Theory* (Mahwah, NJ: Psychology Press, 2002).
24. Earl Miller and Timothy J. Buschman, "Cortical Circuits for the Control of Attention," *Current Opinion in Neurobiology* 23 (2013): pp. 216–22. <http://dx.doi.org/10.1016/j.conb.2012.11.011>
25. Plato, p. 138.
26. Diotima's observers are Aristotle, St Thomas Aquinas, and George Eliot.
27. Timothy Buschman and Earl Miller, "Shifting the Spotlight of Attention: Evidence for Discrete Computations in Cognition," *Frontiers of Human Neuroscience* 4, no. 194 (2010): pp. 1–9. doi:10.3389/fnhum.2010.00194.
28. Dehaene, 2009.
29. Wandell.
30. Thad Polk and Martha Farah, "Functional MRI Evidence for an Abstract, Not Perceptual, Word Form Area," *Journal of Experimental Psychology: General* 131, no. 1 (2002): pp. 65–72. doi:10.1037//0096-3445.131.1.65.
31. Dehaene, 2009.
32. Michael Posner and Marcus Raichle, *Images of Mind* (New York: Scientific American Library, 1994).
33. Dehaene, 2009.
34. Cathy Price, "A Review and Synthesis of the First 20 Years of PET and fMRI Studies of Heard Speech, Spoken Language and Reading," *Neuroimage* 62, no. 2 (2012): pp. 816–47. Hereafter cited as Price. doi:10.1016/j.neuroimage.2012.04.062.

35. Gina Kuperberg, "The Proactive Comprehender: What Event-Related Potentials Tell Us about the Dynamics of Reading Comprehension." In Brett Miller, Laurie Cutting, and Peggy McCardle (eds), *Unraveling the Behavioral, Neurobiological, and Genetic Components of Reading Comprehension* (Baltimore, MD: Paul Brookes Publishing, 2013), pp. 176–92. Hereafter cited as Kuperberg.
36. Dana Gioia, *Interrogations at Noon* (St Paul, MN: Graywolf Press, 2001), p. 3.
37. Jackendoff, p. 69.
38. See Price; also Nina Kraus's excellent work on input from the auditory cranial nerve at the brainstem level; and see Usha Goswami and Jenny Thompson's work on the "speech amplitude envelope" and temporal sampling.
39. Olaf Sporns, "Network Attributes for Segregation and Integration in the Human Brain," *Current Opinion in Neurobiology* 23, no. 2 (2013): pp. 162–71. doi:10.1016/j.conb.2012.11.015.
40. Lau and Kuperberg.
41. Catherine Stoodley, "Distinct Regions of the Cerebellum Show Grey Matter Decreases in Autism, ADHD, and Developmental Dyslexia," *Frontiers in Systems Neuroscience* 8, vol. 92 (2014), pp. 1–17. doi:10.3389/fnsys.2014.00092.
42. Friedemann Pulvermüller, "Brain Mechanisms Linking Language and Action," *Nature Reviews Neuroscience* 6 (2005): pp. 576–82. doi:10.1038/nrn1706.
43. Ho Ming Chow, Raymond A. Mar, Yisheng Xu, Siyuan Liu, Suraji Wagage, and Allen R. Braun, "Embodied Comprehension of Stories: Interactions between Language Regions and Modality-Specific Mechanisms," *Journal of Cognitive Neuroscience* 26, no. 2 (2014): pp. 279–95. doi:10.1162/jocn_a_00487. Hereafter cited as Mar.
44. Natalie Phillips, "Narrating Distraction: Problems of Focus in Eighteenth-Century Fiction 1750–1820" (unpublished doctoral dissertation, Stanford University, 2010).
45. Note I. A. Richards's original use of the term *close reading*.
46. J. Hillis Miller, *Ariadne's Thread* (New Haven, CT: Yale University Press, 1992), p. 19.
47. William Blake, "Auguries of Innocence," *The Pickering Manuscript* (New York: Morgan Library and Museum, 1807), p. 15.
48. Ioulia Kovelman, Elizabeth S. Norton, Joanna A. Christodoulou, Nadine Gaab, Daniel A. Lieberman, Christina Triantafyllou, Maryanne Wolf, Susan Whitfield-Gabrieli, and John D. E. Gabrieli, "Brain Basis of Phonological Awareness for Spoken Language in Children and Its Disruption in Dyslexia," *Cerebral Cortex* 22, no. 4 (2012): pp. 754–64. doi:10.1093/cercor/bhr094.
49. Daniel Levitin, *The Organized Mind* (New York: Dutton, Penguin, 2014), p. 203. Hereafter cited as Levitin.
50. Lau and Kuperberg.
51. Marta Kutas and Kara Federmeier, "Thirty Years and Counting: Finding Meaning in the N400 Component of the Event-Related Brain Potential (ERP)," *Annual Review of Psychology* 62 (2011): pp. 621–47. doi:10.1146/annurev.psych.093008.131123.
52. William W. Graves, Jeffrey R. Binder, Rutvik H. Desai, Colin Humphries, Benjamin C. Stengel, and Mark S. Seidenberg, "Anatomy Is Strategy: Skilled

Reading Differences Associated with Structural Connectivity Differences in the Reading Network," *Brain and Language* 133 (2014): pp. 1–13. doi:10.1016/j.bandl.2014.03.005.
53. Lau and Kuperberg.
54. Norman Geschwind, "The Disconnexion Syndrome in Animals and Man," *Brain* 88, no. 2 (1965): pp. 237–94. doi:http://dx.doi.org/10.1093/brain/88.2.237.
55. Elizabeth Norton, Sarah Beach, and John Gabrieli, "Neurobiology of Dyslexia," *Current Opinion in Neurobiology* 30 (2015): pp. 73–8. doi:10.1016/j.conb.2014.09.007. Also see Joanna Christodoulou, Stephanie Del Tufo, John Lymberis, Patricia Saxler, Satrajit Ghosh, Christina Triantafyllou, Susan Whitfield-Gabrieli, and John D. E. Gabrieli, "Brain Bases of Reading Fluency in Typical Reading and Impaired Fluency in Dyslexia," *PLoS One* 9, no. 7 (2014): pp. 1–14. doi: 10.1371/journal.pone.0100552.
56. Angela D. Friederici and Sonja A. Kotz, "The Brain Basis of Syntactic Processes: Functional Imaging and Lesion Studies," *Neuroimage* 20 (2003): pp. 8–17. doi: 10.1016/j.neuroimage.2003.09.003; also Angela D. Friederici, Sonja A. Kotz, Sophie Scott, and Jonas Obleser, "Disentangling Syntax and Intelligibility in Auditory Language Comprehension," *Human Brain Mapping* 31, no. 3 (2010): pp. 448–57.
57. Mirjana Bozic, Elisabeth Fonteneau, Li Su, and William D. Marslen-Wilson, "Grammatical Analysis as a Distributed Neurobiological Function," *Human Brain Mapping* 36, no. 3 (2015): pp. 1190–201. doi:10.1002/hbm.22696.
58. Davis, p. 28.
59. Mark Seidenberg, *Reading: Our New Understanding of the Original Information Technology* (New York: Basic Books, 2017).
60. Dehaene, p. 41.
61. Sir Edmund B. Huey, *The Psychology and Pedagogy of Reading* (Cambridge, MA: MIT Press, 1908), p. 6.

5

The Deep Reading Brain

> The name, in the realm of language, has as its sole purpose and its incomparably highest meaning that it is the innermost nature of language itself.
>
> ...Man is the namer; by this we recognize that through him pure language speaks...in the name, the *mental being* of man communicates itself to God.[1] (my italics)
>
> Walter Benjamin, "On Language as Such"

> Far the best part, I repeat, of every mind is not that which he knows, but that which hovers in gleams, suggestions, tantalizing unpossessed before him. His firm recorded knowledge soon loses all interest for him, but this dancing chorus of thoughts and hopes is the quarry of his future, is his possibility.[2]
>
> Ralph Waldo Emerson, *The Daemon Knows*

Episteme—connecting the name to the reader's knowledge

Few people have embodied the Platonic concept of *episteme* more fully than the German philosopher, Walter Benjamin, whose life was cut tragically short when he committed suicide in flight from Nazism. Literary critic George Steiner described Benjamin as one of the "master readers of our time."[3] According to Hannah Arendt, Walter Benjamin was one of the first, true literary critics in the first part of the twentieth century. From his early essays like "On Language as Such" to his last works, Benjamin wrote, not unlike Plato, that our words incorporate the "innermost nature of language" and convey the "totality" of human thought—"the mental being of man." In all of his work, saved for the English-speaking world by Harvard University Press editor Lindsay Waters, Walter Benjamin strove to convey how language reflects, embodies, and impels the life of human thought.

In this section I will suggest that something akin to what Plato meant by *episteme* and what Benjamin expressed about the "mental being of man" are linked in a milliseconds-long "potentiation" in the reading act. It is in this tiny moment, which is outside of time as we can perceive it, that the expert reader possesses the ability to connect what our world teaches us about the *word*—during the first 300 to 500 milliseconds of reading—with *what* we have learned as a "totality" of knowledge from the *world*[4] immediately following it. During this impossibly brief moment of time and what follows in quick pace, we *combine and assimilate* these connected knowledge bases using our deep reading processes to pursue what Emerson described as "that which hovers in gleams, suggestions, tantalizing unpossessed." In cognitive neuroscience, this moment contains both the physiological "contents" of the critical N400 window (discussed in Chapter 4) and whatever emerges as the outcome of our prediction processes and their sometimes fertile disruptions. It also represents the cognitive correlative of what I believe Philip Davis means by the "holding-ground" that reading gives the reader for the "contemplation of experience."[5] It is physiologically real, and it is complex mental ground. For, it provides the bridge between the earlier discussed word-level input and an entire range of processes that are not so much Ray Jackendoff's "peepholes" on meaning, as varied lenses on thought—each with its own unique contributions and properties. Together they make up deep reading and all that it beckons us to. In essence, the deep reading processes are, therefore, the lenses that help us peer through those peepholes to our best thoughts.

Let me prepare the way to go below the surface of these processes by referring to how some of these processes have been conceptualized from different, but convergent disciplines. Perhaps the most straightforward descriptions come from education and psychology, where these processes are most often discussed and investigated under the term "reading comprehension."[6] In the field of cognitive neuroscience, a large variety of comprehension-related processes are being studied like conceptual expansion,[7] embodied cognition,[8] inferential, referential, and pragmatic processes, and insight[9] that would all be included under the term *deep reading*.

From within the world of literary criticism, deep reading processes are conceptually related to what I. A. Richards, and then F. R. Leavis and others first called Practical Criticism in the 1920s, when they celebrated systematic, "close," attentive reading by the reader to the varied aspects of the text without undue reference to context or the author. In his now infamous experiment, Richards distributed poems to be read and analyzed by his students without knowing the poet who wrote them.[10] The students, all undergraduates at Cambridge University, were to consider only what they read as the basis for their interpretation and evaluative judgments. The poems were written by a mix of famous poets, including Longfellow, and some decidedly, and at least to Professor Richards, deservedly unknown ones. The result of the experiment did not demonstrate the "greatness" of the more established poets. On the contrary. For Richards, the resulting mix of responses illumined how easily highly educated readers can "misread" text and fail to read with closer analysis and depth. The Practical Criticism movement in literary criticism emerged from Richards's work at the time. More recently, a movement advocating "close reading" has been characterized by a similar adherence to the words of the text and similar attentiveness by the reader.[11] Although the entire thrust of close reading is well aligned with the deployment of deep reading processes, it would be important to make explicit the caveat that these processes can occur with no conscious effort by the expert reader to read *closely*, and indeed that would be a worthy goal.

Philip Davis provides a particularly colorful, albeit ironic twist to current descriptions of close reading by first addressing the current situation in which it is sometimes "impatiently dismissed," presumably because it "sounds no better than what myopic old Mr. Magoo would do." He then proceeds to describe with far more earnestness how close reading involves "wanting to know more of how a piece of writing works.... it is a craft of reading and re-reading for any serious reader who needs to slow and stop, to understand more of the feeling, when something along the lines or the sentences suddenly and arrestingly *matters*."[12] From this perspective, close reading is kin to what Lindsay Waters among others refers to as "slow reading"[13]: "What I am asking myself to do is to step out of the grid of time, to experience works of literature anew. What I am asking you to do is to slow reading down, to preserve and expand the experience of reading."

I would take one step further. Deep reading processes *underlie* our abilities to find, reflect, and potentially expand upon *what matters* when we read. They represent the full sum of the cognitive, perceptual, and affective processes that prepare readers to apprehend, grasp, and assimilate the essence of what is read—beyond decoded information, beyond basic comprehension, and sometimes beyond what the author writes or even intends. My commitment to push forward our understanding of deep reading processes in this book and others is based on the conviction that such a knowledge base will help sustain their continued contribution to the future reading brain.

My own first use of the term *deep reading*[14] years ago stemmed from my wish to bring Proust's insights about the *generative* function within the heart of reading, together with neuroscience's contributions to understanding the reading brain circuit. Since that time, I use deep reading processes as a kind of shorthand to refer to a complete panoply of processes that fall into three temporally interrelated groupings that will scaffold the rest of the chapter: 1) Entry processes like *imagery, perspective taking, background knowledge*; 2) Metacognitive ("Scientific Method") processes in which *analogical thought* functions as the bridge between *background knowledge* and *inferential abilities (observation, deduction, and induction)*, and *critical analysis*; and finally, 3) Generativity processes with *insight* and *contemplation* as vehicles to *novel thought* (note: the term *generative* is used in several different contexts in this chapter).

I am neither the first nor the last to attempt to differentiate these non-exclusive processes. Rather, as alluded to, I see our collective, evolving understanding of the variousness of deep reading processes as the most concrete vehicles for their preservation. It is critical, therefore, for the rest of this book that the reader understand that the range of cognitive and metacognitive processes that I refer to as *deep reading* may or may not be learned by the young reader, as presaged in Chapter 3. Furthermore, and of equal importance to us all, they may or may not be deployed by the expert reader who has acquired them long ago. All of this will depend on many factors that we have encountered or will in various places in this book, including in Chapter 3 on the individual reader's *development*, and in Chapter 6, on both the *medium* and also the *characteristics* of the text that are changing in ways already affecting us all. In what one hopes is the only burst of anxiety-produced hyperbole in this book, I have come to the conclusion that the development of a literate society and the development of a literary mind may well depend on how we conceptualize the importance of deep reading processes, whatever terms we label them with, and act upon this knowledge.

Entry processes—imagery, perspective-taking, and background knowledge

> Yet if neuroscience is fashionable slow, deep, literary reading is not.[15]
>
> Philip Davis, *Reading and the Reader*

Imagery

> Word and image are correlates that eternally search for one another.[16]
>
> Goethe, *Maxims and Reflections*

When we are children, if we are very lucky, we are surrounded by books with illustrations that in the words of Howard Pyle, one of the most famous children's literature illustrators, create "an indelible impression" in the "temple of memory from which the image is never cast to be thrown into the rubbish-heap of things that are outgrown and outlived."[17] Ever so gradually, however, we learn, just as Goethe wrote, to connect words to images which we construct with the guidance and verbal art of authors. As Elaine Scarry evoked in her book, *Dreaming by the Book*, the image-making conjured by our best authors trumps even our most fanciful daydreams.[18]

One of the most interesting, new explorations of imagery's influences is found in *What We See When We Read*. In this book, artist-writer Peter Mendelsund[19] uses Tolstoy's description of Anna Karenina to elicit our own personal images of a character who for many of us is immortalized as one of the most beautiful women of literature. Tolstoy employed a brilliant technique to render an exquisite portrait of Anna in words. He did so by using another character, Levin, to describe his response to a lovingly painted portrait of Anna: "It was not a picture, but a living, charming woman, with black curling hair, with bare arms and shoulders, with a pensive smile on the lips, covered with soft down; triumphantly and softly she looked at him with eyes that baffled him. She was not living only because she was more beautiful than a living woman can be."[20]

Based on Tolstoy's descriptions, Mendelsund did something ingenious to make an important point about the images we construct when we read. He used police composite-sketch software to create a drawing of Anna Karenina! It was lovely, to be sure, but this composite drawing fit neither Mendelsund's visual image of Anna nor my own. This is only as it should be. As Mendelsund emphasized and David Ulin described in his book, *Lost Art of Reading*,[21] we *co-create* images with the author. Paradoxically, the more details are given as in illustrations of the characters, the less we contribute to the process. I for one do not want anyone else to show me exactly how Anna Karenina looked, which is one of the great challenges and hurdles faced in every film version of a beloved work. Thus, despite the exquisite images of Keira Knightley in the recent screen version of *Anna Karenina* and despite the timeless beauty that Greta Garbo brought to earlier film versions, no portrayal supplanted my own first image.

I need only to mention the names of characters you have come to know in books—Robinson Crusoe, Kim, Alyosha and Father Zosima, Madame Bovary, Isabelle Archer, Celie, Mrs Dalloway—and regardless of the edition that you have read, with or without illustrations, these names conjure your own composite images of these characters which are as present in memory's storage as the remembered faces of friends. Indeed, it is from within this interaction that both author and reader contribute to the search between word and image that Goethe articulated long before. Thus when we read a word or a word within a given context, we bring stored images that add to the meanings, the syntactic functions, the knowledge we have about this word and this context, just as Plato glimpsed long ago. All that we see when we read, therefore, may begin with letters and letter patterns, but like the snowballs of childhood it grows to include all manner of visual impressions—some the indelible ones, like Howard Pyle's, some freshly created, each contributing a unique dimension to our ability to envision and feel what "others" see and experience, which is the next topic.

Perspective-taking

Unlike the description for imagery, I want to begin a discussion of the processes involved in perspective-taking by looking first at the brain.

I do so because recent findings from neuroscience on this topic have given me a very different perspective, if you will, from my earlier views. This research shows that perspective-taking capacities utilize the neuronal networks both for what psychologists call our "theory of mind" and also for networks involved in our feelings towards others, like empathy or sympathy and compassion. Early in childhood, as part of the development of a social world that goes beyond ourselves, we gradually construct theories about the "mind" of others, beginning with the realization that "they" have thoughts and feelings, just as we do. Over time both theory of mind and empathy become steadily more sophisticated and complex in their dimensions.

German neuroscientist Tania Singer[22] and her colleagues study the "neural basis of empathy" with several unusual approaches, including the examination of expert and novice meditators and also of romantic partners, who demonstrate very empathic responses with each other. The lovers activate "feeling networks," which include two broad "subcortical" areas immediately below the cortex in the brain that transect and connect many important regions across the brain: the anterior or front sections of both the *insula a*nd the *cingulate cortex*. Both of these areas contain a large type of neuron, the von Economo neurons, which are key to the rapid communication involved across the two areas' long expansive regions. The insula, with its contributory role in empathy, has emerged in Singer's work on mindfulness as a major area of activation during meditation, and indeed appears to be what distinguishes the expert from the novice in meditation practice. Across all their studies, Singer and her group demonstrate how the insula and cingulate cortex form an extensive "feeling network."

These two areas can be thought of as huge connective entities. They link cortical regions in the frontal lobe with the more distant, posterior angular gyrus. They also connect subcortical areas together like the striatum and parts of the *limbic system*, especially the *hippocampus* and little *amygdala*, which are central for memory and for the control of some of our largest human emotions like love and anger. These connective regions underlie our ability to pull together thought and feeling when we read, which is just what perspective-taking demands.

The perspective-taking processes that most of us acquire in reading may not produce the depth of sympathy that Singer's various romantic and/or mindful subjects exhibit towards each other, but they provide important contributions all their own. By widening our experiences through situations we might never encounter, by entering the lives of others for just a while, we learn compassion for people whom we could otherwise never imagine knowing. It is a cognitive force that most of us never come to realize has helped to shape our feeling lives—and perhaps even our moral lives.

Several revered American novelists, like Gish Jen, David Foster Wallace, and Marilynne Robinson, understand the deep significance of this moral force in literature and transmit it through the very different characters they have contributed to contemporary literature. The work of these authors underscores the high stakes embodied in the perspective-taking capacities conferred by the novel and what might happen from the unintended effects of a digital culture on readers today. Jen speaks of what is lost to individuals who never develop their own sense of "interiority" because they have never learned—through the novel's unique transportation—how to enter the spheres of other.[23]

Perhaps one of the most extraordinary examples of perspective-taking is found in Marilynne Robinson's lyrical novels, *Gilead*,[24] *Home*, and *Lyla*, her trilogy about the quiet, unassuming lives of two ministers in an unknown small town in rural Midwest America. There is no sex, no violence, no mystery, save the subtlest forms in human relationships. On the surface, there is little here that would predict the depth of approbation for this work, including the Pulitzer Prize and the Orange Prize. Robinson's genius in these novels is that she is able to make visible her stunning gift for perspective-taking abilities, as each novel is told through the thoughts of a different character on the same small stage of the town of Gilead. It is one of recent literature's most moving examples of the entire worlds to be found in the lives of people we would scarcely ever notice, and would be the less for not knowing.

I want to make a brief synaptic leap here into another meaning of "transport," a concept that allows us to leave our own perspective to encounter another's. In the last chapter's description of articulatory and motoric processes, I referred to the work of Raymond Mar and his colleagues on embodied cognition and on his study of fiction vs non-fiction reading. One of Mar's more intriguing studies involved a comparison of readers who prefer fiction vs those who prefer non-fiction.[25] The fiction readers differed from their non-fiction-preferring cohort in their openness to be "transported," a dimension of feeling that is closely linked to empathy, where we leave our own perspective behind to enter another sphere. I believe Mar's work buttresses not only what happens in perspective-taking, but also the importance of different forms of literature for the development of these processes.

Who would any of us be had we and our children not entered—for some long hours of our lives—the worlds of Frog and Toad, Charlotte and Wilbur, Tom Sawyer and Huck Finn, Elizabeth Bennett and Darcy, Captain Ahab and Ishmael, Dorothea Brooke and Mr Casaubon, Celie and Nettie, Harry Potter and all his friends, not to mention Harry "Rabbit" Angstrom and his various wives? Who would we be without these lives, these perspectives, this ever expanding history of feelings that we might never experience ourselves?

But it is here that neuroscience tells us that we *do* experience these feelings, thoughts, and perspectives of others to a degree, however abstracted, that is physiologically discernible. Not only do words like action and feeling verbs have physiological correlates in the motor and somatosensory areas, Gina Kuperberg's group has shown that the very *pronouns* we use in narrative (e.g. the use of *you* vs *he*) will change our perspective-taking processing. It appears that we engage different areas of our prefrontal cortex when the text refers in some way to ourselves.[26] As Gina and her colleagues probably wrote with their eyes twinkling, there are different activation patterns when "it's all about you." It is another example of reading's nuanced alchemy. Multiple dimensions of knowledge we never consider invisibly add their contributions to whatever we read, including, none too accidentally, background knowledge itself.

Background knowledge

I think of the reader's stored knowledge of the world as the portal to the rest of the deep reading processes, even though bidirectional interactions characterize most reading processes, which will become clearer and clearer as we go. There is a wonderful quotation I have never forgotten from a course taught by the philosopher Joseph Evans, who often said about the subjects that we were studying in Philosophy of Nature: *Ubi amor, ibi oculus* (the more we love, the more we see).

Something very much like that is at work in what and how we read: the more we know, the more we see. Only if we know, for example, something about the horrors of the historical Inquisition and something about the historical Christ will we fully appreciate the spiritually terrifying aspects of the Inquisitor in *Brothers Karamazov*. Only when we know the horrors of what Hitler was doing in Nazi Germany can we understand Anne Frank's *Diary*, or Dietrich Bonhoeffer's *Letters from Prison*, or James Carroll's new work, *Christ Actually*, that was significantly influenced by both Anne Frank's and Bonhoeffer's personal accounts of Nazi Germany.

But background knowledge is not just about the historical knowledge that the reader brings to the text; it is also about the reader's knowledge about the *writing of text* itself. I want to give a most unusual, highly memorable example. In the middle of Heinrich von Kleist's magical nineteenth-century story, *Marquise of O*, there is an unexpected use of the usually innocuous *ellipsis*. Only if we realize that this tiny stylistic device represents a moral…"*lapse*"…by the Russian Count over the sedated Marquise, do we understand everything that happens next. This ellipsis was von Kleist's culturally and linguistically discreet placeholder for the despicable act by the Count that rendered the hapless unconscious Marquise mysteriously *enceinte* two months later! Clearly I have never forgotten the role of the tiny ellipsis in the poor Marquise's ultimate fate, which we will return to later.

Consider a few larger examples from books in science and fiction, beginning with Stephen Hawking's *A Brief History of Time*. Despite a great deal of effort that went into making this book accessible to the larger public by Hawking and his gifted editor Peter Guzzardi, without some basic background knowledge about physics, the reader remains hard-pressed to comprehend it as fully as intended. I have always found it a personal failure that after two readings, I still felt as if I understood only part of what Hawking wanted to contribute to the reader. If there is fault, it lies at the door of my background knowledge of the world of physics, and I felt these lacunae (my own black holes) poignantly in reading Hawking.

By contrast, Robinson's novels of ordinary souls give the reader a foundation for insight which needs little background knowledge, at least the first time one reads them. There is a correlative point. There are in Robinson's created world the kinds of insights that grow in meaning the more "life experience" one brings either to *Gilead*'s gentle tale or to its companions in *Home* and *Lyla*. I believe that the rereading of beloved texts—from the Psalms to the novels of George Eliot—provides us with a very personal mirror to observe the ever developing background knowledge we bring from the different epochs of our lives to what we read.

There are two points here that I wish to underscore, despite their possible obviousness. As we change over time, we bring ever increasing background knowledge to what we read. The young idealistic girl I was who read *Middlemarch* for the first time is very different from the person I am now. Before, my sympathies were directed only to Dorothea Brooke's deep disappointment with the illusory goals and self-centered delusions of her husband, Mr Casaubon.

But now, I will admit that at times I have even come to identify with rigid Mr Casaubon's feelings of being misunderstood by Dorothea, who was too young to appreciate the motivation for his seemingly endless, pointless research that "went nowhither."[27] Only now am I aware that the model for the fictional Mr Casaubon was not the historically real, equally ascetic Isaac Casaubon, who in the seventeenth century also attempted, albeit more successfully, an encyclopedic-like work. Rather, the "truth," as I recently learned it, quite took me aback. For, when Mary Ann Evans (George Eliot's real name) was asked whether the model for Casaubon was someone like Herbert Spencer (the ponderous intellectual who had once rejected her in real life), she responded by pointing with "humorless solemnity...to her own heart."[28] This small historical anecdote enriches my reading of Mr Casaubon with his untoward fear of failure and rejection by others. It was a characteristic that George Eliot understood in all too full measure, as have many, many writers like Virginia Woolf. Perhaps the most important change in my reading of Middlemarch, however, is a more personal one. I can now more fully perceive George Eliot's probing critique of human relationships shining through all the ill-matched marriages in this novel, along with her gently rendered recognition that no one person can fulfill all the expectations for understanding ourselves that we bring to any deep relationship.

The second point is less subtle, but critical to our efforts in this book to understand literacy and non-literacy. The relationship between the reader's background knowledge and an understanding of the author's content is shaped by both unique personal experience and common cultural ones. A simple thought experiment will illustrate this point. Imagine for just this minute the background knowledge that Plato might bring to reading a sentence which contained the words "hero" and "quickness." Now do the same for what a preadolescent boy today from an urban city might bring to the text—our Solomon. Plato might immediately activate thoughts of human heroes like Odysseus and Achilles, the Greek gods Hermes (Mercury) and Artemis, the demigods Atlas and Heracles, and then move quickly to the moral dilemmas confronting the all-too-human characters in Greek dramas where heroism takes very complex, sometimes morally convoluted turns.

Sol, on the other hand, might think first of cultural superheroes who fly "faster than a speeding bullet" like Superman, Batman, and Spiderman, perhaps even the metahuman TV hero Flash, or Zelda, or Derek Jeter (my sole, albeit retired, Yankee hero). But then he might activate thoughts of the feats of Harry Potter or Percy Jackson from Rick Riordan's memorable *Lightning Thief*, both of whom came from books he has just read.

The contrast could not be greater, even if our modern quest for heroes has many an ancient if not phylogenetic root. Plato's world knowledge was filled with Homeric heroes and Greek gods that characterized his emergence from an oral culture, and also, more than likely, the morally heroic characters in the plays of his time. Sol called largely upon the seemingly endless number of superheroes proliferating popular cultural knowledge, and also upon some of the heroes he has read who battle all number of odds. His heroes succeed because they can go beyond all the expectations that circumscribe them with talents that perennially defy normal limitations like human speed.

We need to add one more person to the thought experiment here: the non-literate child, growing up in remote regions of Appalachia— our Susanna. Chances are good that she would have access to the oral stories and tales of heroes in her culture, many of whom, perhaps, come from the Bible. But chances are equally strong that there would be more limits on what she knew than the little boy. Will the limits on what Susanna knows circumscribe her potential to learn more over time and to contribute what is unique about herself? Further, with less knowledge about heroes, would Susanna consider herself less capable of heroic action or never think of it at all? Or, would her oral traditions instill her with other models of heroism? It is less than certain.

Our worries about children who never become literate stem not from any insulting equation, however implicit, that the capacity for heroism or for talents is directly connected to access to contemporary (read Western) culture. Rather, we wish to underscore that literacy plays an irreplaceable role in the advancement of knowledge and that every person who becomes literate has more of an opportunity to use that knowledge for their own lives and the lives of their society than those who have no ready access to it. The real equation is that the more we know, the more we can go beyond our own limits. More specifically, the more we read, the more we bring to whatever we read now and next. The non-literate Susanna does not have less intelligence than Sol; she has less opportunity for adding a wider knowledge of the world's store of learning, which, in turn, gives her less opportunity to use that intelligence in more and more expanded ways over her lifespan.

The murkiest of waters surrounds the significant cultural differences between literate and non-literate persons. My friends and colleagues in anthropology and cultural studies warn me how my message about literacy could be grossly distorted by others into a Western hegemonic argument. Little would depress me more. One can never prevent either misinterpretation or the Procrustean misuses of knowledge, except by ever clearer sharpening of what is essential to know. In this instance the most important point I am making here can be summarized in one simple distillation: literacy adds to the background knowledge of the literate person, which, in turn, changes the way that person thinks, reads, reasons, and dreams, whether about becoming a hero or about a postal clerk in Prague who writes novels and stories that change the way the world views itself.

I want to end this section with one of Kant's insights into the nature of reason as the final "sharpening" of this last thought. Kant believed that concepts without experience are empty; and experience without concepts is blind.[29] I believe a very similar principle holds for the relationship between the individual's background knowledge and the ability to understand the content of written text. Reading the text without background knowledge is often an empty, or far less meaningful, experience. Some would suggest it is virtually impossible. By the same token, having background and experiential knowledge without insights and concepts that provide a scaffolding of meaning for these experiences is equally wanting. Indeed, having a too rigidly held construct of knowledge could itself impede fuller understanding of the text. One of the most powerful contributions of the present reading circuit is that its very construction continuously incorporates expanding, interactive sets of relationships among our background knowledge, the contents of our reading, and our insights into them both. With that said, these same highly reciprocal relationships will increasingly differentiate Solomon and Susanna, and all literate and non-literate children, over their lifespans. We hope this book and all our present work will contribute to changing those differences.

Metacognitive "scientific method" processes—analogical, inferential, and critical analytical abilities

Analogy as bridge

"I drink a liquor never brewed," wrote Emily Dickinson, "from tankards scooped in pearl...Inebriate of air, am I, debauchee of dew."[30] Without a moment's hesitation, the reader knows from the language of metaphor that: a) the shy, retiring poet does not speak of alcohol; b) there are no such things as pearl-lined tankards; and c) the reclusive Ms Dickinson, in all probability, has fallen in love. How do we know any of this?

It is one thing to possess an ever growing corpus of concepts that together make up what I have too blandly labelled background knowledge. It is yet another to be able to retrieve, connect, and represent aspects of these concepts—for example, alcohol's effects and love's effects—and in the process find new relationships among them and new ways of expressing them. This is the stuff of metaphor and simile and figurative language, all of which require a range of the complex processes involved in *analogical reasoning*. Cognitive scientist Dedre Gentner includes four key elements in the use of analogy: the *retrieval* of a past concept/situation that is similar in some way to the present one; the *mapping of* "what goes with what"; an *abstraction* of the new concept or schema that results from this new relationship; and a *re-representation* of this new concept that has emerged from our thoughts about the original concepts and their connections.[31]

Our abilities to make analogies are intrinsically related to our species' symbol-making capacity across multiple learning domains. The roots of these abilities may well begin with the first cognitive *aha*, like the simplest connection between suckling and the mother's breast, and they continue with increasing sophistication as the very young child perceives more and more relationships between known concepts. Gradually, the young child begins to recognize and replicate patterns and after a relatively short time is able to express the perceived relationships between action and language with words as simple as *more*.

I shall never forget one of the most memorable moments in the development of my first son, Ben, when he discovered the word *more*. It was New Year's Eve, and as for many parents with a young child, parties elsewhere were impossible, and the champagne was toasted at home with Ben. Not wanting to give Ben champagne, "someone" poured Ben a tiny glass of beer. After one sip, Ben expressed his first two-word utterance: "More beer!"—pronounced with a perfect Boston accent (both <r>s missing in action). Aside from the untoward excitement I felt about Ben's first signs of syntax, it was obvious that his first use of the word *more* was pointing to a related analogical achievement: the connection between desired action and language.

Some cognitive scientists conceptualize analogical thought as at the very root of human intelligence. To cognitive scientist Douglas Hofstadter, analogical thought represents the "core of cognition": "...every concept we have is essentially nothing but a tightly packaged bundle of analogies, and...all we do when we think is to move fluidly from concept to concept—in other words, to leap from one analogy-bundle to another."[32] Analogy provides us, in this view, with the basis for perceiving, combining, and creating new thoughts our whole lives. Little could be more important in the act of reading. As my anecdote of Ben and the research of Usha Goswami[33] illustrate, the young human being is capable of analogical reasoning from a very early age. This is important because the early development of the reading brain circuit will demand the ability to move from the decoding of information to the assimilation of new concepts to the ability to combine new and old concepts. In other words, young readers must learn to use their analogical abilities to link what they read with their prior knowledge, experiences, and feelings to form new ones.

Indeed, the species' first readers thousands of years ago had to learn to do the very same linkages. I am indebted to Dedre Gentner and her colleagues for bringing my attention to one of the earliest examples of metaphor in the 4,000-year-old epic poem, *Gilgamesh*, in which Gilgamesh mourns the death of his great friend Enkidu:

> ...Gilgamesh covered
> Enkidu's face with a veil like the veil of a bride.
> He hovered like an eagle over the body,
> or as a lioness does over her brood.[34]

The now-ancient readers and the author(s) of *Gilgamesh* employed some of the same analogical processes that the readers and authors of *Divine Comedy*, *Paradise Lost*, and *The Waste Land* used in the domain of poetry or that James Watson and Francis Crick, Gregor Mendel, Thomas Edison, and Charles Darwin used in the domain of scientific discovery. Analogical skills are not unique to written language, but they are honed and accelerated through the development of the literate mind in the individual and in the culture across every domain of knowledge.

I conceptualize the development of analogical thought in written language as the central bridge within deep reading between what we know and the complex metacognitive processes we apply to this knowledge, like inference, deduction, and induction and also insight and critical analyses. It is worth noting once again, albeit in a different context, that in conceptualizing analogy as the central bridge in deep reading, there is no temporal linearity implied by this structural metaphor: the very opposite, as a bridge goes both ways. If, as Hofstadter argues, analogy is the driving force that expands the categories that scaffold our cognition, one of the most important consequences of the *fluidity* of our analogical thought is our ability to use it for new thought and insight. Indeed William James wrote that insight "lies in making creative metaphors or fluid analogies."[35] But that is getting a little ahead of the "storyline" here, which is apropos, given that what we do with all these processes more resembles the spokes within a wheel than any neat and tidy story or linear timeline.

Inferential abilities (observation, deduction, and induction)

Whatever metaphor we might use to try to capture what occurs in the last milliseconds of reading, there is a feed-forward, feed-backward mode of activity that characterizes how our analogical reasoning processes interact with inferential skills like observation, induction, and deduction. The more we use our analogical skills and background knowledge to infer conclusions and insights from what we read, the more informed and accurate will be our inferences, critical analyses, and evaluations, which, in turn, adds to stored background knowledge, sharpens future analogical, inferential, and critical analytic capacities, and so on in the reading life. Our reading brain is an interactive and adaptive prediction machine.

I would like to go somewhat deeper into what a predictive reading brain means for how we read *simply* (the emphases in the last chapter) and how we read *deeply* (the focus here). By now you are prepared to understand that the two are intimately related, but not as you might initially assume. It would be fairly logical to hypothesize a relatively straightforward, linear relationship between the two: that is, that our lower-level, perceptual, and linguistic processes dictate (feed forward) how we think at a higher level about the information they provide. One of the most important shifts in our understanding of the reading brain concerns how intimately connected, non-linear, and constantly adapting the relationships are between what we see and what we know.

Andy Clark, a scholar in Edinburgh best known for his interdisciplinary work in philosophy on the extended mind, wrote one of the most thought-provoking articles in the cognitive sciences on "predictive brains." In this article he described what is referred to as a *hierarchical generative model* for understanding the relationship between what we perceive and what we do and think. To illustrate the bidirectionality within the hierarchy of relationships between the lower- and higher-level processes, he gave a wonderfully apt quote by cognitive scientists Richard Hawkins and Sandra Blakeslee: "As strange as it sounds... your predictions not only precede sensation, they determine sensation."[36]

As seen in the last chapter, Gina Kuperberg brings this conceptualization of cognition to life in her work on language comprehension in both speech and reading. She argues that our higher-level predictions feed down to our lower-level representations, including visual and acoustic input, as well as lexical or word-level representations, in a highly iterative way that helps us deal with the inevitable *uncertainty* in a text or in an author's mind. In her words, "the process of comprehension can be conceptualized as an incremental cycle of inference and prediction, based on prior beliefs and unfolding bottom-up input."[37] Within this bidirectional cycle we are constantly updating our information. And where our predictions do not match the input—the prediction errors—we construct new hypotheses and sometimes change our underlying "generative model." Some of our most important insights emerge from the further processing that such errors require of us, while suspended within the extra milliseconds in Davis's "holding-ground."

And indeed, some of the most important work in the cognitive neuroscience of language focuses on how these hierarchical generative models operate on the "uncertainty" in the author's mind (or speaker's) and in the varied texts which change from text to text in their cognitive demands. In Kuperberg's view, we are constantly adapting: "Every time we read a scientific manuscript, a sci-fi chapter, or a novel by Jane Austen, we will be exposed to quite different statistical structures in our linguistic inputs. The type of generative framework we have…is…uniquely suited for dealing with such variability in our environments." It is through this adaptive framework that we develop the prediction capacities inherent in "proactive comprehension." I would further suggest that the steady elaboration of the literary mind over time emerges in part from the generation of the innumerable hypotheses that accompany our reading over time. This cumulative set of hypotheses from all the reading that went before serves to help us predict and/or resolve predictions that sometimes "go nowhither"—like the many garden paths of thought in poor Mr Casaubon's mind.

I have labeled some of the metacognitive processes involved in the inferential aspects of deep reading as the "scientific method" processes, because they are mutually engaged in many of the steps we follow in science: observations; hypothesis-generation; testing; evaluating results of our hypotheses. There is, however, an important caveat. In many but not all areas of science, we are testing hypotheses based on observable facts. Not so with everything we read. Indeed, much of what we read, particularly in works of poetry and fiction, requires methods more akin to those in physics, where the task is to deduce the presence of an entity—like an unknown particle—based on its minute effects on known entities.

This is the uncertainty principle in literature that authors employ when they "tell the truth, but tell it slant//Success in circuitry lies," as

Emily Dickinson wrote long ago. We are equipped to deduce her obliquely given meanings by virtue of the adaptive, hypothesis-generating nature of our predictive processes. Thus, when she writes of "wild nights, wild nights" from her (almost) never departed-from home in nineteenth-century Amherst, Massachusetts, we infer there is some beloved figure, albeit only from his effects on her poems. Whether or not "he" was the elusive Mr Hutchinson from Boston who read a few of her poems, we are privy only to the effects on her as deduced from her poems' unmistakable, abandoned longing.

By the same token, whether or not the unconscious Marquise of O was remotely aware of the Russian count's seduction, *we* are. Our knowledge is based on two separate "clues": first, our *observation* of the anomalous, unexplained ellipsis; and second, our *deductions* following the disclosure of the "effects" later on of what happened during the unexplained ellipsis—the clueless Marquise's pregnancy, which forced the hapless woman to write a public letter asking who might be responsible!

But how does the reader come to know how to infer these clues? There is much to learn about inference not only from cognitive science, but also from the act of reading mysteries, whether about the heart or about a crime, which are, often as not, connected. Mysteries teach us to observe, to ferret below the surface, to imagine, to construct scenarios and hypotheses, to analyze the data, and when very lucky, to experience the great *aha* moment, when we solve the mystery before the author reveals it. In other words, mysteries give us a literary case study of Bayesian probabilities in action.

Let us take an example. I would hazard a semi-informed guess that when you read Agatha Christie's mysteries, you are your own versions of Miss Marple and Hercule Poirot (whose name I suddenly realized might be based on the name of the great mathematician, Henri Poincare). Like them you search for the anomalous remark, the unexplained behavior that when questioned leads to the generation of one testable hypothesis after another. In so doing, you activate networks described earlier for *empathy* and *theory of mind*, alongside a formidable set of networks in regions involved in cognition, including in particular our left and right prefrontal cortex. The latter are holding areas which provide us with our uniquely *global, neuronal workspace*.[38] The left prefrontal region allows us to connect our observations and move back and forth from one self-generated hypothesis to the next. The right prefrontal cortex allows us to test and evaluate the worth of each of them. Someone should write a story about a neuroscientist who discovers exactly what occurs in the brain when it solves a mystery, and then...vanishes.

On that note, it is just as well that I do not provide further detail, though I hope you seek it elsewhere. Rather, I would like to suggest that solving mysteries in both literature and science employs some of the same strategic uses of our metacognitive prediction powers and similar amounts of focused attention. This may well be what *prepares* us for the hoped-for insights that emerge from reading, but they are not the same thing. Indeed, it may well be that after the prefrontal cortex's preparations of our analogical and inferential skills, the brief *cessation of focus* is exactly what allows us to make totally new connections leading to insight, a topic we will return to shortly.

Critical analyses

Before doing so, however, it is important to consider what happens immediately to Hercule Poirot's "little grey cells" after we assemble our observations and inferences into them. Just as analogy provides a critical bridge between our background knowledge and these inferential processes, our capacity for critical analysis creates a bridge between the data from our deductions and inductions and the powerful judgments and immersion into the text that can change us. It is what Alan Jacobs described in his beautiful apologia for reading:

> to decide to read something...is to choose a particular form of attention. That choice creates simultaneously silence and receptiveness to a voice; the reader acts imaginatively, constructing meaning from...words on a page, but also ideally, strives to assume a posture of charity toward what he or she reads. This choosing reader is never merely passive, never simply a consumer, but constantly engages in critical judgment, sometimes withholding sympathy with a thoughtful wariness, and then, in the most blessed moments...giving that sympathy wholly and without stint.[39]

This view of reading is everything that comes when our critical judgments allow us to immerse ourselves. With Jacobs's permission, I would elaborate upon the "blessed moments" that can occur in the last moments of immersive reading. Some will reflect the careful results of our analytical, problem-solving processes, and some will be the stuff of insight and generativity processes.

They are different. Cognitive scientists like Mark Jung-Beeman and John Kounios demonstrate that these two types of processing can "co-occur, overlap, and interact, yet they are phenomenologically, behaviourally, and neurologically distinct," with differences in the brain mechanisms underlying both.[40] The processes underlying critical analysis involve a methodical evaluation of the cumulative information gleaned from text. During this process, readers probe, assess, and ultimately judge the content of the text—from its proximity to truth to its elegance of expression. It is time well spent: just this extra effort ultimately contributes to whether these analyses become incorporated and consolidated in our memory *or not*. Without the imprimatur of critical analytical processes on what we have decoded and comprehended, the reader does not reach the intellectual closure in memory that is possible for the cognitive processes embodied in reading.

One of the great concerns expressed about the transition into a digital culture is that reading could become more superficial, if less time is allocated to close, deep reading. As will be elaborated in the next chapter, I worry that without the allocation of time specifically to critical analytical processes, the entire reading circuitry will come to a cognitive dead end. Such an aborted circuit would mean that there would be less transfer of knowledge gained from the text and less basis for insight, both of which are often primed by critical analytical contributions.

It is here that I hope the reader will think back once more to Solomon and Susanna. One of the most important contributions that literacy makes is the development and refinement of critical analytical skills. I have different worries for each child. For Solomon I am concerned that he will not learn to use his beginning analytical skills if their formation and deployment (think time) are not sufficiently emphasized by our culture in whatever medium(s) found in his school. Further, as he becomes more and more accustomed to the numerous distractions in his environment, I worry that he will have less motivation (or learned ability) to expend the time to use these processes when it is important to do so. Without formal literacy, I worry that Susanna will not have the opportunity to develop either her potential or her nascent analytical skills. Her intelligence is never the issue; its development and its future contributions are. There is a wonderful remark by Stephen Gould that hangs in the entry to our research center in which he writes that it is less important to know the convolutions of Einstein's brain than to know that people just like him are spending their daily lives in sweatshops around the world.

An understanding of the relationship between the growth of critical analytical processes and the development of literacy is of critical importance for Susanna and every non-literate person on our interconnected planet. An understanding of the relationship between critical analytical processes and the development of insight is of critical importance for the literate Solomon and all the children like him who will become, in a temporal breath, our future leaders.

To be sure, I have never decided whether critical analysis processes belong as much in the next generative phases of deep reading, as in the present metacognitive category. Just as the literary works of Walter Benjamin and Harold Bloom inhabit a space that lies between the worlds of literary criticism and of literature, so also do these important intellectual processes inhabit both the analytical and the generative aspects of deep reading that come next.

Generativity processes: the time for insight and novel thought

"Towards a neural signature of insight"

> An insight is so capricious, such a slippery thing to catch *in flagrante*, that it appears almost deliberately designed to defy empirical inquiry. To most neuroscientists, the prospect of looking for creativity in the brain must seem like trying to nail jelly to the wall.[41]
>
> Arne Dietrich and Riam Kanso

If I sometimes stop in wonder at the ineffable beauty of those works of literature that make us all pause in sheer appreciation for their creativity and insight, I also appreciate very much neuroscientists like Mark Jung-Beeman and John Kounios from Northwestern University, and Arne Dietrich and Riam Kanso from the American University in Beirut who strive to help us understand what lies beneath. The above quote, with its own eloquence, captures the difficulty in pinpointing the physiological basis of "insight," one of the major goals of deep reading. For insight is surely a "slippery thing," whether from the standpoint of its neural signature or from the perspective of the reader.

Characterizing what happens in the brain's processing of insight during the last milliseconds of reading cannot be neatly summarized at this moment in the neuroscience literature. There is little consensual agreement about the particular networks, regions, or even hemispheres that are most active during insight processes. As Katz declared almost two decades ago with little apparent effect, "The claim that creativity is located 'in' the right hemisphere should be dispelled with at once."[42] Since then, Katz's admonition has fallen like the proverbial unnoted tree in the public's oblivious forest. Most people continue to associate and "locate" creativity in any form with the right hemisphere.

Dietrich and Kanso have contributed a great deal to help dispel and refine that oversimplification through time-intensive meta-analyses of many available studies. Underscoring the lack of consensus in our knowledge about what our brain does during moments of creative insight, at one point they concluded, "It might be stated that creativity is everywhere!" Despite this understandably exasperated pronouncement, they and a few other researchers are beginning the hard work of distinguishing the component aspects of insight from highly related cognitive functions like divergent thinking and artistic creativity.

For example, Mark Jung-Beeman and John Kounios seek to uncover what the brain does en route to insight.[43] They show how Pasteur's famous remark—"Chance favors only the prepared mind"—could not be more correct in the physiology of insight. There appear to be discrete brain structures deployed for preparation and also for search. Just as we discussed in the section on critical analyses, the prefrontal neural networks involved in the evaluation of our cumulative inferences *prepare our mind* for what happens next—whether coming to summative conclusions or the rare, desirous leap into a whole new level of understanding. Along the way, Jung-Beeman and Kounios suggest that when we are working methodically on problem-solving, we often activate the visual and attention areas, along with the well-known prefrontal areas. When we are en route to insight, however, we actually *inhibit* or *turn off* the visual regions and make the "leap" to activate a rather unlikely, still too little-known region in the right hemisphere's superior temporal gyrus. Of the limited things we know about this area, it appears to be activated during the processing of literary metaphor, and also during the later semantic processes.

More detail is gradually emerging. Not only does insight appear to activate this right temporal region after the preparation phase in the prefrontal areas, but 300 milliseconds *before* this insight, there is literally a spike in the brain's gamma waves (the highest electrical frequency we have). It is as if the preparation for insight lights up the cortex over this small convoluted fold in the right temporal lobe. And then, a more metaphorical form of illumination occurs milliseconds later. We feel with intuitive certainty that this insight is correct and worthy of our continued thought. Just as in the last steps of the critical analytical processes when the prefrontal areas give their imprimatur, they do so here as well. We have thought something new.

From a physiological perspective, these findings underscore the need to allocate sufficient time in milliseconds for the processes that lead to insight, particularly the time en route and immediately following it. Many thoughtful individuals in different disciplines write about the relationship between *time* and insight processes from a different but very related perspective. Lindsay Waters writes: "slowing down can produce a deeply profound quiet that can overwhelm your soul and in that quiet you can lose yourself in thought for an immeasurable moment of time."[44] Apologists for slow reading like Waters and others emphasize the relationships that thread together how we read, how we think, and what we value. At the center of their efforts is the hope that thoughtful readers will enter an entirely different temporal framework—one that is at odds with the present milieu's emphases on speed, immediacy, and multitasking—so as to enter a place where attention and contemplation can coexist. From the perspective I hold, what Waters, Ulin, and others call *slow reading* represents the temporal sanctuary where deep reading can take place. It is what Davis conceptualized as the moment where writer and reader meet to co-create *"a holding-ground for the contemplation of experience."*[45]

Although the intention of those who advocate slow reading could not be better directed, the term itself can be misleading, or worse, off-putting to less informed readers—as if they only have to slow the speed of their reading (a potential proxy for slowing themselves down) to capture the essence of the author's intent and to immerse themselves

The Deep Reading Brain

in the reading experience. In reality, the extra time to apply deep reading processes amounts to *imperceptible* milliseconds in the brain's time. Advocates of slow reading know this, but many well-meaning readers do not. The point that I wish to make explicit here is that the goal of slow reading is not reached by one's perception of speed, but rather by the reader's intention to reflect on the meanings of what is read and to go one step further—to germinate one's own insights into it.

In describing this last grouping of deep reading processes, I have offered neither definitive categories for conceptualizing insight, nor consensual descriptions of its underlying physiology. Both remain elusive. In his superb *New Yorker* essay on the "Eureka experience," Jonah Lehrer[46] described the quicksilver nature of what we try to capture when we speak of terms like the *aha moment* and *eureka*. And yet we know exactly when it happens. Often as not, these moments are elicited by the author, sometimes directly (e.g. through characters), and sometimes obliquely, as seen in Shakespeare's advice from Polonius to Hamlet, "And thus do we of wisdom and of reach...By indirection find direction out."[47]

I wish to highlight one example of the insight process by describing one of the more remarkable scenes and characters in literature and my ultimate grasp of what this scene meant when I was a young would-be English major. The phantasmagoric snow scene in Thomas Mann's novel, *Magic Mountain*, exemplifies *received insight* by a character that is meant to be imparted to the reader. Set in an alpine, mountain air sanitarium for treating tuberculosis, the very structure of the novel has the protagonist Hans Castorp, a kind of Jedermann, regularly thrown between two fierce intellectual antagonists, Setembrini and Naphta. These two men hold passionately debated, divergent perspectives, which Castorp feels incapable of judging.

At one point, Hans leaves the sanitarium to ski in the surrounding mountains and finds himself in a snowstorm of unbelievable power and wonder, with the unmistakable potential to kill him. Time ceases for him. Within this moment, Hans Castorp experiences visions of breathtaking beauty: a translucent rainbow appears over a landscape that dazzles his senses, and reminds him of what he has already experienced in his past. His perceptions of timelessness and beauty lead to thoughts that transcend the dialectical views of the two "pedagogues."

Suddenly Hans Castorp's world is opened to a view of life far beyond his static notions of time and death. Until this point he perceived himself as a piece of insignificant matter, regularly torn between the more intellectually elaborated and sophisticated viewpoints of others, with little to offer of his own thinking. He lived his life narrowly and, if not thoughtlessly, with little comprehension of either life's or death's meaning for him. The confrontation with the storm and his seemingly imminent death gave Hans Castorp a transforming insight:

> Man is the master of contradictions, they occur through him, and so he is more noble than they. More noble than death...that is the freedom of his mind. More noble than life...that is the devotion of the heart....I have...dreamed a poem of humankind. I will remember it. I will be good. I will grant death no dominion over my thoughts. For in that is found goodness and brotherly love, and in that alone.[48]

On the surface it would seem that Mann, whose pedagogical propensities sometimes overwhelm one, leaves little for the reader to think for themselves. Yet, more than three decades have passed since I read that spellbinding scene in nature, and I can still "see" the blizzard in my mind. I can still "see" the small quilt-covered bed in my real home where I read this scene. I can still feel what the young, torn, and insignificant-feeling Hans Castorp experienced from despair to conviction and joy. I can, therefore, still "feel" what I experienced while reading this passage. Despite or perhaps because of the transparently pedagogical element in Thomas Mann's novel, I came to understand something about life's transitoriness that I never understood before. I was still twenty years old, but it was as if I had been given a glimpse— of the inescapability of my own death, and of what trumped it: the goodness and the love that are to be searched for—within the crevasses in nature and in mind, and in the heart's uncertain reach. I was transported from a little town in Illinois to a sanitarium in the Alps, and I was changed by insight into and from that passage.

Generativity

Experiences of insight like this one from my youth are the very stuff of deep reading and what we hope for every young person and for the reader of any age. But such transformative insights are not the only aspect in what I mean by the *generative* dimension that is at the acme of reading. The psychologist Erik Erikson characterized the last stages of human development as a time when we can experience the greatest potential for generativity and going outside ourselves. The last processes in deep reading provide a fitting analogue to Erikson's depiction. Sometimes if we are very fortunate, we move from personal insight into the creation of thoughts that reach outside ourselves. Reading's developmental arc reflects our life: the successful deployment of Plato's four dimensions of words leads us to the point when we the readers have the potential to go outside them all, to approach the last category in Plato's taxonomy, *On* or Being. Plato did not believe that words were adequate for conveying this "fifth" dimension, which he conceptualized as the "real essence" behind the word. Neither does Ray Jackendoff, whose cognitive perspective on language urges us to examine the limits of our words for reflecting thought, while simultaneously understanding the powerful expansions in these very efforts.

It is in this moment of trying to describe what happens next in deep reading that I most wish I could show Plato the final figure of Diotima's brain that ends this chapter. If Plato could watch what the brain does during an actual enactment of *eidolon*, *onoma* (with its meanings and functions), *episteme*, and *on*, in real time and actual cerebral space, he would glimpse what I hope the reader now is prepared to appreciate: the full beauty of the reading brain's capacity to use all the processes that contribute to understanding the written word as the basis for generating new, never before encountered or shared thought. In this context, the *generating of new thought* represents a slightly different meaning than in Kuperberg's and Clark's accounts of *hierarchical generative* frameworks, in which we produce hypotheses in order to infer the text's or author's meanings. But they are surely related to the underlying creative capacity that undergirds both uses of the word.

There is a still earlier use of the word discussed in Chapter 2: Chomsky's paradigm-changing description of the *generative nature* of grammar—how the finite structures of our grammar can permit infinite numbers of utterances. The origins for my own thinking about the *generativity* at the heart of written language began without doubt with this view. But my thinking gradually changed over the years, in no small part due to the contributions of Ray Jackendoff into the generative dimensions within semantic and phonological language functions. I believe that each of these language functions contributes to a unique, convergent form of creativity and generativity that written language provides the reader. Within such a construct, grammatical functions provide the conceptual scaffolding for generativity, while semantic, morphological, and phonological contributions provide the expanding conceptual substance and content.

With this as context, beginning and ending with the frontal and prefrontal areas, the structure of the reading brain provides the reader with a global, neuronal workspace where the assimilation of input from perception, language, and affect meets our prediction capacities and propulses our knowledge—for ourselves and sometimes for others. It is the place where the written word meets the sum of our world knowledge and deepens our understanding of both. In this sense, generativity in written language has its *origins* in the intrinsically creative aspects of all its linguistic components and its *expression* in thoughts that go beyond the author and the text. The end of each truly deep reading, therefore, prepares for the beginning of the next.

Proust's thoughts on this endpoint of reading (or, in essence, its next starting point) have guided my thoughts for two decades, even to the title of my last book. Lovingly rendered in a brief, little-known essay "On Reading" a century ago, Proust wrote that at the essential core of the reading process, we go beyond the "wisdom of the author" to discover and give our own wisdom, within "that fertile miracle of communication that takes place in the middle of solitude."[49] It is this fertile miracle between author and reader that is the ultimate end of the generativity processes and the beginning of whatever comes next: our personal "quarry" of thoughts and hopes.

Catherine Stoodley's last drawing of the reading brain represents our final, but unfinished effort to render a snapshot of the reading circuit at this moment in time (see Figure 5.1). It is based on research discussed here and in the most recent meta-analysis of more than forty imaging studies by Anna Martin, Matthias Schurz, and their associates in Salzburg.[50] It is a work in progress, which illustrates the potential for some of the multiple, possible pathways and redundant, parallel paths that words can take along their way to being understood. We have depicted St Thomas Aquinas, the humble

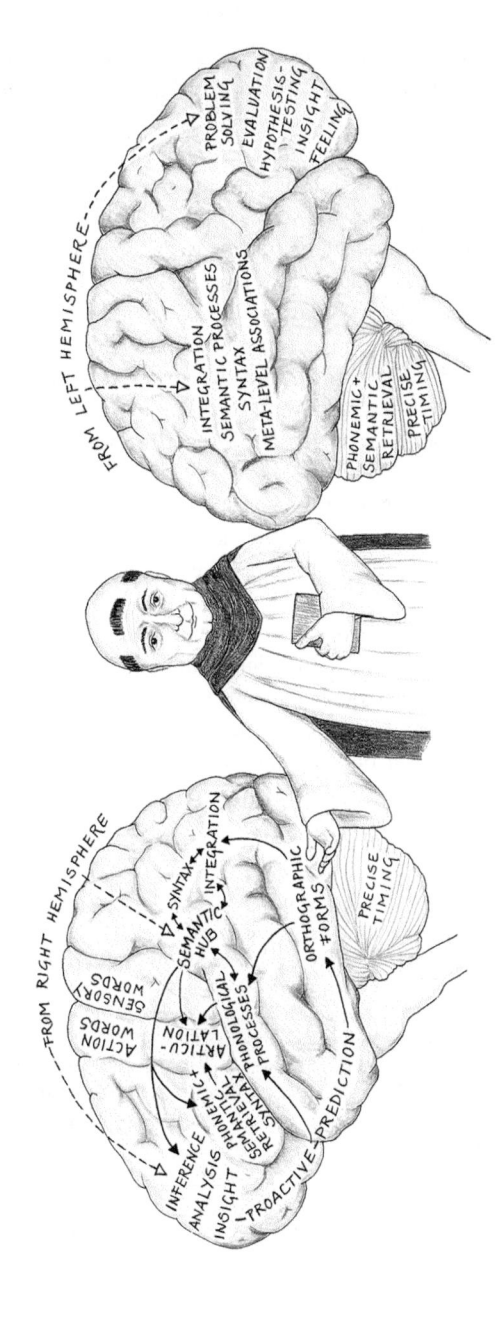

Figure 5.1. Full reading brain circuit with St Thomas Aquinas

author of one of the world's greatest works, *Summa Theologica*, alongside this reading brain for several reasons. First, we think he would look upon our "unfinished" efforts with a personal understanding that this sum of the reading brain research, not unlike the never finished summary of his own thought, can only be one, time-locked effort to depict what we know. Second, we believe he would delight to know just how complex and elaborate the process is that he cherished in his lifetime. There is an apt passage from G. K. Chesterton's endearing portrait of St Thomas: "When asked for what he thanked God most, he answered simply, 'I have understood every page I ever read'." We would like to think that this drawing and indeed the whole chapter are visible testimony to the enormous, multifaceted gift that reading bestows on readers from St Thomas Aquinas to Susanna and Solomon.[51]

Still, as I wrote at the start of these chapters, at the end there remains much mystery, particularly about the next iterations of the reading brain. These will be shaped to an unknown extent by present and future digital mediums. Both the advances in our technical ability to image the reading circuit *and* the many lacunae still missing in our knowledge are the objective correlatives of the reading brain's continuously evolving complexity and plasticity. Soon enough, the ongoing changes in our culture will be reflected in the next iteration of the reading brain. Whether or not we will preserve the deep reading processes in that brain will be at the center of the critical issues we turn to now.

Notes

1. Walter Benjamin, "On Language as Such." In *Selected Writings: Volume 1, 1913–26* (Cambridge, MA: Harvard University Press, 1996), p. 65.
2. Ralph Waldo Emerson. I am indebted to Cynthia Ozick for this quote in her "'The Daemon Knows' by Harold Bloom," *New York Times Book Review* (May 18, 2015).
3. George Steiner, *Real Presences: The Leslie Stephen Memorial Lecture at University of Cambridge* (Cambridge: University of Cambridge Press, 1986).
4. Our *word* knowledge can take more activation time, particularly when there is the need for correction and re-evaluation, as shown in the ERP P600 findings by Gibson et al. Our *world* knowledge includes what cognitive scientists refer to as event knowledge.
5. Davis, p. 16.
6. The roots of this work stem from mid-twentieth-century educator Benjamin Bloom's taxonomy of thinking skills from extraction of information to critical analysis.

7. Anna Abraham, Karoline Pieritz, Kristin Thybusch, Barbara Rutter, Sören Kröger, Jan Schweckendiek, Rudolf Stark, Sabine Windmann, and Christiane Hermann, "Creativity and the Brain: Uncovering the Neural Signature of Conceptual Expansion," *Neuropsychologia* 50, no. 8 (2012): pp. 1906–17. doi:10.1016/j.neuropsychologia.2012.04.015.
8. Mar.
9. Karuna Subramaniam, John Kounios, Todd B. Parrish, and Mark Jung-Beeman, "A Brain Mechanism for Facilitation of Insight by Positive Affect," *Journal of Cognitive Neuroscience* 21, no. 3 (2009): pp. 415–32. doi:10.1162/jocn.2009.21057. Hereafter cited as Jung-Beeman and Kounios.
10. Karin Littau, *Theories of Reading* (Cambridge, UK: Polity Press, 2006). Hereafter cited as Littau.
11. Littau.
12. Davis, pp. 84–5.
13. Lindsay Waters, "Time for Reading," *The Chronicle Review* 53, no. 23 (February 9, 2007): p. B6. <http://chronicle.com/article/Time-for-Reading/10505>. See also work by Alexander Olchowski, David Mikics, and Thomas Newkirk.
14. Recently, I learned that Sven Birkerts may have been the first to use the term in his *Gutenberg Elegies* to describe one aspect of deep reading, its contemplative dimension. I am indebted to Nicholas Carr for including my more elaborated use of the term in his book, *The Shallows*.
15. Davis, p. 23.
16. Johann Wolfgang Goethe, *Maxims and Reflections* (London: Penguin Classics, 1999).
17. Quoted in Nick Clark, "Imagination, Invention, and Appropriation in Twentieth-Century Picture-Book Art." In Jill Shefrin (ed.), *One Hundred Books Famous in Children's Literature* (New York: Grolier Club, 2014), p. 49.
18. Elaine Scarry, *Dreaming by the Book* (Princeton, NJ: Princeton University Press, 2001).
19. Peter Mendelsund, *What We See When We Read* (New York: Vintage, 2014). Hereafter cited as Mendelsund.
20. Quoted in Mendelsund.
21. David Ulin, *Lost Art of Reading* (Seattle, WA: Sasquatch Books, 2010).
22. B. Bernhardt and Tania Singer, "Neural Basis of Empathy," *Annual Review of Neuroscience* 35 (2012): pp. 1–23. doi: 10.1146/annurev-neuro-062111-150536.
23. Gish Jen, personal correspondence, 2014.
24. Marilynne Robinson, *Gilead* (New York: Farrar, Strauss & Giroux, 2004).
25. Mar.
26. Eric Fields and Gina Kuperberg, "It's All About You: An ERP Study of Emotion and Self-relevance in Discourse," *Neuroimage* 62, no. 1 (2012): pp. 562–74. doi: 10.1016/j.neuroimage.2012.05.003.
27. George Eliot, *Middlemarch* (New York: Penguin Classics, 1998; originally 1874).
28. I am indebted to Philip Davis for this fact, based on a question George Eliot was asked by F. W. H. Myers. See also the play *A Dangerous Woman* by Cathy Tempelsman on George Eliot and this topic.
29. Quoted in John S. Dunne, *Love's Mind: An Essay on Contemplative Life* (Notre Dame, IN: University of Notre Dame Press, 1993).

30. Emily Dickinson, *Complete Poems of Emily Dickinson* (Cambridge, MA: Harvard University Press, 1960).
31. Dedre Gentner, Keith J. Holyoak, and Boicho N. Kokinov (eds), *The Analogical Mind: Perspectives from Cognitive Science* (Cambridge, MA: MIT Press, 2001). Hereafter Gentner. See Dedre Gentner and Ken Forbus, "Computational Models of Analogy," *WIREs Cognitive Science* 2 (2011): pp. 266–76. doi: 10.1002/wcs.105.
32. Douglas Hofstadter, "Analogy as the Core of Cognition." In Gentner, pp. 499–538; see also Paul H. Thibodeau, Stephen J. Flusberg, Jeremy J. Glick, and Daniel A. Sternberg, "An Emergent Approach to Analogical Inference," *Connection Science* 25, no. 1 (2013): pp. 27–53. doi:10.1080/09540091.2013.821458.
33. Usha Goswami, "Analogy and the Brain: A New Perspective on Relational Primacy," *Behavioral and Brain Sciences* 31, no. 4 (2008): pp. 387–8. doi:10.1017/S0140525X08004561.
34. Gentner.
35. William James quoted in John G. Geake and Peter C. Hansen, "Neural Correlates of Intelligence as Revealed by fMRI of Fluid Analogies," *Neuroimage* 26, no. 2 (2005): pp. 555–64. doi:10.1016/j.neuroimage.2005.01.035.
36. Andy Clark, "Whatever Next? Predictive Brains, Situated Agents, and the Future of Cognitive Science," *Behavioral and Brain Sciences* 36, no. 3 (2013): pp. 1–73. Hereafter cited as Clark. doi: 10.1017/S0140525X12000477.
37. Gina Kuperberg and T. Florian Jaeger, "What Do We Mean by Prediction in Language Comprehension?" In *Language and Cognitive Neuroscience*, in press. Hereafter Kuperberg.
38. Dehaene.
39. Alan Jacobs, *The Pleasures of Reading in the Age of Distraction* (New York: Oxford University Press, 2011), pp. 149–50.
40. Jung-Beeman and Kounios, p. 419.
41. Arne Dietrich and Riam Kanso, "A Review of EEG, ERP, and Neuroimaging Studies of Creativity and Insight," *Psychological Bulletin* 136, no. 5 (2010): pp. 822–48. doi:10.1037/a0019749.
42. Quoted in Dietrich and Kanso.
43. Jung-Beeman and Kounios.
44. Waters.
45. Davis.
46. Jonah Lehrer, "The Eureka Hunt," *New Yorker* (2008).
47. William Shakespeare, *Hamlet*.
48. Thomas Mann, *The Magic Mountain*, trans. John Woods (New York: Knopf, 1996), p. 487.
49. Proust, p. 67.
50. Anna Martin, Matthias Schurz, Martin Kronbichler, and Fabio Richlan, "Reading in the Brain of Children and Adults: A Meta-Analysis of 40 Functional Magnetic Resonance Imaging Studies," *Human Brain Mapping* 36, no. 5 (2015): pp. 1963–81. doi: 10.1002/hbm.22749.
51. G. K. Chesterton, *St. Thomas Aquinas* (New York: Image Books, 1933/1956), p. 21.

6

A Second Revolution in the Brain

> We transgress not because we try to build the new, but because we do not allow ourselves to consider what it disrupts or diminishes.[1]
>
> Sherry Turkle, *Alone Together*

> We will ultimately multiply our intellectual powers by applying and extending the methods of human intelligence using the vastly greater capacity of non-biological computation.... We have the ability to understand our own intelligence—to access our own source code, if you will—and then revise and expand it.[2]
>
> Ray Kurzweil, *The Singularity is Near*

That both Turkle and Kurzweil represent vitally important perspectives on technology and the future of our society confronts us head-on with the complex realities in the present transition from a literate to a digital culture. As cautioned by Turkle, we are en route to becoming *cultural bystanders*, whose detachment prevents awareness of the potential loss of qualities essential to our humanity. As foretold by Kurzweil, we have the possibility to participate in exponential leaps of knowledge that technology will make available in the century ahead and that could drive human society forward. Both of these views are conceivable, which makes our collective wisdom about what lies within these scenarios all the more vital.

I want to begin this chapter with my greatest fear and my highest hope about the intrinsically linked futures of the reading brain, literacy, and the literary mind in the present transition. I will then unpack some of the unique affordances of print and screen in the next two chapters as a way to approach the divergent views of the future represented by Turkle and Kurzweil. The earlier parts of this book presented readers with a particular foundation of background knowledge from linguistics, child development, and the cognitive neurosciences.

It is the reader's preparation for this moment in the book. I wish, just as depicted in the last chapter, for readers to combine this book's content with their own background knowledge; to come to their own conclusions about these filial, but sometimes contradictory, cultural realities; and then, as at the apex of deep reading, to go well "beyond the author."[3]

First, my greatest fear. It is a triptych. I worry about the formation of deep reading capacities in the young; about the deterioration of these capacities in expert readers; and about the indifference and/or lack of knowledge about the consequences of both. Whether or not these fears become reality, the present reading brain circuits will ineluctably change to reflect the different emphases in digital reading mediums, with the concomitant changes in digital readers. The fear is that these new capacities will replace, rather than complement, our present capacities. Within such a scenario, it is more than likely that there will emerge a culturally altered version of what connotes the literary mind, which will alter literature itself. It is an open question as to what will emerge, but there will be a changed reading brain. In Chapter 3 we described how Castro-Caldas and Reis referred to the reading circuit's formation as a "revolution in the brain."[4] We are embarked on its second revolution.

Second, and simultaneously, I look with keen excitement at another way of viewing the effects of the exact same scenario: that is, the new dimensions of cognition and perception that are already evolving for the species, and the stunning progress in communication that will make literacy and learning available to massive numbers of human beings who would otherwise have no opportunities to become literate. This unleashed human potential cannot be calculated.

All of this is not so much a Cassandra-like dilemma, as our own twenty-first-century struggle between the culture of print and the culture of screen and the differing emphases in the latter. Like Turkle, I consider our society better prepared for innovation than the preservation of core human values. Like Kurzweil, I believe there has never been more cause for optimism for the intellectual expansion of our species. Therein lies the problem and, perhaps, the solution that the Viennese have long solved. When confronted with two choices at Cafe Oper in Vienna, one should always inquire if there is a third possibility that combines the others. Graphic novelist Mark Danielewski[5] makes a similar point when asked about future emphases on words vs images in literature and the graphic novel: "I think there's a common point between both worlds, and there's a point of departure where they each demonstrate their own sort of possibilities."

In this chapter, I wish the reader to consider a similarly differentiated and integrative option for the future reading brain. It begins with a dispassionate examination of the most critical factors for the next generation's formation of a reading brain. For ultimately, it is about what the members of our next generation will *become* that is the leitmotif of this chapter and indeed all of my research. The principles underlying our youth's formation should never be left to chance, which, too often, is not chance, but rather the effects of cultural trends that can be based more on profit for the few, than the good of the many. As Walter de la Mare once wrote, "Only the rarest kind of best in anything can be good enough for the young."[6]

Within that context, let us look first at the changing world of the young and their emergent capacities as they assimilate and adapt to a digital culture, and then at the changes many of us are experiencing as adult readers. From a developmental perspective, several, intimately connected questions press upon us: first, what is the reality of our *digital habits* from the earliest years on? Second, what are the consequences of these digital habits for the *nature of attention*? Specifically, what are the relationships between *how we attend* and *how and what we read* (e.g. decisions about text length and complexity for both reader *and* writer)? And third, given the immediacy and overwhelming volume of easily accessed information, what are our relationships to this *information overload*, and its effects? These highly interrelated questions and their varying offshoots will structure this chapter.

Habits of the young and old

In her thorough and very valuable book, *Words Onscreen: The Fate of Reading in a Digital World*,[7] Naomi Baron summarizes the varied studies about young people's online habits and the effects on their attention and on memory and cognition. Baron writes that about two-thirds of the children in America from two to thirteen are using digital devices, with many children online an average of seven hours a day, every day of the week, and an ever increasing number of youth online as much as twelve or more hours a day. In a study in 2013, Common Sense Media reported that children's use of digital devices increased from 52 per cent to 75 per cent just in the two years between 2011 and 2013. During this same period, 93 per cent of older youth, between twelve and seventeen years old, reported having computer access in their homes. Such large exposure has a potential influence greater than time in school with teachers or time at home with parents and families.

The everyday reality in many households, however, now includes the youngest of our children. A recent British study indicates that 51 per cent of children between three and four years have a tablet.[8] Many babies and toddlers under two are exposed to various digital devices despite the recommendations by noted pediatrician Barry Zuckerman and the American Academy of Pediatrics[9] that children under two should have restricted amounts of time only. The reasons for such recommendations are related to both conceptual and linguistic development. For example, Katherine Hirsh-Pasek studies the language development of infants and young children, including those who are exposed to the now almost typical barrage of baby videos and programs with all manner of bells and whistles—most of which implicitly (or explicitly) suggest that everyone's child has a chance to become the new Alan Turing or Amadeus Mozart. In this work, Hirsh-Pasek[10] along with a number of other important developmental researchers[11] suggest that very young children who are simply in the presence of ordinary language stimulation by ordinary humans like parents and caretakers demonstrate better, early, oral language development. It is an unsurprising finding that few parents appear to know.

Baron cites both a Bowker study and one by Scholastic that indicate that the vast majority of parents of children aged eight and under want their children to be encountering more books than digital devices, but they do not want to exclude the latter. There are reasons both good and ill for parents who are, often as not, overwhelmed with the challenges of raising children in a time of cultural transition. Clinical psychologist Catherine Steiner-Adair[12] has written persuasively about the need for parents to "disconnect" from technology in reasonable ways, so as to navigate between overuse (which amounts to digital addiction for some youth) and cultural alienation in their children. Reminiscent of all the fears our society has had over the emergence of each technological innovation in the last century—from radio and film to television and now the digital world—parents worry, but appear to believe they can do little to "stem the tide." Steiner-Adair argues eloquently both for a new role for parents in which they reclaim stewardship of their young's development and also for new relationships among our youth who are often seeking *meaning* in their devices rather than in each other.

With regard to the development of oral and written language, many parents, particularly those who purchase programs that seek to develop early reading in the very young, are insufficiently knowledgeable about their own roles in imparting what young children need most: to *be spoken to, listened to, and read to every day*.[13] The research is unequivocal on the importance of these three, cost-free, invaluable contributions to early child development.

Such a fact, however, does not mean there should be no exposure to the digital world. I would like to invoke what I have long called "the grandmother's principle," which amounts to using simple, but informed common sense in the gradual introduction of any medium of communication, from television and video, to laptop and tablet. If the child is set in front of any one of these mediums for hours with no guidance, and/or if the medium becomes used as a surrogate caretaker, the ever increased domination of the medium over other influences (from parent to school) should come with little surprise. Nor should the invisible cognitive, perceptual, and social changes that accompany this amount of exposure to any medium. The most transparent, medium-influenced change seen in young and old alike is a primary one in cognition: attention itself.

The changing nature of attention and its effects

As described in Chapter 4's account of the reading brain, the first essential component in the reading circuitry is attention in all its forms. Before ever focusing on the matter at hand, the reader must use one form of attention (the orienting system) to move from its previous stimulus, another to redirect itself, and yet another to focus with laser precision on what is to be attended to as long as necessary. The attentional systems are critical to everything we read. More important for this discussion, it is the *nature of attention* that separates the casual perusal of surface information from the deep reading processes necessary to be critical analysts of that information.

Herein lies the problem. Attention, which changes naturally across the development of the child, is changing still further, and perhaps less naturally, in its adaptation to the characteristics of the mediums of communication. The term *continuous partial attention* is as apt and worrisome a depiction of what is occurring today as when Linda Stone first used the term in 1998. For example, in one study cited by Baron and conducted by Time Inc., young people switched media sources twenty-seven times in an hour. In another study, students reported using, on average, three to four digital devices at a time, rapidly switching their attention from one to another.

Distraction and its sources

The very idea that many of our young are basically switching their attention every two to three minutes is or should be a wake-up call to everyone who wishes to understand how to ensure not only the deepening intellectual development of each child, but also the preparation of the citizens of our society. In her book *Distracted: The Erosion of Attention and the Coming Dark Age*, Maggie Jackson writes that all of us are "air-traffic controllers now."[14] Jackson based some of her work on distraction on the extensive research conducted by psychologist David Meyer on the cognitive effects of *multitasking*. In one of the more memorable quotes on the topic of multitasking, Meyer stated that despite all the training one can do, no one can "be as good as if you just focused on one thing at a time. Period."[15]

It is one thing to be less proficient at multiple tasks, it is yet another to be aware of the *costs* to multitasking. Meyer's research demonstrates the "switch costs" to the brain that occur when the attentional systems have to change goals midstream, learn or recall the "rules" for the new task, repress or inhibit whatever is still streaming as input from the previous still activated task, and then attempt to complete one or both or more tasks still. Further, the more complex the tasks, the "steeper the costs." Neuroscientist Daniel Levitin[16] buttresses Meyer's conclusions with research showing the corresponding increase of the stress-related hormones cortisol and adrenalin, during the hyperattention states induced during multitasking. It is, not unlike Maggie Jackson's "air-traffic controllers" metaphor, as if children and indeed many of us are unknowingly shifting the attentional systems of the brain into a heightened *fight or flight* mode for enormous amounts of our days.

As both Levitin and Meyer argue, such a state is hardly conducive for most learning. And that, of course, is one of the central issues. What does it mean for the intellectual growth and learning of children that their attentional systems are "always on"?[17] What are the cognitive advantages and disadvantages to them as they hone their increasingly adept, impresario-like skills in monitoring multiple devices? Not that long ago, I used the past research of Stanford neuroscientist Russ Poldrack to underscore how inefficient multitasking can be, if one of those tasks requires particular attention and thought. Poldrack's earlier research illustrated how we can perform several tasks at once at a *surface* level, but that we must return to each one, if there is more serious cognitive effort required.

More recently, however, he and his colleagues refined this conclusion with an added pertinent factor. They looked at task switching when one task is well learned (e.g. reading) and the other untrained.[18] They found different neural substrates not only for the trained and untrained tasks, but also for what is involved in switching itself. In contrast to their former work, a very important finding is that when a task is well trained, the negative effects of multitasking can be diminished. Thus an important caveat in the multitasking and task-switching literature involves how automatic or trained each individual task is. Given our collective dependence on air traffic controllers, it is a welcome conclusion, but not one to generalize from too quickly, particularly for the young.

This is because the human attentional systems are evolutionarily predisposed to move immediately to any new or novel stimulus.[19] In other words we are wired to attend to whatever new sensory input attracts (distracts) our attention, which makes a multi-stimuli context almost impossible for our children to override. It is, for example, a very sobering finding by Baron that 90 per cent of young people report they would always multitask when reading on screens. By contrast, only 1 per cent of these youth would do so when reading print. To be sure, in the not-that-distant past, this adaptive perspicacity protected our ancestors from predators, as well as provided them with food for their survival. In the fairly recent past in 1939, Walter

Benjamin wrote that we are becoming a "neurotic population with urgent needs for stimuli."[20] One can only imagine how he might view today's population, whose members have moved still further into a virtually *continuous* use of their *hyper-attention* systems.[21]

How we attend affects how we read: the "new norms" in reading

One of the shifts that most people appear oblivious to concerns the striking changes in their own current reading habits.[22] Reading researcher Ziming Liu describes the "new norms" for reading as skimming, word-spotting, and moving from topic to topic without necessarily adhering to the linear sequence originally constructed by the author.[23] These behaviors are the objective correlative of our fragmented attention. Indeed, many digital readers appear to follow either an F or Z zigzag pattern where they read the first lines, a few words in the middle, and then, if they get to the end, the concluding lines. Others appear to move from the beginning to the end, which, if found engaging, results in a backwards zigzag to pick up supporting elements in the middle.

Imagine for just a moment what might have happened if readers in the last century used a *zigzag browse mode* for Virginia Woolf's *To the Lighthouse* or word-spotting for Proust's *Remembrance of Things Past* or Joyce's *Ulysses*. These works, with their evocation of the "stream of consciousness" of our thinking life, might well have appeared unreadable and/or uninteresting to most readers and thus been lost to all of us. As Sherry Turkle discusses in her most recent book, *Reclaiming Conversation*,[24] more and more digital-reading students "graze" at what they read, which "makes it hard to develop a narrative to frame events." It is a recipe for missing not only a plot's sequence, but also the beauty of a writer's painstakingly chosen *mot juste*,[25] and the *multisensory* richness of the reading experience itself, beginning with its physicality.

Anne Mangen[26] hypothesizes that the importance of the physical dimensions of print does not represent some emotion-laden adherence to past mediums, but rather plays a vitally important role in the facilitation of comprehension, particularly in following the *sequence* of the plot. Her research highlights how students are less able to apprehend important aspects of text while reading a story when they read it on digital screens, rather than in print. In one of her studies, college-age students read the same story in two mediums. The students reading on screen could not report plot details as well as students reading with print. Further, the reading comprehension of the screen readers showed a lack of sequential thinking, that may well be the consequence of the non-linear zigzag reading behaviors often reported for digital readers.

The material *physicality* of the book, as opposed to the inherently transient nature of visual images on digital screens, is conceptualized by researchers from very different disciplines as an antidote to the new modes of reading. Andrew Piper, in *Book Was There*,[27] writes perceptively about the importance both of the *redundancy of information* in text that adds to our understanding, and also of the *physicality* of books that conveys a sense of touch and concrete solidity to our thoughts. In stark contrast to the book and the more permanent quality of its pages, the page on a digital screen is, Piper bemoans, a "fake," with no real existence. Along similar lines, feminist literary critic Karin Littau[28] highlights how the "materiality and physical organization" of books sharpen the reader's "sense and sensation" when encountering text. She worries, therefore, that the lack of physicality in screen reading will diminish sense and sensation and in the process *distance* the affect and engagement of the reader. Expressing a view that is increasingly noted, Piper and Littau fear that the more time reading on screens, the less time will be spent experiencing the multiple dimensions of words and text—including their physicality—all of which contribute to the deeper, slower processing of information.

Recall that Natalie Phillips and her colleagues found that their students activated motoric areas mirroring the actions of Jane Austen characters when they were instructed to engage in *close* reading, but not in more casual reading. I would suggest that the finding of motoric activation in the *close readers* for the physical descriptions also suggests that the "physicality" *evoked* by the text itself presents an additional dimension to its comprehension. Further, this may occur regardless of medium, since these readers were all reading digitally in the magnet when imaged. We will return to this point shortly.

Second, comprehension, whether it be directed to the reconstruction of plot or to the interpretation of scientific findings, is the product of multiple contributions from both internal and external sources—from the reader's background knowledge to the author's abilities to evoke "sense and sensation" in the reader, and more than likely, to the *influence* of the medium's characteristics (like the physicality of print forms) on the *individual* reader. For some readers, particularly those whose formation as a reader involved the physical mediums of print, the contribution of the medium's physicality may add an additional facilitating element to the threshold that governs their comprehension.

What we do not know fully is whether the physicality of print makes the same types of contributions to the young "digital natives," who themselves are anything but homogenous. There may indeed be not only a developmental formation difference here for digital natives (and print natives), but also an individual preference difference that is based on the unique characteristics of the learner. I recently observed videos of children at the Denver Academy who were first taking a survey on their print vs screen preferences, and then reading a passage (the identical one) on screen or in a book.[29] There were striking differences in what was perceived by individual children to be more helpful to their reading and also on what the children viewed as the weaknesses of both mediums. For example, one student memorably wrote: "A weakness of print books is that they catch on fire really easily"! Yet another, however, thoughtfully wrote: "I read e-books and paper equally... I don't think one is better than another. I don't judge a book by how I read it. I judge it by what I read." If the sentiments and reflective capacities of this second student were universally shared among his age group around the world, we would have no need for the concerns in this chapter.

The results of the Denver Academy survey indicated that most children there preferred print, just like the results from a far more comprehensive study by Baron of today's digital natives. That said, a clear number of the Denver Academy children (all of whom were diagnosed with dyslexia or other learning differences) demonstrated clearer strengths in screen reading, in part because they could control font size and length of text on a page. There are three interrelated issues here: first, individual reader differences and the reader's particular preferences, self-perceptions, and the individual's "set" towards reading; second, the question of text length and the associated issue of text complexity; and third, the complex, important relationships between the changing nature of the reader's attention and the demands of the text (e.g. length and conceptual density).

Before disentangling these issues, I want to return to a point briefly mentioned earlier. All of Phillips's subjects were undergoing an fMRI and thus reading inside the magnet on a screen under both close reading and surface reading conditions. In this study, therefore, close reading was not related to the medium, but to the instruction to adopt a particular "set" or approach to the text. The critical question that follows is whether the noted tendency to read more shallowly on screen and to read with *more time and closer attention* with print could be decoupled in some future research studies and investigated for the potential resolution of some concerns raised here. In other words, would both screen and print reading groups have more similar results if they were instructed to do "close reading"? Would such a set towards close reading or deep reading be able to override the often observed propensity to read more quickly and more distractedly on the screen (an issue we will elaborate in the next section)?

This is an important point if we as a society are to recognize the possible threats of what screen reading pushes the reader towards, and use this knowledge to address those threats in the future, regardless of medium. Gamification expert Katherine Isbister and I hope to tackle these issues head-on, by studying whether we can find ways to change how children direct their attention digitally and whether we can help redress the threats to close, deep reading by changing some aspects of digital screen attention in the viewer interface. It is a critical, unanswered question that is influenced by the next topic: what we read.

The relationship between how we attend and what we read

A major issue to this point in the chapter is whether the ability of an author to use every word, every complex concept necessary to assure true perception and comprehension by the reader is being curtailed—implicitly or explicitly—by the ever shorter attention spans in the reader and the new norms of skimming and browsing in reading styles. Think back to the discussion of syntactic development and how influenced it is by age, exposure to sentences of greater complexity and sophistication, and medium use. Very soon sentences—even like the last two—may be less likely to be fully read or, more importantly, completely understood. Certainly the concept-dense sentences of Henry and William James have already begun to be avoided by otherwise excellent students of literature,[30] who report that they don't have the *patience* to read such long, demanding sentences. Similarly, Katherine Hayles[31] reports how teachers of literature lament that because many of their students don't want to read long novels, they are turning more and more to short stories for their students. At what price are the changes in these students occurring?

I have written on what I call *cognitive patience* elsewhere,[32] therefore, I will only summarize a few thoughts here. Whether we trace the original Latin root of patience to *patior*, which translates "to suffer," or look elsewhere at the Greek word for patience, *hypomone*, which could be equated to *perseverance in the moment*, there are two insights from these etymological roots that need our notice. If a growing number of our best and brightest students of literature have begun to shun some of the finest works in our past literary legacy because the texts are too long, and because the students no longer possess the perseverance to "suffer through" them, who will *we*, the rest of us, become? Who will we be if huge portions of our past literary traditions become less incorporated in the corpus of what the educated person reads and writes and *is taught*? I do not suggest that every person needs to read Henry James or James Joyce or Joyce Carol Oates to be a member of a civilized society.

But the inclusion of patience in this discussion is not only about the formation of past and future literary minds. All educated individuals of our societies need to be able to exert cognitive patience, which translates into the extra milliseconds necessary for denser, more demanding texts, regardless of discipline. And what may begin as a discussion of patience and text density is ultimately about the structure and meanings of language and the nature of thought itself in today's culture. Decisions by a society over its future leaders and its laws require a citizenry prepared to think through and with complexity.

Great discernment and rigorous research, therefore, are essential both now and in the future to ascertain whether the potent combination of diminution of attention span and reduction of text length are actually reducing the underlying complexity of what we read and how we comprehend. We do not know this with certainty. What we know, however, is that our ability to understand ever more sophisticated text furthers our ability to comprehend the varied, often complex, and cognitively demanding issues that are at the heart of human character, and indeed of a democratic society. We need to know, in Turkle's earlier quoted words, what we are *disrupting* in those human capacities and values and what to do about it. There are few more obvious places to look than in another large set of related questions, concerning the role that the surfeit of information plays in our lives.

Information: how much is too much? Knowledge: how much is too little?

Fundamentally connected to issues surrounding diminished attention, changing reading behaviors, and their combined influences on the shifting characteristics of reader and text are the effects of the quite literally mind-boggling increases of information. Kurzweil describes these leaps as the vehicle for exponential advances in many aspects of our lives. But not all. How the individual learns to approach and use this tsunami of information is critical, lest it become the impetus to reduce critical analysis rather than to promote it. As most of us (and certainly Google) know, when faced with a plethora of information, many people opt for the simplest or sometimes simply the first, most conveniently available piece of information. This means that much of our information is either adjudicated by nothing more than being the entry with the most hits, or sometimes the one that was paid most for by a company to assure pride of place on the first half of the first entry page.[33] In other words, our present knowledge is being influenced by popularity (which might mean the simplest common denominator or form of that knowledge) and sometimes by a profit motive.

Few of us would ever want to lose the extraordinary contributions made by Google to our daily lives, but that does not abnegate the need to understand the extent to which we are ceding our critical analytic powers, and the consequences of doing so. The excesses of information's availability will only increase. One of the more disturbing discoveries I made while researching this topic came from a study conducted by the Global Information Industry Center at the University of California in San Diego. In a single year,

> Americans consumed information for about *1.3 trillion hours*, an average of almost 12 hours per day. Consumption totaled 3.6 zettabytes and 10,845 trillion words, corresponding to 100,500 words and 34 gigabytes for an average person on an average day. A zettabyte is 10 to the 21st power bytes, a million million gigabytes.[34]

Because these data are several years old, one must only infer that a more current estimate would go well beyond these already staggering figures. How can any one of us process this much incoming information that reflects numerous, competing sources, all vying for our increasingly shortened attention? The book you are reading is probably around 70,000 words plus a few more. Most of you would blanch at the prospect of trying to read it in a single day. Yet you are consuming more than that day in and day out in one interrupting fragment after another.

There are antidotes. Information specialists like David Levy are working towards "informational environmentalism," where

> just as we fight to save marshlands and old-growth forests from development and pollution... so we need to fight to save ourselves from the "pollutants" of information overload; the overabundance of information that turns us into triagers and managers, rather than readers; the proliferation of bad or useless or ersatz information; the forces that push us to process quickly rather than thoughtfully.[35]

Many of the most important contributors to the future of the expert reading brain are captured in that passage: our inability to process the overwhelming quantities of that much information (most of it unnecessary), leading to the inescapability of rapid, superficial processing in a hyper-attentional triage (*fight and flight*) reading mode, leading to the gradual deterioration and demise of thoughtful, deep reading. In Naomi Baron's perspective, all of this leads away from reading "long, connected texts towards short excerpts"[36] that can be immediately retrieved, quickly digested and, more than likely, only cursorily incorporated in the reader's intellectual wheelhouse. In British psychologist

Susan Greenfield's perspective, this cycle not only produces readers with shorter attention spans, but it also promotes text with less abstract content, resulting in more literal-minded readers—which, in turn, will ultimately change writing itself.[37] In my perspective, such a shift would change the nature of deep reading's deployment in which both extra milliseconds and the reader's intentions are necessary to link internal background knowledge with the reader's inferential, analogical, and critical analytical processes.

Deep reading and what comes next

Thus, we return to my initial "worst fear." *The most important issue in the transition from a literacy-based culture to a digital one* is whether the time- and cognitive-resource-demanding requirements of the deep reading processes will be lost or atrophied in a culture whose principal mediums advantage speed, multitasking, and the continuous processing of the ever-present next piece of information. Further, the question that is the leitmotif of all my current research is whether children, confronted with the overwhelming and intrinsically distracting glut of immediately accessible information, will *develop* either the cognitive capacities or the *motivation* to expend the time to think through the layers of meaning, syntactic structure, and inferred insights in what they read.

By cognitive capacities, I refer to the processes integral to the development of the expert reading brain circuitry in the earlier chapters: attention and short-term memory, long-term memory use of background knowledge, analogical and inferential thought, and the cognitive underpinnings of insight and novel thought. I do not doubt for a moment that the richness of knowledge that is at the disposal of our youth will have a profoundly positive impact on what becomes possible in our near futures. But will children—who are continuously flooded with stimulating, sensorial images (visual, tactile, and auditory) and volumes of information—learn to use their own imaginations and steadily build their own internal platforms of knowledge?

The state of the research on these questions at the moment of writing this book is mixed, as Baron's comprehensive review demonstrates. Such a mixed and sometimes contradictory picture is inevitable in the beginning of any field of study, when researchers cannot yet control for all the differences in their subjects—from technological exposure to learning preferences—and the many different possible outcomes. Paradoxically, I find this mixed picture a positive sign; for, when I began my own research in this area while writing *Proust and the Squid*, findings about the effects of digital reading were largely negative. In this final section, I have selected one ongoing research direction that is not found in many overviews, but is representative of some of the emerging, varied aspects of the work in the "new literacies."[38]

Reading researcher Julie Coiro has written a fascinating dissertation in which she studied a group of average seventh graders in both their online reading and offline print reading.[39] Her study exposes something very important that I am observing more and more: individual variation and its importance for learning on different mediums. What she found, almost by accident when examining the necessary scatter plot of her data, was that some of her lowest performing readers of print were the highest performing online readers, and some of her highest performing print readers were the lowest performing online readers. Furthermore, in various analyses she found no significant relationship between reading abilities for online tests and print-based reading tests. In other words, we are dealing with at least two diverging types of reading in our young. My translation: we are observing the emergence of differently formed reading circuits in different kinds of readers.

I highlight this only somewhat surprising finding because it embodies the three central premises that began this book and will end it. We humans were never genetically programmed to read. The reading brain circuit is the product of a cultural invention and as such, is extremely *malleable* to a variety of influences. At a minimum, it differs according to: the writing system's requirements; the medium's emphases within the circuit (e.g. from decoding skills to deep reading processes); the type of instruction and formation of the reader; the differences in text (e.g. style, length, and density); and individual differences (e.g. age, language background, learning profiles, preferences). Specifically, there are different reading circuits for individual readers, as we already know from brain-imaging of children and individuals with dyslexia, that may be more or less compatible with print vs online reading requirements. (Recall, for example, the subgroup of Denver Academy students with dyslexia who were more proficient online.) I believe what we are seeing in Coiro's study is the formation in action of differently wired reading circuits. We are, in other words, seeing our futures begin to form. Before we are prepared for them.

A first algorithm for what comes next

As forecast at the outset, there are at least three cultural options immediately available to us: the vigilant maintenance of the advantages of a print-based culture; increasing adaptation to the affordances rendered by a predominantly digital-based culture; and the pursuit of an iteratively responsive, hybrid culture informed by incoming research on the advantages and disadvantages of print and digital reading for particular individuals and for particular types of text. I have no doubt shown my hand. The very wording of those options and likewise the structuring of this chapter and the next reflect my biases. Just as Alan Lightman and his colleagues indicated early on in their aptly titled book of essays, *Living with the Genie: Essays on Technology and the Quest for Human Mastery*,[40] there is neither the possibility of putting digital culture back in its original bottle, nor is there wisdom in doing so.

Indeed, wisdom should be the ultimate goal in any societal move forward. In this, we recapitulate something close to what Plato confronted as he assessed, in part through Socrates' objections, the advantages and disadvantages in moving from oral to written culture. It was never then, nor is it now, about a choice between two technologies of knowledge. Rather, the primary issue concerns how we humans can use our combined biological and non-biological cultural tools for the collective good in the future, particularly of our children. I began this chapter by referring to two very different visions of that future—one that warns us of the potential loss of our most essential human qualities; and one that asserts the possibility of an "enhanced" intelligence that goes beyond any evolutionary leap by yoking our present biological with our future non-biological (technology-driven) capacities.

We are literally and virtually in uncharted waters, a metaphor that is suggestive of a modest, albeit interim solution: *tacking*. Just as the knowledgeable sailor must vigilantly tack to and fro when confronted by unknown conditions, I believe we must do something quite similar, if we are to avoid the Scylla and Charybdis of either lurching blindly forward without sufficient knowledge, or becoming fixated on the past.

I believe that an understanding of how the reading brain develops prepares us to "tack" through the present transition and guide the next iteration of the reading brain in our children. It illumines three sets of factors that must be entered into any algorithm for the future and three principles for their analyses: the entire range of perceptual and cognitive processes affected; the different affordances of the mediums; and text-based factors. The principles for working with these factors include: preserving the best-known aspects of our present reading brain, while simultaneously helping to form the new cognitive and perceptual capacities necessary for twenty-first-century culture; ensuring best uses of the different affordances of the available mediums for specific phases in the individual's development; and finally, preserving and promoting different forms of literature and text.

Among the non-exclusive factors included in each of these variable sets are the following factors, beginning with the individual's cognitive capacities: attention (the ability to attend, focus, concentrate); memory and retrieval (short-term capacities and long-term storage); automaticity of decoding skills; formation of deep reading skills (from perspective-taking to insight); "imagination"; developmental and individual learning preferences; and history and *nature of instruction*. The second set of factors incorporates distinct, developmentally important affordances of print and screen mediums including: physicality; emphases on personal knowledge-building; elicitation of attention, background knowledge, and imagination; imagability; uses of memory; engagement; ease of access to information; expansion of internal platform of knowledge; and democratization of access to information. The third set involves essential characteristics of text to be considered, including: the text's length; genre; conceptual and linguistic density; and word and/or visual image-based emphases (e.g. emerging literary options like the graphic novel).

It is in the context of all these variables that I envision the development of a *biliterate brain* in which we as a culture provide a carefully reflected and researched developmental trajectory for the formation of reading. By my own reckoning, our research has not progressed sufficiently to present a fully formed proposal that is based on rigorous

A Second Revolution in the Brain

evidence about what would be best for the formation of the next reading brain. Nevertheless, my next book will begin to sketch such a scaffolding because our children are already outpacing our research. In both this book and my next, the literacy agenda I foresee for our children represents a *biliteracy agenda* that will incorporate what we view as the best characteristics of each medium for different cognitive capacities and different types of text at specific developmental epochs in the child's life. It is an agenda that I hope will become a bridge to far more elaborated, better informed blueprints and more longitudinal-based research on these issues and the *multiple literacies*[41] of the near future. There is little doubt there will be more forms and more mediums than print and screen around the virtual corner.

Within that context, there has *never* been one ideal method for teaching literacy, even when it was a far simpler time, with only print reading necessary for the children to learn. Two decades of my life were devoted to designing and researching one of those methods, called RAVE-O, based on simulating the reading brain. My colleagues and I devised materials and strategies that would enhance every major component in the reading brain circuitry from letter pattern recognition to deep reading skills.[42] Although the goal of this method was and is specifically to benefit struggling readers, the principles within it are more universal and the large empirical, randomized treatment control evaluations are very supportive of its efficacy. My personal evaluation of all the years of work that went into RAVE-O, however, is that this method, *any* evidence-based method or intervention, is only as good as the teacher's knowledge, engagement, and ability to implement it.

A similar reality tempers all present and future efforts at describing what a hybrid developmental trajectory for literacy should include for the next generation. There is little doubt that we need to develop better and more sophisticated blueprints for what comes next, but it is essential to bring teachers' knowledge and engagement into whatever we do. We can place all of the ongoing research into ever more precise, multivariable equations based on the factors we know are important going forward, but if we do not include the teacher, school, and family variables into our equation, we will waste much time and effort.

For those who argue that we need methods, especially digital-based ones, that are "teacher-proof," I do not believe that any form of technology, no matter how well designed, should ever replace the role of human teachers in learning. As you will soon see in the next chapter, I am not saying how old these teachers should always be. Rather what I stress is that cultural inventions like literacy, by virtue of the fact they have no genetically determined sequence of development, need the culture to help children acquire them. No one needs to be "taught" language; immersion in a linguistic environment is enough to trigger the biological sequence. Reading, whether in books or on screens, is radically different and requires our best forms of cultural nurturance and prodding.

The forms of this *prodding*, however, are changing in startling ways, in amazing places around the world, including places where there are no physical schools and no formal teachers. Of all the affordances of the digital culture, I believe that the single most important one for the expansion of literacy involves the *democratization of knowledge* that is made possible through technology. This affordance provides heretofore unheard-of access possibilities for non-literate people who would never otherwise become literate. In the next chapter, we will examine this and other affordances of screen culture in one of the most unique experiments in reading development in our lifetime.

Notes

1. Sherry Turkle, *Alone Together* (Cambridge, MA: MIT Press, 2009), p. 284.
2. Ray Kurzweil, *The Singularity is Near* (New York: Viking, 2005), pp. 4, 128.
3. Marcel Proust, *The Days of Reading*, trans. John Sturrock (London: Penguin Books–Great Ideas, 2008), p. 70.
4. Castro-Caldas.
5. Quoted in Kim O'Connor, "Finally, an Enhanced E-Novel that Isn't Just a Gimmick," *Slate* (December 3, 2012). <http://www.slate.com/articles/technology/future_tense/2012/12/mark_z_danielewski_s_the_fifty_year_sword_enhanced_e_book_will_change_kindle.single.html>.
6. Nick Clark, "Imagination, Invention and Appropriation in Twentieth-Century Picture-Book Art." In Jill Shefrin (ed.), *One Hundred Books Famous in Children's Literature* (New York: Grolier Club, 2014), p. 49.
7. Naomi Baron, *Words Onscreen: The Fate of Reading in a Digital World* (London: Oxford University Press, 2014). Hereafter cited as Naomi Baron, 2014. See also Naomi Baron, *Always On* (Oxford: Oxford University Press, 2008). Hereafter cited as Naomi Baron, 2008.
8. Ofcom, *Children and Parents: Media Use and Attitudes Report* (London: Ofcom, 2013).
9. Ari Brown, "Media Use by Children Younger Than 2 Years," *Pediatrics* 128, no. 5 (November 2011): pp. 1040–5. doi: 10.1542/peds.2011-1753.

10. Kathy Hirsch-Pasek and Roberta Golinkoff, with Diane Eyer, *Einstein Never Used Flashcards* (Emmaus, PA: Rodale, 2003).
11. J. R. O'Toole and Madonna Stinson, "Drama, Speaking, and Listening: The Treasure of Oracy." In Michael Anderson and Julie Dunn (eds), *How Drama Activated Learning: Contemporary Research and Practice* (London: Bloomsbury, 2013); see also Sally Ward, *Baby Talk* (London: Arrow Books, 2004).
12. Catherine Steiner-Adair, *The Big Disconnect* (New York: Harper Collins, 2013).
13. See discussion in Chapters 4 to 6 in Maryanne Wolf, 2007.
14. Maggie Jackson, *Distracted: The Erosion of Attention and the Coming Dark Age* (Amherst, NY: Prometheus, 2008), pp. 79–80. Hereafter cited as Maggie Jackson.
15. Quoted in Maggie Jackson.
16. Daniel Levitin, *The Organized Mind: Thinking Straight in the Age of Information Overload* (New York: Viking Press, 2014). Hereafter cited as Levitin.
17. Naomi Baron, 2008.
18. K. Jimura, F. Cazalis, E. Stover, and Russ Poldrack, "Neural Basis of Task Switching Changes with Skill Acquisition," *Frontiers in Human Neuroscience* 339 (2014): pp. 1–9. doi:10.3389/fnhum.2014.0033; also see related work on "attention deficit trait" by Edward Hallowell.
19. Frank Schirrmacher, personal correspondence, August 2009.
20. Quoted in Karin Littau, *Theories of Reading: Books, Bodies, and Bibliomania* (Cambridge, UK: Polity Press, 2006), p. 4. Hereafter cited as Karin Littau.
21. N. Katherine Hayles, "Hyper and Deep Attention: The Generational Divide in Cognitive Modes," *Profession* (2007): pp. 187–99. Hereafter cited as Katherine Hayles. doi:10.1632/prof.2007.2007.1.187.
22. Maria Konnikova, "Being a Better Online Reader," *New Yorker* (July 16, 2014). <http://www.newyorker.com/science/maria-konnikova/being-a-better-online-reader.>
23. Ziming Liu, "Reading Behavior in the Digital Environment: Changes in Reading Behavior over the Past Ten Years," *Journal of Documentation* 61, no. 6 (2005): pp. 700–12. Hereafter cited as Liu. <http://dx.doi.org/10.1108/00220410510632040>.
24. Sherry Turkle, *Reclaiming Conversation* (New York: Penguin, 2016).
25. Italo Calvino, *Six Memos for the New Millennium* (New York: Random House, 2008), p. 48.
26. Anne Mangen, Bente Walgermo, and Kolbjorn Bronnick, "Reading Linear Texts on Paper versus Computer Screen: Effects on Reading Comprehension," *International Journal of Educational Research* 58 (2013): pp. 61–8. doi:10.1016/j.ijer.2012.12.002.
27. Andrew Piper, *Book Was There* (Chicago, IL: University of Chicago, 2012).
28. Karin Littau.
29. Jolene Guttierez, *Denver Academy Survey*. Personal correspondence: Philippe Ernewein, July 29, 2015.
30. Personal correspondence from Chair of the Department of English Literature at a prestigious university, 2010, who requests anonymity; also multiple professors of literature since then.
31. Katherine Hayles quoting from H. Jamali, D. Nicholas, and I. Rowlands, "Scholarly E-books: The Views of 16,000 Academics: Results from the JISC National E-Book Observatory," *Aslib Proceedings* 61 (2009): pp. 33–47. doi:10.1108/00012530910932276.

32. Maryanne Wolf, *Letters to the Good Reader* (New York: HarperCollins, in preparation).
33. Nicholas Carr, 2008.
34. Robert Bohn and James E. Short, "How Much Information: American Consumers Report" (University of California, San Diego: Global Information Industry Center, 2009).
35. Quoted in Judith Shulevitz, *The Sabbath World* (New York: Random, 2010). From David Levy, "More, Faster, Better: Governance in an Age of Overload, Busyness, and Speed," *First Monday*, Special Issue (2006). <http://dx.doi.org/10.5210/fm.v0i0.1618>.
36. Naomi Baron, 2014.
37. Susan Greenfield, *Mind Change* (London: Rider/Embury/Random House, 2014).
38. D. Leu, W. O'Byrne, L. Zawilinski, J. McVerry, and H. Everett-Cacopardo, "Expanding the New Literacies Conversation," *Educational Researcher* 38, no. 4 (2009): pp. 264–9. doi:10.3102/0013189X09336676. See e.g. James Gee, *What Video Games Have to Teach Us about Learning and Literacy* (New York: Palgrave Macmillan, 2005); D. Fox Harrell, *Phantasmal Media: An Approach to Imagination, Computation, and Expression* (Cambridge, MA: MIT Press, 2013); Katherine Isbister's forthcoming book.
39. Julie Coiro, "Predicting Reading Comprehension on the Internet: Contributions of Offline Reading Skills, Online Reading Skills, and Prior Knowledge," *Journal of Literacy Research* 43, no. 4 (2011): pp. 352–92. doi:10.1177/1086296X11421979.
40. Alan Lightman, Daniel Sarewitz, and Christina Desser (eds), *Living with the Genie: Essays on Technology and the Quest for Human Mastery* (Washington, DC: Island Press, 2003).
41. Bill Cope and Mary Kalantzis, *MultiLiteracies* (London: Routledge, 2000). See also Margaret Weigel and Howard Gardner, "The Best of Both Literacies," *Educational Leadership* 66, no. 6 (2009): pp. 38–41. <http://www.ascd.org/publications/educational-leadership/mar09/vol66/num06/The-Best-of-Both-Literacies.aspx>.
42. Robin Morris, Maureen Lovett, Maryanne Wolf, Rose A. Sevcik, Karen A. Steinbach, Jan C. Frijters, and Marla B. Shapiro, "Multiple-Component Remediation for Developmental Reading Disabilities: IQ, Socioeconomic Status, and Race as Factors in Remedial Outcome," *Journal of Learning Disabilities* 45, no. 2 (2012): pp. 99–127. doi:10.1177/0022219409355472. Hereafter cited as Morris, Lovett, Wolf; also see Maryanne Wolf, Catherine Ullman-Shade, and Stephanie Gottwald, "The Emerging, Evolving Reading Brain in a Digital Culture: Implications for New Readers, Children with Reading Difficulties, and Children without Schools," *Journal of Cognitive Education and Psychology* 11, no. 3 (2012): pp. 230–40. <http://dx.doi.org/10.1891/1945-8959.11.3.230>.

7
A Tale of Hope for Non-Literate Children

> I work with severely traumatized children everyday.... I see places and go places everyday that many of you will never see. My advice to all of you who teach is to resist your good, natural, maternal, parental, protective impulse to save these children from what surrounds them.... You will not save them. Instead, understand that teaching them, and especially *teaching them to read* is the salvation you have to offer and the salvation they most need. Don't let their poverty, stories, and circumstances distract you from that, not for a minute.[1]
>
> Steve Dykstra, *A Passage on Don Meichenbaum*

> Although the students certainly faced challenges, the teachers faced at least as many if not more... There were no books. The children were reciting from memory a story that they had read with their teacher over and over.... I prepared to read them a story... To my delight, Joe said, "Let me try." Try he did, and with sheer determination, he succeeded. The look on his face was one of pure joy as he loudly proclaimed, "I can read!" My joy matched or probably even exceeded his.[2]
>
> Sr Leonora Tucker, *I Hold your Foot: The Story of my Enduring Bond with Liberia*

One of the most endearing expressions used in Liberia is "I hold your foot," which means "I beg you," or "I plead with you." As recounted by Sr Leonora Tucker in one of the most touching and humorous memoirs by a teacher in Africa, the parents of young children would use this expression on their knees before her and the other courageous School Sisters of Notre Dame, as the mothers tried every means they knew to get their child into a "school" that would have challenged any teacher on the globe. Sr Leonora's description of Joe's joy and her own captures a moment like none other in a non-literate child's life...or in a teacher's. It would be fair to say that one of the most powerful, life-changing, professional experiences either Stephanie Gottwald or I have ever had is the content of this chapter which describes work that we hope will make literacy possible for children and families in some of the most remote regions of the world.

As discussed by Steve Dykstra, the work of Don Meichenbaum, a leading international trauma and mental health expert, gives a particular context for situating this chapter. Like Meichenbaum and Dykstra my group has long believed that literacy is the single best foundation we can give children, whether traumatized by war, impoverished by harsh environments, or simply growing up in our own backyards. But I never imagined that one day I would be asked one of the most audacious questions: would it be possible, based on the collective knowledge about the reading brain, to create a digital learning experience for non-literate children who have no schools, to teach themselves to read? Could work on the reading brain and on intervention with struggling readers in the US be applied in the design of digital tablets for children who would never otherwise become literate? This chapter will describe the still-unfolding story of our efforts to confront this question and in the process approach literacy and technology in a whole new way. But first a prefatory caveat.

In the last chapter the affordances of print reading were both defended and extolled, while the affordances of digital reading were given less than their due. From the outset of this chapter, the reader will be asked to make a 180-degree cerebral turnabout as we examine one of the most transformative and most promising affordances of digital reading: its ability to be used as a tool for the democratization of knowledge. Unlike the issues described in the last chapter concerning the comparative affordances of print-based and digital-based mediums, the more than 200 million children in this world who will never attain full literacy do not have the luxury of choice. For most of these children there are few or no books or paper, few prepared teachers, and very few adequate schools. These are the young that world governments call "pastoral children" in rural environments, or "street children" in urban areas, terms that cannot hide the extreme poverty in which most of them live out their lives. Pope Francis minces no such words. He calls them the "disenfranchised children of the world" and asks society three Kantian-like questions: what do we know? What can we do? What do we hope?

My group was asked a version of the first two questions: do we know whether relatively inexpensive digital materials—from tablets to cell phones—could help these disenfranchised children learn to read in the absence of teachers and adequate schools? There is no discussion here of replacing print or teachers with technology, but rather of directing the great potential of technology to helping children learn, particularly when there are no materials and no or too few teachers to guide them. And now to the unlikely history of this initiative.

History of the project

The project began as a collaboration amongst our Tufts Center for Reading and Language Research group, Nicholas Negroponte and Cynthia Breazeal from the MIT Media Lab and their teams, including Matt Keller from an earlier technology-based initiative,[3] and soon after, Robin Morris from Georgia State University. We began to discuss what were then radical ideas about whether our insights into the formation of the young reading brain, particularly our intervention research with children with dyslexia, could provide the basis for a digital approach to literacy. For example, would it be possible to curate, and/or create apps and activities that target all the important areas in the reading brain circuit and place them on an engaging mobile device for children who have never seen a pencil, much less a tablet? Would children be able to teach themselves and each other on this device with no adult instruction or help? There are few literate adults in the remote regions that need literacy most. Could mobile technologies prove capable of delivering not only apps, but also assessments to ensure the efficacy of the approach? How could we implement these technologies and evaluate the children in the difficult, remote regions where most of these 200 million children live? In other words, we asked ourselves whether it is humanly possible to create a digital learning experience that will help children learn to read in places and situations where schools and teachers are either unavailable or insufficient, where few adults are literate, and where typical communication and assessment possibilities are practically nil.

These were only the questions addressed to ourselves about what *we as researchers* could do. The four major hurdles that the children in any remote area face were and are of a far more overwhelming nature. First, they have no exposure to any form of technology or electricity, and must become computer-literate at a basic level for any digital learning to occur. Second, many of the concepts that would typically appear on any of the available apps and activities would be unfamiliar to the children (e.g. the verb *swim* is close to a foreign concept to children who have no easy access to water). Third, the children have no exposure to the English language, and there were few to no appropriate apps or digital activities available at the outset of our project in most pastoral children's native languages. Fourth, the children have no exposure to writing or to any other form of symbolic representation. Any one of these hurdles, much less all four, could prove insurmountable.

Several factors finally trumped our collective doubts and convinced us to go forward. First, our increased understanding of the young reading brain and how to teach it made the curation and development of innovative digital content a conceivable goal. Our experience with innovative reading interventions like the RAVE-O Program[4] encouraged us. Our long-term collaborations with Robin Morris in Atlanta and Maureen Lovett in Toronto had demonstrated through tough, randomized treatment–control design studies how targeted emphases in systematic reading interventions can help young, struggling readers learn to read.[5] We knew first-hand how the applied aspects of knowledge can change the lives of students whose childhoods would have otherwise been maimed before they even began their lives. From these intervention studies, and related ones, we were prepared to try to apply the collective knowledge based on traditional school settings to non-readers in very difficult non-school settings.

Second, the constant breakthroughs in technology were making new mobile devices both affordable and available around the world, thus making the financial basis of digital learning more feasible for large numbers of children. Even in the time from our first deployment to our most recent one, the costs for tablets have decreased dramatically, while their battery life and screen quality have increased.

Third, the growing ubiquity of connectivity, along with advances in cloud computing and big data analytics, enabled completely new forms of assessment, both of children's individual usage and progress and also of the performances of large populations (e.g. from the level of the village to the country to more global levels of analysis). If we could create a tightly iterative design in which a child's performance could be immediately analyzed, we believed we could eventually provide ever more targeted individualized instruction on the specific areas of need for a given individual. Such an adaptive learning design could provide one of the most important means for advancing learning on digital technologies in the remote areas of the world.

These three factors became the theoretical and applied framework for beginning our initiative with one overarching goal: to investigate whether our evolving knowledge of the young reading brain, big data analytics, child development (particularly child-driven learning), and new technologies could be successfully applied to mobile devices in areas deemed impossible for teaching children. We were cautiously hopeful.

Principles and framework for first deployments

In the fall of 2011, the consortium began our first, still ongoing initiative in two remote regions of Ethiopia. Ethiopia was selected as the first pilot for several reasons, beginning with the fact that it represents one of the ten countries with the highest rates of illiteracy. Over half of its population of 91,196,000 people are non-literate, with more Ethiopian women being non-literate than men. (Note: the statistics for non-literate women represent one of the great, changeable problems in many underdeveloped countries and one of our particular concerns.) The Ethiopian government at the time allocated less than $100 per person a year on education, making it one of the lowest rates in the world, and something they wished to change.

With the critical support of the government and local leadership, two village sites were selected, as representative of Ethiopia's most inaccessible populations. The reason for such dramatically difficult settings for our first deployment was that if we were able to demonstrate that children in these most difficult of conditions could make significant progress towards literacy, then there would be a strong rationale for assuming that the millions of children in similar, seemingly impossible conditions for learning could also learn to read using digital devices.

The first village, Wonchi, is found on the rim of a volcanic crater at 11,000 feet and is an agrarian community with relatively good access to well water. It is astonishingly beautiful, settled in the hills near Lake Wonchi in rural Ethiopia. It is a place that has "access" to almost nothing. For a visitor to get there, one has to leave the overland vehicle far behind, and walk across paths bordering on gulches that drop hundreds of feet below. It is another of the world's places where no one goes without intent, but one is richly rewarded for the effort.

The second village, Wolenchite, is located at the edge of the Great Rift Valley which stretches across vast territories of parched, dry land. There is little that softens the eye's first impression of a stark, harsh landscape for humans and animals alike. The frequent sight of wild, scrawny, rib-showing camels in the distance seemed the correlative of the sparse human habitations along the road that led to the turnoff to Wolenchite—where there was no road. To ensure that we could reach their village by overland vehicle, the parents and grandparents of the village removed at least one half-mile of large volcanic rocks to allow passage from the nearest road to their settlement. I will never forget my first sight of the size of those rocks and boulders to the side of the path. I instantly understood the resolve and the herculean efforts the villagers must have taken to remove them, all the while avoiding the asps and much worse crawling creatures evicted in the process.

Children and the adults in these two villages have neither electricity nor running water nor sanitation nor easy access to any form of transportation or communication. To the best of our knowledge, the children had never seen books or paper or pencils before our arrival; nor had they seen any form of technology. Perhaps most importantly for this work, the children speak Oromo, one of several languages in Ethiopia, and have never, or very rarely, heard English, or seen written language in either Oromo (which uses a Latin script) or English.

With no connectivity available, the tablets required a solar-charging system that was provided to each village by funds from Negroponte's previous initiative and its foundation. Before we began, the villagers could not have been more supportive. In both sites the adults worked together to build a small structure for the solar-charging units. Unlike the thatched roofs of all their huts, they built the structures with wooden stakes and a tin roof. Light shines continuously through small open spaces between the stakes, and two hand-hewn benches furnish the inside of the structure. Perhaps unsurprisingly, the new places served almost immediately as gathering spots for the children. Two computer engineers from the University of Addis Ababa, Michael Girma and Markos Lemma, were the first to visit the villages. They taught the adults to use the solar power units so that the tablets could be recharged every night.

Most importantly, Markos and Mike were the first to give the tablets to each of the forty children, twenty in each village. Because we needed to know—particularly for future deployments in even more remote places—whether children could learn unaided to turn the tablets on and use them without a teacher, Markos and Mike had to assiduously avoid teaching the children how to turn the tablets on or problem-solving for them. The stories of the "first digital experiences" by the children are now the stuff of legend in our group, and have even been the subject of several media articles and films.[6] For us the whole project began in earnest when the first boy in the first village took the tablet, explored it from front to back *for all of four minutes*, and then shouted in Oromo, "I got mine on! I'm the lion!"

This feat was the first of many epiphanies by the children and by us. The little boy, who came to be called the Lion Prince by us, proceeded to teach all the other children how to turn their tablets on. Within a short time, the whole group of children were immersed in tablets that took the first author four times longer to turn hers on for the first time. Within a month every app and activity had been turned on by the children.

Mike and Markos were as grateful as we were when a similar, albeit slower version of this scenario was replicated in the second village. Over time the two young men developed strong, important relationships with the children and their families in the villages. Then and now they visit the villages twice a month, maintain the equipment, and in the beginning, swapped memory cards so that researchers in the consortium could study how the tablet contents were used from minute to minute by each child.

With the entry of technology expert Tinsley Galyean, now at the helm of our efforts, the MIT and GSU teams over time developed an automated method for data collection and remote app updates. The tech team continues to pioneer a tightly iterative, evidence-based approach in which we collect data (cross-sectionally and longitudinally) through the tablets to track how children use the tablet and apps. These data give us information every time a child turns on an app or touches a word on the interactive apps and enable us to assess both different aspects of the children's learning and also their engagement in every app on the tablet. Both of these forms of data help to improve, adapt, and revise the apps and tablet experiences.

Tablet content principles and the *app map*

One of the most important steps in our work involved the selection of apps and activities. In the beginning, we hoped to select apps based on the described components of the reading brain circuit for written English—what we came to call the *app map*. This map was designed to designate the most important skills necessary for the formation of pre-reading, with emphases on the well-known and not-so-well-known language, perceptual, and attentional processes in the young reading brain circuitry described in Chapters 2 and 3. For example, some skills included in the app map are those commonly associated with learning to read: that is, phoneme knowledge or sound awareness, vocabulary growth, conceptual knowledge, letter-naming and letter-sound knowledge, sight word recognition, decoding, and comprehension skills. Other skills, less commonly emphasized, involve auditory perception of phonemes and rhythmic patterns known to foster phoneme awareness, knowledge of the multiple meanings of words, learning syntactic functions of words (e.g. action verbs), etc. All of this comprised our first ideal template for apps.

The reality, however, was that what we selected and what we sought were not the same. At the time of our first curation, there was a paucity of high-quality apps and activities for the Android tablet that targeted the multiple components of our ideal app map. We chose, therefore, a group of apps which were approximations of the apps we hoped someday to use; a large group of e-books of well-known children's stories; videos of topics that taught early conceptual development; and selected segments of educational television devised for young pre-readers through the cooperation of our public television broadcaster, WBGH, in Boston.

In our first iteration there were over 325 apps, videos, and activities for the children to select from on the tablets; these were eventually reduced considerably on the basis of the data. The basic processes that were addressed with these apps and activities included: alphabetic knowledge, letter name knowledge, letter–sound correspondence principles, early conceptual knowledge, early language learning in the English language, some basic decoding principles, and some sight word recognition. What we found during still evolving curation efforts was that while there has been much work in the last four years in developing educational apps, the skills and abilities that they promote still represent a relatively small portion of the entire app map that we envision. This will be a major goal for us in the next few years.

One app created by Cynthia Breazeal and her then PhD student Angela Chang is a prototype for future development of apps for concept development, and proved particularly engaging to the children in both villages. Called a TinkrBook, this app presents a new kind of interactive story that supports and invites children to "tinker" with text and graphics and to explore how these changes impact the narrative.[7] One key design principle is called textual *tinkerability*, where an interactively reinforced association links the written word, the spoken word, and the graphical depiction of the concept.

Immediate first goals

After the children began using the tablets, we were better able to re-examine the four seemingly insurmountable hurdles that the children initially embodied. In the process we set four goals for our work with them. The first goal of the project—getting the children to a level of computer literacy, without human direction or instruction—was the quickest attained. We could see from the outset that the children in the two villages were able to use the tablets almost immediately. To this moment, the four-minute learning by the Lion Prince boy is a powerful reminder of the intelligence and natural curiosity of children in every setting around the world. It is also a gut-wrenching example of the waste of much of that potential in children who will never have an opportunity to develop it.

The other aspect of the first goal involved curating apps that would both address the major processes in the reading brain circuit, and also engage the children. Some apps that we thought were far too simple (e.g. a set of toddler blocks with letters on them) turned out to be extremely engaging and instructive for the pre-literacy levels of the children. Other apps and activities (including e-books) that we prejudged exciting were opened only once or twice and left behind. They proved to be largely inappropriate for that stage of the children's development.

The second goal was to include apps that could help the children understand concepts of child development less known or unknown in their culture. For example, categories and concepts that we consider *basic* with regard to color, time, number knowledge, home and family environments in Western cultures are not necessarily known in villages like Wonchi or Wolenchite. Because the content of our apps included many of these basic concepts, it was important to ensure sufficient exposure to these categories of conceptual knowledge, so that the children could learn new concepts and words that would be helpful to pre-literacy skills.

Our third goal comprised activities to help the children begin an understanding of oral English. At the time, it was more important to the parents that the children would learn some English, than that they would learn to read. The parents felt that their children would have more opportunities for future employment if they knew English. From the perspective of the Ethiopian government at that time, if their pastoral children began to learn English, this might enhance the chances, at least for some children, for future educational opportunities. Based on these reasons and the lack of apps in Oromo, we focused on the deployment of an English language-based literacy curriculum.

Because this choice continues to prompt many questions for us, we want to add a parenthesis here. Although there were pragmatic reasons for this initial choice of using English apps, it is one that we hope quickly to shift to include apps in the native languages. The Ethiopian government now holds similar views. From their viewpoint and from a linguistic perspective, it is conceptually easier to learn to read in one's own language than to learn to read in an unfamiliar one. Towards that end, we have begun to create Oromo–English vocabulary apps that are based on two principles: that children learn words most easily in their own language, and also that they learn words more quickly when they represent things (animate and inanimate) in their immediate environments. Thus, we asked our Ethiopian counterparts to take pictures of the children holding their own personal objects with the words spoken and written in both Oromo—the children's language—and English.

We all released a collective sigh at the first pictures, which included a little boy from Wonchi holding up his favorite, very skinny chicken, and a beautiful, smiling older girl from Wolenchite with her arm affectionately curled around a dust-matted, furry donkey.

Our fourth and most difficult goal was to introduce the children to the precursors of literacy. Discussed in Chapter 3, these included learning the most important elements of alphabetic knowledge from learning the alphabet to a working knowledge of letter shapes and sounds. We also hoped that some children might acquire rudiments of very basic sight word recognition for the words that were most frequently seen on the apps, like *father*, *mother*, *dog*, and *cat*.

Our thinking throughout this early phase of our deployment was that if we can someday achieve the first four goals, the next goals would involve basic decoding of simple words and basic reading comprehension of brief passages. Indeed, for the last year and a half, we have been working with both several app designers and graduate students at Tufts, MIT, and the Rochester Institute for Technology with Gordon Goodman, to create apps that introduce the next phases of reading development, a critical, ongoing aspect of our work.

An old maxim in reading research, used by the late renowned reading researcher Jeanne Chall, is that children must learn to read, so that they can "read to learn."[8] Our ultimate objective for these children has been and continues to be that we want to enable them to move along a continuum of literacy pre-reading precursors through early reading development to the critical reading transition that involves fluent decoding and deep reading processes.[9] If children can attain this latter stage of literacy, they can enter a whole new world of learning across multiple domains. It is our hope to ensure that we are building the kind of open-source platform that will someday allow many types of learning from numeracy, science, and health/hygiene to ethical development. But that is getting too far ahead of the story of our first deployments and our first assessments that were administered nine months after we began.

First assessment

The stories of the Desert Fathers remind me of my experience when first entering the tiny community of Wonchi to evaluate the children's progress. Through the Desert Fathers' stories we come to realize that the monks came to *see* the vast beauty of the world and feel the joys and sorrows of multitudes of people through the experience of looking out of single, tiny, cave-like crevasses in the rocks that were their hermitage homes. They wrote and prayed and felt they had nothing and everything. Something like that occurred to me as I looked on at the sheer, natural beauty of the tiny grouping of thatch-roofed huts called Wonchi, nestled in their rolling terrain above Lake Wonchi. Being in the midst of the small group of human beings there helped me to understand the reality—both the beauty and the hardships—of many other places. Wonchi was beautiful, but the beauty did not obfuscate the reality that Wonchi has "access" to almost nothing, beginning with roads. At one point before our arrival, my intrepid driver wanted to continue driving on what was a narrow donkey path down one steep hill and then up another to the Wonchi settlement. On one side of the path was the wall of the hill and on the other was a gulch that dropped hundreds of feet below. I will never forget that my equally intrepid guide, Matt Keller (who had been in every war zone I had ever read about), opted to leave the overland vehicle very quickly, and walk the rest of the way. The driver only laughed as he continued on, and I hopped out to…give Matt company on the ground!

When the children first saw that a woman visitor was coming, they raced to the top of their hill to greet me with the loud, animated cries of childhood. That is, they screamed and shouted until suddenly they stopped. Confronted with an unknown woman who couldn't stop smiling or speaking in a language they could only, eventually, laugh at, utter silence reigned for two minutes. After those two minutes, childhood won out, and the same range of personality types, the same mix of different forms of intelligence, and the same assortment of body shapes and sizes in children everywhere began to surface before my eyes.

There was the shy, slightly overweight older girl who would later become the resident teacher of all the young, girls and boys alike. There was the fearless, gregarious, wiry, little girl who would have tested the patience of any teacher in the world with her non-stop chattering. There was the boy who said nothing, but who looked with barely suppressed excitement at the pencils and paper I was bringing,

A Tale of Hope for Non-Literate Children

which he had never seen nor used before. You can guess that this was the Lion Prince.

The almost invisible gathering of humans in Wonchi, who live in the traditional thatched-roof huts of one's imagination, inhabit an area very near where archeologists believe the birthplace of humanity began. I felt something akin to walking inside our human past *and* our world's future as I began to interact with the children and families of Wonchi. They are just...us. That was and continues to be my strongest impression. It should not have come as an epiphany to anyone working in child development, but I think it is important to state that I had anticipated more differences than commonalities between the young children in Wonchi and the children of Boston. This is despite the fact that I have taught thousands of undergraduates about nature and nurture's intrinsic interaction across all human beings across every culture.

I make this admission with more than a little professional humility. I think many people carry within themselves the unarticulated thought that children who are literally "out of the world's sight" are significantly different from their peers in other parts of the world, possibly even less gifted intellectually because they have less access to the many forms of knowledge found in more populated and more educated areas of the world. What I want to underscore by describing my personal, unexpected responses is that these young children are just like ours—with the same bell-shaped curve of distributed intelligences and personalities as children anywhere. I begin with this simple fact because it exemplifies how the children of Wonchi possess the same *potential* as all children to contribute their unique talents to the world. The less simple, correlative fact is that as they grow older, the children of Wonchi *will* begin to change from children in other places. They will never receive the opportunity to contribute in the same ways that other children do, simply because they, like 50 plus million similar pastoral children, are non-literate.

It is within this larger context of children's potential for intellectual development that I wish to describe the progress these children made. The first behavioral assessments were made in the single worst and most endearing testing conditions of my professional life. There were no quiet testing rooms, and there was no privacy—at all. Ultimately I sat with each child practically tucked under my arm during testing, as the rest of the village watched, listened, and tried to decide to clap or not to clap after each child finished one of the tasks. The best I could do from a "clinical" perspective was to draw a circle in the dust around the child and me and ask (through the laughing interpreter) that everyone stay on the other side of the line. Despite these worst of clinical testing conditions, the children did their best on these "games" and gave us important data on the progress the children were making in the four areas we set. These included technological familiarity; basic conceptual growth; English vocabulary development; and literacy precursor skills.

Except for two children whose mother decided that children cannot learn without a teacher, all the other children became completely computer-literate with the tablets. As mentioned, in Wonchi, all the children were able to turn on their devices within the first day without instruction or direction; in Wolenchite, by the second day all were engaged. Thus our first hurdle was surmounted more easily than any of us might have anticipated: the children became quickly at home with these technologies.

With regard to our second and third goals for growth in concepts and vocabulary, all of the children knew some of the small sample of basic English vocabulary words we tested; over half of the children knew the meaning of over half of the words. This result is encouraging when one takes into account two facts: 1) the words on the vocabulary assessment were randomly chosen from the apps on the tablet to represent basic concepts; and 2) the children had no environment to practice their knowledge of these words. Despite the fact they spoke no English, most of the children learned many basic vocabulary words.

It also became apparent in the course of the testing that the children from Wolenchite were not progressing as consistently or as quickly as children from Wonchi. We hypothesized that the amount of time needed for getting their water (two and a half hours each way) might have caused two sources of impediment for the children from Wolenchite. First, the sheer time expended by many of the children to pick up water would give them less time on the tablets. Second, and more insidious, were the possible, deleterious effects on the children's cognitive development caused by not having enough water in their daily intake. Although the government had assured us that there was no malnutrition in either site, our eyes were sufficient to see the differences in the children.

Despite that contrast, there was unexpected, anecdotal observational evidence about the children in Wolenchite that we learned from the interpreter. It turned out that the interpreter's "day job" was to bring truant children in the nearest real town to school. It was his firmly held observation that the children in Wolenchite were progressing better than the town children in school in learning precursors like the alphabet. He was adamant in his conviction. We have no way to judge this, but it was simultaneously encouraging and discouraging to hear.

The fourth "precursors of literacy" goal turned out to be both the most challenging and the most surprising. Many children achieved remarkable precursor literacy skills with the tablets in the first year. All of the children were able to recite all of the letters of the alphabet. Most of the children recognized most letters in any array—serial or mixed. Most were able to write their letters, despite not having had paper or pencil before the testing. Earlier in the year Markos and Mike had sent back pictures of the children writing letters with sticks. It appears that the children were able to generalize motoric skills from writing with their finger on the tablet, to writing their letters with long sticks on the dust-covered ground. Then, when asked to write on paper, they were able to use their analogical skills to write (draw) their letters with a pencil. It was extremely touching to watch how they used every tiny space on the pages of the small blue "test" books to show their expertise in writing, and to save room for writing more in their books later.

A small percentage of the children knew letter–sound correspondence rules. This latter group could recognize almost all English letters in any array. They could write letters from memory. Most impressively, they could read a group of sight words like *mother*, *father*, and *baby*, along with animal words like *cat* and *horse*. I was initially stunned when I first heard the older female *teacher* read these words without faltering. She had not been able to perform earlier on the relatively simple decoding measure, so I had not intended to test her further. Markos insisted, however, that I test her on sight words. I was gobsmacked by her performance. To be sure that she and the other two children who could sight-read knew the meanings of these sight words, we asked them to show Mark, Mike, and me pictures of the words they were sight-reading. They quickly pulled out their tablets and showed us apps with images corresponding to these words, like the family app with a mother, father, and baby. The top performers, therefore, were and remain at the time of writing on the cusp of beginning to read.

It is noteworthy that in both villages, the older girls were among the most advanced and were actively teaching the other children. It was like watching the creation of a teacher. What was so striking is that this was a place in which there had been no teacher before to observe and imitate. It was akin to watching the emergence of the "first school."

Mike and Markos elaborated in their biweekly visits how the child-driven learning dynamic in both settings created a natural collaborative atmosphere. The children with greater learning ability appeared compelled and excited to help the other children by taking a leadership role. If expanded and reinforced over time, we believe that such positive, collaborative roles among children create a natural environment for the development of leadership capacities, empathy, a sense of interconnectedness, and a stronger awareness of self and other. Certainly the young Lion Prince, who taught everyone in Wonchi how to use the tablets, became the unlikely hero of the village. Along with the older girls, he took on the role of teacher in his village. He literally was transformed from being the shyest child in the village to the most admired.

Perhaps the crowning, albeit ironic, "teaching moment" for the intervention researchers in our consortium happened when we saw videos of the older girls "drilling" their younger charges. Many of us in reading intervention research have been accused of fostering "drill and kill" practices by having children engage in repetitive learning behaviors, particularly in the key learning of letter–sound correspondence rules. Until now I have explained to hundreds of teachers that many children need "multiple exposures" to letters, letter patterns, and their phoneme correlatives, so that these visual and auditory patterns become "represented" in the reading brain. There are obvious physiological reasons for why this is so, but after seeing the girls of Wonchi, I may just use their video to demonstrate that intuitive, good teaching utilizes repetition everywhere.

When taken as a whole, the behavioral data in the Ethiopian deployments chronicle the emergence of literacy in a group of children who have never before been exposed to symbolic text. They also demonstrate a first proof of concept to show how mobile devices like the tablet can give children access to the precursors to literacy and to beginning to learn another language. What we have not achieved at this point is the most difficult, Helen Keller epiphany—the move from sight word recognition to true decoding and comprehension. No child in either village was able to decode the words in the decoding task in our first assessments.

Thus the ultimate question we asked—whether digital technology can help pastoral children in remote areas learn to read on their own—has only a partially positive answer. We may discover that the last insights into discovering how decoding works will require very different apps, or more direct human intervention, even if on an itinerant basis. We may discover like Sugata Mitra describes[10] that the presence of one adult, like a non-literate grandmother, has a significant effect on the children's learning.

At this point in our work on global literacy, the questions raised in the Ethiopian pilot are guiding us in ever new directions. Maureen Lovett, our intervention partner of many years and an expert on child and adult literacy, has joined these new efforts, along with new technology experts, while Nicholas Negroponte has gone on to another of his visionary projects. Our new and growing team is concentrating its efforts on more targeted app content and on varied deployments to be described next. We want to know how newer iterations of the tablets function in wholly different educational contexts (from no schools, to overcrowded schools, to preschools of varying formats); for different ages of non-literate children; and perhaps someday, for non-literate adults.

Next steps

> It was touching to see these three big men, with the marks of their hard labour about them, anxiously bending over the worn books and painfully making out, "The grass is green," "The sticks are dry," "The corn is ripe"—a very hard lesson to pass to after columns of single words all alike except in the first letter. It was almost as if three rough animals were making humble

efforts to learn how they might become human. And it touched the tenderest fibre in Bartle Massey's nature, for such full-grown children as these were the only pupils for whom he had no severe epithets and no impatient tones. He was not gifted with an imperturbable temper, and on music-nights it was apparent that patience could never be an easy virtue to him; but this evening, as he glances over his spectacles at Bill Downes, the sawyer, who is turning his head on one side with a desperate sense of blankness before the letters d-r-y, his eyes shed their mildest and most encouraging light...[11]

George Eliot, *Adam Bede*

Regardless of what happens next, the children of Wonchi and Wolenchite have given us a never expected petri dish for studying the beginnings of literacy. We do not know whether we can replicate the same early learning curve we saw in Ethiopia in children in different environments which may be equally difficult in some ways, but more hostile to learning itself. For example, the parents of the children in both villages could not have been more supportive. What of children in a Mumbai undercity, like those described so eloquently by Katherine Boo,[12] who have no such supportive families and whose basic goal must be to survive? What of children who have schools, but schools which are so overpopulated and understaffed that 60 to 100 children may be taught in a single classroom by one insufficiently prepared teacher?

And what of children in our own backyard in the rural US, where poverty and inadequate language environments render them at risk for school failure before they even enter the kindergarten door? Could the same sets of principles on our tablets in Ethiopia be employed to help diminish the insidious educational gap in the US that begins well before school, but grows every year after? What of the non-literate parents themselves? Just as George Eliot portrayed in the touching passage in *Adam Bede*, many a non-reading adult would give a great deal to learn to read. Would some of our work, using differently designed interfaces, provide a way for the non-literate adults to teach themselves to read?

To address these and related questions of generalizability, we have begun new deployments in each of the following settings: in urban and rural populations in India; in settlement schools in South Africa; and in language-impoverished, rural populations in Georgia and

Alabama.[13] Our school-based deployments include an area north of Durban, South Africa and soon sites in Peru. Our preschool deployments are taking place in the rural US—in Georgia and Alabama, in India, and in a preschool in an urban slum in Kampala, Uganda.

Each of these deployments brings unique challenges to our work and provides us with unique opportunities for increasing the utility of our platform and the comprehensiveness of our literacy apps for increased numbers of children. We work with on-the-ground NGOs to distribute the tablets to children in these places. All of our "new" children range in age from four to eleven years of age, and if in a school setting, typically use the tablets at the schools for approximately one hour per day. In each of these settings the children are assessed prior to receiving the mobile devices on an adaptation of standard pre-literacy, vocabulary, and early literacy skills tests. We collect information on how well they have learned the meanings of words, phonemic awareness skills, the names and sounds of letters, and if they can read a simple list of words. As from the start, the platform is designed to collect extensive data on the children's usage patterns of the apps.

In the US deployments, the students in preschools and kindergarten classes use the tablets about an hour a day and bring the devices home once per week. The districts participating in the project are classified as rural and most of the families living there have little income. Preliminary data suggest that when compared to children who did not have access to the tablets upon kindergarten entry, the children with tablet exposure outperformed those without the tablets on vocabulary knowledge, letter identification, and letter-sound identification. This project is set to expand to many more children in the rural South and is viewed by the school systems as a genuinely hopeful means of reaching children who are unlikely to have access to preschool in the immediate future.

Interestingly, we are seeing very similar results in Uganda and South Africa. Children in Uganda face an enormous challenge at a very early age. When children enter school at the age of six, they are already tested on early math and English reading skills. Only children who do well on these tests and whose parents can afford it are accepted into the private schools. For those children who do not have access to a preschool, they have no option but to enter the public schools where more than eighty children are often crowded into a single classroom with one teacher. In cooperation with the Clover Foundation, we have made tablets available to forty children from four to six years of age. They can use the tablets for as much as an hour a day. Our assessment results there tell us that the children are quickly learning their letters and numbers and are expanding their knowledge of English vocabulary. What we have learned from informal discussions with their mothers is that the children at the preschool come home and teach their younger siblings alphabet songs and stories that they have learned from the tablets in school. It is another example of contagious learning in action.

Before adding more deployments, we are simultaneously working towards the curation and/or development of better designed, more comprehensive apps, that can target components of the reading brain circuitry in a more precise and developmentally scaffolded manner. A major challenge throughout is to help children move more seamlessly from one skill to the next, while still giving them maximum choice and powerful engagement, so that they persevere. Towards those ends, we are working to combine our evolving app map with a new *mentoring system* that will connect the child's performance to sequenced learning goals. Two converse examples illustrate. Children often spend less time in an area of their perceived weakness, like vocabulary. These children will be identified through usage and performance data and encouraged to select from a group of apps emphasizing diverse approaches to learning new vocabulary. Another group of children may excel at vocabulary, but struggle to understand basic letter–sound relationships. They will be encouraged through the mentoring system along a different path—with apps that enhance their weaker decoding skills, at the same time that they continue to develop their linguistic strengths. In the near future we want to be able to go beyond usage and engagement data to measure specific behaviors, both on apps and on new assessment apps (disguised as games). Our goal-directed, iterative process, therefore, continues to build towards an adaptive, dynamic, individualized learning system that promotes literacy development in multiple ways for all children—wherever they live, whatever their first, second, or sometimes third language.

Ultimately, we wish to provide a template—a more universal app map—that represents the best perceptual, linguistic, and cognitive principles needed for the development of the reading circuit, with specific recommendations for different languages and orthographies. We are, for example, attempting to construct principles for the choice and/or creation of apps that address the full repertoire of the phonemes in whatever language the children are learning to read, as well as pivotal, basic concepts in early child development. In the coming years, we hope to work with linguists, neuroscientists, and educators in different languages to create an ever more specific template and app map directly related to what we know at this moment about the reading brain, and its variations that reflect a particular language and a particular writing system's unique emphases. Just as different reading circuits are needed for alphabets and Japanese syllabaries and Chinese logosyllabaries, so also are different apps for their acquisition.

Along similar lines, we hope to collaborate with similar-minded groups and initiatives around the world to encourage teachers, researchers, and designers to contribute educationally, socially, and culturally relevant materials for their societies. Within this context we hope to contribute to the development of shared repositories of apps, photographs, and picture collections, as well as stories, fables, and children's books that can be uploaded into interactive storybooks. As discussed, in one example in our most recent deployments, we hope to inspire children in the rural US to create material for vocabulary and stories that can be sent to our international sites, and vice versa in an exchange of words for beloved objects.

Such exchanges not only expand and reinforce children's understanding of vocabulary and their own oral language traditions and written culture, but just as importantly, such communication between groups fosters a growing understanding about another culture. Children who become connected to each other through such digital sharing are better prepared to understand and empathize with other children from around the world. Thus the development of apps for literacy and an open-source platform for other forms of literacy and learning represents the means for disenfranchised children to attain a far wider, deeper learning experience, one that can embody principles of ethical and character development at the same time that it helps them learn to read and count and code.

By the time we have learned how to help children reach the stage in which they are reading fluently across varied domains, we will ask the third Kantian question: what do we hope? Our earnest hope is to contribute to a global open-source platform with digital materials available from around the world, for many areas of learning, at every developmental level. We envision this platform as a *global hub* that will help bring about a new, intellectual/technological movement in which an international community of users, developers, technologists, scientists, education practitioners, policymakers, and families work together to create a place where the digital assets, findings, and methods of best practice can be shared by all, to help all children have their best chances to reach their potential.

Important international collaborations by researchers, NGOs, policymakers, and educators are already happening in inspiring ways in different places and across various disciplines. For example, such collaborative efforts are integral to the goals of several recent meetings initiated by Pope Francis and the Pontifical Academy of Sciences, that range in their foci from malnutrition and brain development for disenfranchised children, to the UN's Sustainable Development Goals and their implications for education, economics, ecology, and the health of children at the periphery of human society.[14] Similarly, at an international meeting of neuroscientists, educators, and policymakers organized by Ken Pugh, the Director of Haskins Laboratory at Yale, interdisciplinary collaborations have begun that have the potential to change both the way knowledge is disseminated and also the speed with which it is applied to the most profound problems of our "common home."[15]

Summary and next directions

> Without a solution to the problems of the poor, we cannot resolve the problems of the world.[16]
>
> Pope Francis

The leitmotif of this chapter, and indeed of all our work, is that literacy can open the mind of a person to knowledge in all its varieties, and, in the process, to creativity, personal growth, critical thought, and ethical reasoning. Such forms of thinking in a society can fuel discovery, productivity, and innovation, which, in turn, can drive economic growth, public health, and the well-being of that society. The

A Tale of Hope for Non-Literate Children

beginnings of a literate mind, we believe, go hand in hand with the development of a literary mind and an engaged citizenry.

If our combination of a theoretically based, digital-learning experience can be successful across such diverse cultures and settings, we estimate that millions more children could become literate in the next generation through similar initiatives. The implications of such an advance in literacy and its sequelae would be extraordinary, beginning with the UN estimations of dramatic decreases in poverty and mortality rates, and extending to expanded connections across vastly different cultures. Literacy does not ensure a conflict-free world; but its absence almost certainly assures the existence of conflicts between the literate and the non-literate and the increased likelihood of exploitation of those who cannot read, whether they are women or the poor or the defenseless young. Perhaps the mere acquisition of literacy has never prevented a war, but the sequelae of literacy—from better economic development to lower mortality rates—give fresh reason not to engage in conflicts that would destroy what people have achieved.

For, at the most basic level, literacy changes the brain of every literate person, which allows new forms of thinking and learning to flourish in a society. Each new generation of readers passes these skills and their accompanying expectations on to their children and grandchildren, thus potentially ending the cycle of illiteracy and, very importantly, changing its insidious correlate—poverty. Higher rates of literacy empower young women to seek greater educational, economic, and even entrepreneurial challenges, which, in turn, make them more likely to raise healthy, literate, economically independent children.

With the most basic of tools, individuals with an adequate to advanced level of literacy can become full-fledged members of society and can become involved on an equal basis in social and political discourse. As the world around us changes the way information can become available to anyone with access and the ability to read and understand it, there is a potentially revolutionary leap forward possible for the citizens of our world, wherever and whoever they are. There has never been a time in human history when literacy has been more important to a child's future, or more possible.

To be sure, until we demonstrate that children in our villages and preschools can learn to read, our acknowledgedly bold goals at the time of this chapter's writing will remain unmet. Nevertheless, what we have already learned from the literacy initiatives in two tiny villages in remote Ethiopia, in the slums of Kampala, and in the rural farmlands of Alabama and Georgia inspires us to continue until we do. From the start of our work to the still removed moment when we can give this work over to others, our constant goal is to elicit in children everywhere a desire to use literacy to go beyond their own knowledge and to help each other in the process. We want the next generation to learn to read and to think in ways that render the new readers capable of the highest forms of creativity, reflective thought, and also ethical judgment. Our Lion Prince now wants to be a computer engineer. Our oldest female Wonchi "teacher" wants to be a pediatrician. Both of these professions were unknown to them a short while ago.

The too-little-understood reality is that in seeking to release the potential of children who might otherwise be exploited, underutilized, or completely ignored, we help millions of other people around our world. If efforts like the global literacy initiative described here can achieve even some part of our stated goals, we predict that more initiatives will quickly follow suit with more contributions to make.

Indeed, even as we write, the new X Prize for Global Learning was based in part on the promising results from the children of Wonchi and Wolenchite. If all the 200 teams that are now competing across forty countries to win the $10 million X Prize could work together in bringing whole new forms of literacy and literature to children in their respective countries, we believe that there will emerge a never-before-seen increase in the connectedness among people around the world. New avenues of empathy and compassion may be opened for human beings who would never otherwise have encountered each other in their daily lives in Mumbai, Wonchi, Wolenchite, Bangladesh, Uganda, Blakely, Georgia, and Roanoke City, Alabama. Certainly the dissemination and application of knowledge we possess today will exponentially increase and become open to all, as the recent meetings at the Vatican and Haskins Laboratory presage.

Notes

1. Don Meichenbaum, as discussed by Steve Dykstra in a post to *Spelltalk*, February 2, 2014.
2. Mary Leonora Tucker, SSND, *I Hold your Foot: The Story of my Enduring Bond with Liberia* (Lulu Publishing Services, 2015), pp. 125–6.

3. One Laptop Per Child.
4. See Maryanne Wolf, Mirit Barzillai, Stephanie Gottwald, Lynne Miller, Kathleen Spencer, Elizabeth Norton, Maureen Lovett, and Robin Morris, "The RAVE-O Intervention: Connecting Neuroscience to the Classroom," *Mind, Brain, and Education* 3, no. 2 (2009): pp. 84–93.
5. Morris, Lovett, Wolf.
6. See CuriousLearning.com.
7. Angela Chang and Cynthia Breazeal, 2013.
8. Jeanne Chall, *Stages of Reading Development* (New York: McGraw-Hill, 1983).
9. Wolf and Barzillai.
10. Sugata Mitra, personal correspondence during meeting at MIT on global literacy, 2012.
11. George Eliot, *Adam Bede* (New York: Modern Library, 2006; first published 1859), p. 21.
12. Katherine Boo, *Behind the Beautiful Forevers: Life, Death, and Hope in a Mumbai Undercity* (New York: Random House, 2012).
13. Smithsonian.
14. Pontifical Academy of Sciences Meetings: *Bread and Brain*, 2014; *Socially Excluded People*, 2014; *Children and Sustainable Development: A Challenge for Education*, 2015. See in particular, paper presented by Daniel Wagner, "Learning, Literacy and Sustainable Development: Inclusion, Vulnerability, and the SDGs," November 13, 2015. See also chapters by Maryanne Wolf, Stephanie Gottwald, Tinsley Galyean, and Robin Morris <http://www.casinapioiv.va/content/dam/accademia/pdf/sv123/sv123-wolf.pdf>; Maryanne Wolf, Stephanie Gottwald, Tinsley Galyean, Robin Morris, and Cynthia Breazeal <http://www.casinapioiv.va/content/dam/accademia/pdf/sv125/sv125-wolf.pdf>.
15. Pope Francis, *Laudate Si Encyclical* (May 24, 2015). <http://w2.vatican.va/content/francesco/en/encyclicals/documents/papa-francesco_20150524_enciclica-laudato-si.html>. Ken Pugh, *Haskins Global Summit. Early Development, Health, and Learning among at-Risk Children: Seeking a Global Perspective.* December 1–3, 2015.
16. Jim Yardley and Simon Romero, "Pope's Focus on Poor Revives Scorned Theology," *New York Times* (May 23, 2015). <http://www.nytimes.com/2015/05/24/world/europe/popes-focus-on-poor-revives-scorned-theology.html>.

Epilogue

In the last analysis, all of us involved in literacy—whether in remote regions, our own cities, or in brain-imaging labs—hope to bring to the world's collective attention the vast communicative potential and profound generativity at the heart of reading. In so doing, we seek to expose the *great waste* when children never experience either. If the next generation of children begin to develop deep reading skills like perspective-taking, critical analysis, and novel thinking, they will be building an internal platform for their own contributions both to ever new forms of knowing and to time-honored ones like literary knowledge. The editor of the Literary Agenda series, Philip Davis, has written that "the *'literary'* offers to human discourse something more than the opinionated, the informative, the finished and the explicit—an extra dimension achieved in the processes of thinking out into language, with both its hesitations and its surprises; in the contextual feeling of a thought—its nuance, resonance and richness for further development; and thus in the increased capacity for realization and discovery."[1]

Like the repurposing of many a "reading-neuron," I would be happy to have Davis's descriptions of the *literary* reused now to describe the apex of *literacy*—deep reading, the penultimate goal of all our work. Thus, perhaps, it is not too great a surprise that, like T. S. Eliot, we discover "at the end of all our exploring"[2] that *literacy* and *the literary* are separated twins possessing not only similar features, but close to identical goals for this generation and the next. Together they point the way to the third revolution in the human brain. To bring such a set of goals to reality will need the vision and the efforts of many people: *we hold your foot.*

Notes

1. Davis, Proposal to *Literary Agenda* series.
2. T. S. Eliot, *Four Quartets* (New York: Harvest/Harcourt Brace Jovanovich, 1943), p. 59.

Acknowledgments

No one ever writes a book like this one without the help of many colleagues, friends, and family, and in the case of this book, without the help and hopes of families in villages in many places. I want to begin, however, with the person who helped more than anyone else, Stephanie Gottwald, who provided much of the content in Chapter 3 and, as I said at the start, looked over my shoulder in Chapter 7, and visited every site in our projects. I am deeply indebted to her for all the years she has been the Assistant Director of the Center for Reading and Language Research, and now the Director of Content in the global literacy initiative, Curious Learning. In both roles, her commitment to children and to the research base that underlies our work has been a continuous gift to us all.

The next individuals I wish to thank are the members of the Tufts Center for Reading and Language Research, past and present, particularly the PhD, Masters, and undergraduate students whose research is represented here—Mirit Barzillai, Terri Benyareh, Kathleen Biddle, Ellen Boiselle, Joanna Christodoulou, Katharine Donnelly Adams, Patrick Donnelly, Yvonne Gill, Eric Glickman-Tondreau, Tami Katzir, Lynne Miller, Cathy Moritz, Elizabeth Norton, Melissa Orkin, Ola Ozernov-Palchik, Catherine Ullman-Shade, Laura Vanderberg, and many others who should be mentioned but for text length, which we have long exceeded. We thank Niermala Singh-Mohan for her wonderful patience and perseverance with the manuscript preparation. Catherine Stoodley deserves her own special acknowledgment because she inhabits so many roles: former undergraduate student, esteemed colleague in neuroscience research, and the most amazing illustrator one would imagine. Cat is unique in all the world!

The second "we" includes the extraordinary work of the members of the Curious Learning global literacy initiative with board members Tinsley Galyean, Robin Morris, Cynthia Breazeal, and contributors and staff Scott Webb, David Gibbs, Edgar Wharton, Eric Glickman-Tondreau, and new recruit Maureen Lovett. The work and dedication of this team under the leadership of Tinsley Galyean and Stephanie Gottwald underlies the last chapter of this book and the hopes for many of our future directions. We also would like to thank all of our on-the-ground deployment partners—Michael Girma, Markos Lemma, the Italian Development Council, the Clover Foundation, Creesen Naicker and the MRP Foundation, Prayog in Bihar, the Human Welfare Association, Early County and Roanoke County Schools, UTEC and Maba, and all those groups and organizations who share this vital mission with us.

I wish to thank two Tufts University colleagues in particular for their immense contributions to my thinking in Chapters 2, 4, and 5: linguist Ray Jackendoff and neuroscientist/psychiatrist Gina Kuperberg. I am truly in their debt for their many kindnesses and the depth of their knowledge. Few people have contributed more to the writing of this book. Except for Barbara and Brad Evans. The personal commitment of Barbara Evans to the work of our Center, whether in Africa or Boston, has made all of our research possible in the last years. Our gratitude to Barbara and Brad Evans is not to be measured.

I am also deeply indebted to Philip Davis for urging me to contribute this book to his Literary Agenda series and for helping to guide me during the entire process. No one could have a more articulate or wiser editor.

And now I wish to say something most authors should not say. To meet the timely schedule of this Oxford series, I agreed to complete this book in one year. I should never have been so foolhardy and will always wish I had two more years. I was able to meet this commitment *only* because of the fact that I spent my sabbatical in one of the single best environments that exist for scholars: the Center for Advanced Studies in the Behavioral Sciences at Stanford University. Under the directorship of Margaret Levi and associate director Sally Schroeder, the Center offered me and all of the Fellows an interdisciplinary haven for writing, research, and unrivalled intellectual exchanges among colleagues from different disciplines. From the tenacious, sometimes Sherlock Holmesian help of the librarians (Amanda Thomas) to the superb technology assistance (Ravi Shivana and Patrick Goebel) to the graciousness of *every* staff member, the Center supported the work of the Fellows so that we could accomplish seemingly unattainable goals in a relatively brief period of time. The Fellows themselves provided daily, often inspiring input and feedback to each other. I am especially grateful for discussions in the area of technological innovation with Fox Harrell and Katherine Isbister, and in the area of philosophy and literature with Jenann Ismael and Anne Coiro. Simply put, I could not have finished this book without the entire staff of the Center, the atmosphere and support they provided, and the rare fellowship of all the Fellows of the 2014–2015 year.

Finally, both Stephanie and I wish to thank our families and friends. The support of Heidi Bally, Cinthia Coletti, Paul and Ulli Grossman, and Aurelio Maria Mottola, a ring of friends like no other in my life, cannot be measured. I will always be grateful to Victoria Munroe whose generosity of spirit gave me a "local habitation" for my thoughts for the past several years. My gratitude to my two sons, Ben Wolf Noam and David Wolf Noam, goes beyond what I want to put in words for the world. I will simply say that they have given my life love, support, and surprises daily! Recently, they have been contributing in wonderfully innovative ways to the work in this book on global literacy and to work on dyslexia. And now Stephanie wishes to give her own acknowledgments.

I wish to extend my deepest gratitude to my mentor and teacher, Maryanne Wolf. From the very first day of my time at the Center she has expressed the utmost confidence in my contributions, frequently when I myself had no idea that I could do it. She is for me a striking example of human and intellectual generosity that serves as a daily reminder of the nature of our shared mission.

And to my family, in particular my husband Matthias and my girls, Maria and Lydia, I am deeply grateful. It would not be possible to do this work without your love, support, fashion guidance, and pie.

Finally, we wish to thank the editors at Oxford University Press, particularly Jacqueline Baker and Eleanor Collins, for helping to guide this book through all its stages. We are most grateful.

Every effort has been made to trace and contact copyright holders prior to publication. If notified, the publisher will be pleased to rectify any omissions at the earliest opportunity.

Selected Bibliography

Naomi Baron, *Always On* (Oxford: Oxford University Press, 2008).
Naomi Baron, *Words Onscreen: The Fate of Reading in a Digital World* (Oxford: Oxford University Press, 2014).
Nicholas Carr, *The Shallows* (New York: W. W. Norton & Co., 2010).
Philip Davis, *Reading and the Reader: The Literary Agenda* (Oxford: Oxford University Press, 2013).
Stanislas Dehaene, *Reading in the Brain* (New York: Penguin Viking, 2009).
Stanislas Dehaene, *Consciousness and the Brain* (New York: Penguin Viking, 2014).
Michael Dirda, *Book by Book* (New York: Henry Holt and Co., 2005).
Mark Edmundson, *Why Read?* (New York: Bloomsbury, 2004).
Susan Greenfield, *Mind Change* (New York: Random House, 2015).
Lisa Guernsey and Michael Levine, *Tap, Click, and Read: Growing Readers in a World of Screens* (New York: Jossey-Bass, 2015). (Note: although Guernsey and Levine's book appeared after the present book was written, it is a superb reference.)
Eva Hoffman, *Time* (New York: Picador, 2009).
Philip Holcomb and Jonathan Grainger, "Watching the Word Go By: On the Time-Course of Component Processes in Visual Word Recognition," *Language and Linguistics Compass* 3, no. 1 (2009): pp. 128–56. doi:10.1111/j.1749-818X.2008.00121.x.
Ray Jackendoff, *A User's Guide to Thought and Meaning* (Oxford: Oxford University Press, 2012).
Maggie Jackson, *Distracted: The Erosion of Attention and the Coming Dark Age* (Amherst, NY: Prometheus, 2008).
Ray Kurzweil, *The Singularity is Near* (New York: Viking, 2005).
Ellen F. Lau, Alexandre Gramfort, Matti S. Hämäläinen, and Gina R. Kuperberg, "Automatic Semantic Facilitation in Anterior Temporal Cortex Revealed through Multimodal Neuroimaging," *Journal of Neuroscience* 33, no. 43 (2013): pp. 17171–81. doi:10.1523/jneurosci.1018-13.2013.
Daniel Levitin, *The Organized Mind* (New York: Dutton, Penguin, 2014).
Alberto Manguel, *A History of Reading* (New York: Penguin Press, 1996).
Mark Seidenberg, *Reading: Our New Understanding of the Original Information Technology* (New York: Basic Books, 2017).
Catherine Steiner-Adair, *The Big Disconnect* (New York: HarperCollins, 2013).
Sherry Turkle, *Reclaiming Conversation* (New York: Penguin, 2016).
Brian Wandell and Jason Yeatman, "Biological Development of Reading Circuits," *Current Opinion in Neurobiology* 23, no. 2 (2013): pp. 261–8. <http://dx.doi.org/10.1016/j.conb.2012.12.005>.

Maryanne Wolf, *Proust and the Squid: The Story and Science of the Reading Brain* (New York: HarperCollins, 2007).

Maryanne Wolf, Mirit Barzillai, Stephanie Gottwald, Lynne Miller, Kathleen Spencer, Elizabeth Norton, Maureen Lovett, and Robin Morris, "The RAVE-O Intervention: Connecting Neuroscience to the Classroom," *Mind, Brain, and Education* 3, no. 2 (2009): pp. 84–93.

Maryanne Wolf, Stephanie Gottwald, Tinsley Galyean, and Robin Morris, "Global Literacy and Socially Excluded Peoples" (*The Emergency of the Socially Excluded Meeting:* Pontifical Academy of Science, 2014). <http://www.casinapioiv.va/content/dam/accademia/pdf/sv123/sv123-wolf.pdf>.

Maryanne Wolf, Stephanie Gottwald, Tinsley Galyean, Robin Morris, and Cynthia Breazeal, "The Reading Brain, Global Literacy, and the Eradication of Poverty" (*Bread and Brain, Education and Poverty Meeting:* Pontifical Academy of Science, 2014). <http://www.casinapioiv.va/content/dam/accademia/pdf/sv125/sv125-wolf.pdf>.

Index

Figures are indicated by an italic *f* following the page number.

acquired alexia 88
alphabets 30–2
analogical thought, and deep reading 122–4
Anderson, Michael 70, 78
Annoni, Jean-Marie 74
Aquinas, Thomas 136–7
Arendt, Hannah 109
Aristotle 81, 86
Aronoff, Mark 19
attention 8, 83–6
   continuous partial attention 146
   distraction 146–8
   impact of digital culture 145–6
   impact on what we read 151–3
   multitasking 146–7
   orienting attention system 85
   screen vs print 148–51

background knowledge, and deep reading 117–22
Baron, Naomi 143–4, 146, 147, 154
Benjamin, Walter 61, 109–10, 130, 147–8
Beowulf 12
biliteracy agenda 159
biliterate brain 158
Blake, William 97
Blakeslee, Sandra 125
Bloom, Harold 130
Bolger, Donald 73
Booth, James 59
Breazeal, Cynthia 165, 171
Broca's area 93–4, 96, 98, 102
Brown, Roger 20
Buschman, Timothy 85

Carreiras, Manuel 5–6
Carroll, Lewis 19, 25
   "Jabberwocky" 23–4
Casaubon, Isaac 119

Castro-Caldas, Alexandre 58–9
cells:
   retinotopic organization 77–8
   working groups/cell assemblies 79–81
Chall, Jeanne 9, 39–40, 173
Chang, Angela 171
Chang, Bernard 83
Changeux, Jean-Pierre 85
Chaucer, Geoffrey 12
Cherokee 29
Chesterton, G. K. 138
child development:
   analogical thought 123
   comparison of literate/non-literate children 55–8
   differently formed reading circuits 156
   environmental print 50–1, 52
   imagining thoughts of others 48–50
   impact of exposure to language in home 47–8
   learning letters 52–4
   literacy and children's play 60–2
   logographic reading 51–2
   reading to children 40–7, 50, 51
   use of digital devices 143–5
   vocabulary knowledge 47
Chinese writing system 29, 30
   nu shu writing 30
Chomsky, Carol 22–3, 40, 103
Chomsky, Noam 21, 22, 26, 135
Christie, Agatha 127
Clark, Andy 125
close reading 96, 111, 151
coarticulation 17–18
cognitive patience 152
Cohen, Laurent 54, 59, 75
Coiro, Julie 156
Collins, Billy, "On Turning Ten" 37–8
Common Sense Media 144

comprehension, screen vs print reading 148–50
connectivity, and reading brain 72–4
Constantine, David 67
continuous partial attention 146
critical analysis, and deep reading 128–30
cummings, e. e. 18–19

Danielewski, Mark 142–3
Davis, Philip 3, 7, 103, 110, 111, 113, 132, 188
deep reading 7, 105, 110–12
  analogical thought 122–4
  background knowledge 117–22
  critical analysis 128–30
  future of 142, 155–7
  generativity 134–8
  generativity processes 111, 130–8
  imagery 113–14
  importance of 112–13
  inferential abilities 124–8
  insight 130–4
  metacognitive processes 111, 122–30
  novel thought 135
  perspective-taking 114–17
Dehaene, Stanislas 54–5, 56, 59, 75–6, 78, 85, 90, 104
Dejerine, Jules 101
De la Mare, Walter 143
Dennett, Dan 77
Devlin, Joseph 90
Dickinson, Emily 14, 93, 122, 126–7
Dietrich, Arne 130, 131
digital culture:
  attention 145–6
  development of cognitive capacities in 155–6
  distraction 146–8
  impact on deep reading 155–7
  screen vs print reading 148–51
  young people's use of digital devices 143–5
digital reading 150–1
  comprehension 148–9
  democratization of knowledge 164
  development of different reading circuits 156–7
  impact on what we read 151–3
  reading habits 148
  use of digital devices 143–5

Diotima 81, 82
Diotima's brain 82–3, 84 f, 137 f
  phonological and semantic processes 95 f
  visual system 87 f
distraction 146–8
Dykstra, Steve 163, 164
dyslexia 53–4, 60
dysnomia 92

eidolon:
  attention 83–6
  vision 86–92
Eliot, George 95 f, 97, 179–80
  Middlemarch 119
Eliot, T. S. 188
embodied cognition 96–7, 116
Emerson, Ralph Waldo 109, 110
empathy 115, 116
  imagining thoughts of others 48–50
English:
  alphabet 30–2
  changes in 12–13
  writing system 30–1
entry processes, and deep reading 113–22
  background knowledge 117–22
  imagery 113–14
  perspective-taking 114–17
environmental print 50–1, 52
episteme 68, 105, 109–10
Epstein, Joseph 4
Erikson, Erik 135
Ethiopia, literacy project in:
  first assessment 173–9
  goals of 171–3
  sites for 167–9
  see also global literacy project
Evans, Joseph 117

false-belief task 49
Farah, Martha 88
Fischer, Kurt 92
Fitch, W. Tecumseh 21
Flaubert, Gustave 15
Francis, Pope 10, 164–5, 184
Friederici, Angela 70, 101–2

Gabrieli, John 60, 98, 101
Galyean, Tinsley 169

Index

Gazzaniga, Michael 71
generativity processes, and deep reading 130–8
  insight 130–4
Gentner, Dedre 122, 124
Geschwind, Norman 101
Gidney, Chip 27–8
Gilgamesh, Epic of 124
Gioia, Dana 92
Girma, Michael 169
Gleason, Jean Berko 20
Global Information Industry Center 154
global literacy project:
  app development 182
  data collection 169–70
  deployments in different settings 180–2
  in Ethiopia 167–9
  first assessment 173–9
  future development 182–3
  goals 171–3, 186
  mentoring system 182
  tablet content principles 170–1
Goethe, Johann Wolfgang von 113
Goodman, Gordon 173
Google 153
Goswami, Usha 17, 123
Gottwald, Stephanie 6, 164
Gould, Stephen 130
Grainger, Jonathan 77
graphemes 30–1
Greenfield, Susan 154–5
Guzzardi, Peter 118

Harsdoerffer, Georg 18
Hart, Todd 47–8
Hauser, Marc 21
Hawking, Stephen 118
Hawkins, Richard 125
Hayles, Katherine 152
Heaney, Seamus 12
Hebb, Donald 79
Henry, Marcia 31
High, Pam 40
Hirsh-Pasek, Katherine 144
Hofstadter, Douglas 123, 124
Holcomb, Phil 77
Huey, Edmund 104

imagery 113–14
inferential abilities, and deep reading 124–8
infixes 19
information overload 8, 153–5
informational environmentalism 154
insight, and deep reading 130–4
invariant visual object recognition 54–5
Isbister, Katherine 151

Jackendoff, Ray 13, 16, 24, 26, 66, 69, 92, 103, 110, 135, 136
Jackson, Maggie 146
Jacobs, Alan 128
James, William 42, 124
Japanese writing system 29
Jen, Gish 116
joint attention, and reading to a child 42
Jung-Beeman, Mark 129, 130, 131

Kanso, Riam 130, 131
Kant, Immanuel 121
Keller, Matt 165, 174
Kennedy, Rebecca 20, 43
Klass, Perri 40
Kleist, Heinrich von 118
Kolinsky, Regine 59
Korean *Hangul* 32–3
Kounios, John 129, 130, 131
Kuperberg, Gina 71, 91, 99, 100, 117, 125–6
Kurzweil, Ray 141, 153
Kutas, Marta 99–100

language skills, comparison of literate/non-literate children 55–7
learning to read:
  impact on the brain 58–60
  learning letters 52–4
  mirror invariance 53–4
  visual cortex 54–5
Leavis, F. R. 111
Lehrer, Jonah 133
Lemma, Markos 169
Lessing, Doris 13
Levitin, Daniel 98–9, 146
Levy, David 154
Liberman, Isabelle 18
Lightman, Alan 157

linguistics:
  linguistic systems 14
  morphology 18–20
  orthography 28–34
  phonology 14–18
  pragmatics 27–8
  semantics 23–7
  syntax 21–3
literacy:
  additive effects of 39, 40
  advancement of knowledge 121
  children's play 60–2
  critical analysis skills 129–30
  as cultural invention 3–4
  definition 2
  impact on the brain 55, 58–60
  implications of advances in 184–5
  literacy gap 38–9
  reading brain 4–5
  thought 3, 103–4
literary mind, future of 142
Littau, Karin 149
Liu, Ziming 148
logographic reading 51–2
logographic symbols 28–9
Lovett, Maureen 166, 179
Lyytinen, Heikki 54

McCandliss, Bruce 90
Mangen, Anne 148–9
Manguel, Alberto 2
Mann, Thomas, *Magic Mountain* 133–4
Mar, Raymond 96, 116–17
Martin, Anna 136
meaning 97
  semantic contributions 97–101
  syntactic contributions 101–3
Mehler, Jacques 16
Meichenbaum, Don 164
melody 16
Mendelsund, Peter 113–14
metacognitive processes, and deep reading 117–22
  analogical thought 122–4
  critical analysis 128–30
  inferential abilities 124–8
  scientific method 126
metalinguistic awareness, comparison of literate/non-literate adults 58, 59
Meyer, David 146

Miller, Earl 79, 85
Miller, J. Hillis 97
Milne, A. A., *Winnie the Pooh* 46–7
mirror invariance 53
Mitra, Sugata 179
Molfese, Victoria 52
Morais, Jose 59
morphemes 19–20
morphology 18–20
Morris, Robin 165, 166
Mueller, F. Max 46
multitasking 146–7

N400 99–100, 110
names, and word retrieval 92–7
National Assessment of Educational Progress 38
National Survey of Early Childhood Health 40
Negroponte, Nicholas 165, 168, 179
neuronal networks 70
neuronal niche 75
neuronal recycling 22, 75–6
neuroplasticity 72
  reading brain 74–7
nonsense words 24
Norton, Elizabeth 60

Ogunnaike, Yomi 57–8
onoma, and word retrieval 92–7
orthography 28–34
  alphabets 30–2
  Korean *Hangul* 32–3
  syllabary 29–30
  writing systems 29–31

Pasteur, Louis 131
pastoral children 4, 8–9, 164
Perfetti, Charles 33, 73, 74, 90
periventricular nodular heterotopia 83, 85
perspective-taking 114–17
Petersen, Steve 89
Phillips, Natalie 96, 149
phonemes 15, 17–18, 93
  awareness of literate/non-literate adults 58
phonetic systems 17
phonics 15
phonological systems, and word retrieval 93–4

phonology 14–18
　coarticulation 17–18
　four tiers of sound 15–18
　melody 16
　phonemes 15, 17–18, 93
　phonetic systems 17
　syllabic structure 16
Pinker, Steven 21
Piper, Andrew 149
Plato 24, 66, 67–9, 81, 82, 105, 110, 135, 157
play, impact of literacy on 60
Poldrack, Russ 98, 147
Polk, Thad 88
polysemous words 24–5, 27
Practical Criticism 111
pragmatics 27–8
prediction 69, 91, 100, 110, 125–6
prefixes 19, 20
pre-reading 39–40, 170, 173
　environmental print 50–1, 52
　imagining thoughts of others 48–50
　impact of exposure to language in home 47–8
　learning letters 52–4
　logographic reading 51–2
　reading to children 40–7, 50, 51
Price, Cathy 90
print reading 148–51, 156
prosody 16
Proust, Marcel 3, 38, 136
psycholinguistics 13, 34 n. 3
Pugh, Ken 73, 90, 184
Pulvermüller, Friedemann 96
Pyle, Howard 113, 114

Raichle, Marcus 89
Ramachandran, V. S. 71
RAVE-O Program 159, 166
Reach Out and Read (ROaR) program 40
reading:
　definition 2–3
　generativity 26
　screen vs print 148–51
reading brain 4–5
　attention 83–6
　connectivity 72–4
　convergent research approaches 70–1
　different reading circuits 52, 73–4, 156
　future of 142, 157–9
　impact of learning to read on 58–60
　malleability of reading circuit 156
　neuronal networks 70
　neuronal recycling 75–6
　neuroplasticity 74–7
　prediction 69, 91
　speed of recognition 77
　vision 76–7, 86–92
　word retrieval 92–7
Reis, Alexandra 58–9
retinotopic organization 77–8
Richards, I. A. 111
Risley, Betty 47–8
Robinson, Marilynne 116, 118–19

Scarlett, George 60
Scarry, Elaine 113
Schneider, Walter 73
Schurz, Matthias 136
See, Lisa 30
Seidenberg, Mark 100, 104
Sejong, King 32–3
semantic facilitation 99
semantic neighborhood 25, 97
semantic networks 97–101
semantics 23–7
Sequoyah 29
Shakespeare, William 46, 66
Shankweiler, Don 18
Shaw, George Bernard 32, 36 n. 29
Singer, Tania 115
slow reading 111, 132–3
Snow, Catherine 40
Socrates 5, 69, 81–2
Sonnevi, Göran 1
speech amplitude envelope 17, 107 n. 38
Spencer, Herbert 119
Sporns, Olaf 94
Steiner, George 109
Steiner-Adair, Catherine 144–5
Stone, Linda 146
Stoodley, Catherine 82, 94, 136
suffixes 19, 20

Swinney, David 27
syllabary 29–30
syllabic structure 16
syntactic networks 101–3
syntax 21–3, 103
  universal/particular grammar 22

Tagalog language 19
theory of mind 49, 115
Thomson, Jenny 17
Tolstoy, Leo 113–14
tonotopic organization 93
Toro, Juan 16
Tucker, Leonora 163–4
Turkle, Sherry 141, 148, 153

Uganda 62, 181–2
Ulin, David 114

vision 76–7, 86–92
visual cortex 54–5
  retinotopic organization 77–8
  working groups/cell assemblies 79–81
visual word form area (VWFA) 54–5, 68, 90–1
vocabulary knowledge 47

Wallace, David Foster 116
Wandell, Brian 70, 78, 88, 90
Waters, Lindsay 109, 111, 132
Wells, H. G. 10
Wernicke's area 93–4
Woolf, Virginia 119
word retrieval 92–3
  phonological systems 93–4
  syntactic/meaning-based systems 96–7
words 24
  attention 83–6
  Plato's five dimensions 67–9
  polysemous words 24–5, 27
  semantic contributions to the meaning of 97–101
  syntactic contributions to understanding 101–3
  visual processing 86–92
working groups/cell assemblies 79–81

X Prize for Global Learning 186

Yeatman, Jason 70
Yoruba 57–8

Zuckerman, Barry 40, 144